THIRTY YEARS
ON THE
LINE

Also by Leo D. Stapleton

COMMISH
FIRE AND WATER

THIRTY YEARS
ON THE
LINE

LEO D. STAPLETON

dmc associates, inc.
Boston

Publisher's Note

I first read Leo Stapleton's *Thirty Years on the Line* in manuscript twelve years ago when I was editorial director of a small publishing company in Boston. I thought *Thirty Years* was a great book that told tales of truly heroic professionals, courageous people who risked their lives for the general public but who were also largely unappreciated by these same people. I thought fire fighters deserved some wider, greater recognition from the citizenry they served, and I thought *Thirty Years* would be a good place to start. Unfortunately for me, the owner of the publishing company could not see the promise of Leo's manuscript. Fortunately — for all of us — another publisher could. *Thirty Years* was a great success. The original publisher went back to press six times and sold the rights for a mass market paperback edition.

Publishing in Boston is not a large world; Leo's and my paths crossed from time to time over the years. I had set up dmc to develop book projects for publishers, and Leo . . . well, Leo was appointed Commissioner and Chief of the Boston Fire Department. He called me one day in November of 1989 and told me he had finished working on another manuscript; he wondered if I'd be interested in reading it, maybe even publishing it. I know I am many things, but I like to think I am not a fool. "Of course I would, Leo," I said.

Seven months later, in May of 1990, dmc published *Commish.* In May of 1992 we published *Fire and Water,* Leo's first novel. And now we have published this reprint edition of *Thirty Years on. the Line.* It took some time . . . but I finally got to publish Leo Stapleton's first book, just as I wanted to do a dozen years earlier.

We've published this reprint edition of *Thirty Years* for a very simple reason: people asked us to. Countless fans at fire musters, shows and expos across the country would ask where they could get a copy. These people were usually young men and women, new to the fire service. They'd heard of the book, of how good it

The Commish

was, of its great humor and basic truths. They were a new generation of fire fighters and they wanted *Thirty Years on the Line.*

Leo retired as Commissioner and Chief of the Boston Fire Department in January of 1991 after thirty-nine years of service. His friends held a testimonial for him in April. The hall was packed; I suspect the fire marshall should have imposed a fine of some type. The crowd, a bit shy of 2000 people, resembled a convention as I looked around the hall. I guess in a way we were; for we were united by the respect and admiration we gave Leo Stapleton — a jake from Boston who always gave his best to the job.

Leo and his wife, Doris, still live in South Boston; they have now been married forty-three years, and the number of their grandchildren has increased to an even dozen. Leo is still writing; he is still lecturing and teaching; and he is still trying — with great determination — to improve his golf game.

His fans — you and I — wish him the best.

Dennis Campbell

This book is dedicated to my wife, Doris, for her truly magnificent performance throughout thirty-three years on the marriage line.

It is also dedicated to all Boston Fire Fighters, past and present but to four in particular: My father, John V. Stapleton, my sons, Leo and Garret, and to Moe Cunniff, the best aide I ever saw.

Acknowledgements

I would like to acknowledge the following:

My other son, Edward, the first supporter and most severe critic.

My daughters, Jenny and Amanda, for their critique with the woman's touch.

My brother, Jack, who always supports me, right or wrong.

Msgr. Matthew P. Stapleton for his objective review and benevolent acceptance of the vernacular — with proper chastisement, of course.

Kathy Downs, who typed the manuscript, cheerfully corrected the spelling and translated fractured phrases.

Photographer Bill Noonan for his superb selection of photographs from his inexhaustible supply.

And David Stapleton McEttrick; cousin, confidante, conscience, critic, advisor, agent and friend. Without his persistence and true professional help, this book would be buried forever in a bottom bureau drawer.

The incidents in this book are all true although some locations and identities have been altered where necessary. I have tried to report those incidents I did not witness as accurately as possible.

Contents

Introduction

This is a book about fire fighting in the City of Boston, Massachusetts, covering a thirty year period from the 1950's into the 1980's.

Boston was incorporated as a town in 1630 and has one of the oldest established fire departments in the country. While it is only forty-nine square miles in area, it has over 100,000 buildings and an extremely high population density. The nighttime population is around 600,000 citizens, but since it is the hub of a great metropolitan area, the daytime population is approximately 1,500,000.

Most of the buildings were erected before the twentieth century and the construction methods used, combined with the narrow streets, steep hills, and severe winter weather, make it a uniquely difficult city for fire fighting.

While the outlying districts of the city have many single family dwellings, most of the citizens live in apartment houses that range from three to six stories high. There are thousands of four, five, and six-story townhouses or brownstones that are constructed of wood with brick exterior walls and inadequate division walls between adjoining structures. As many as twelve such buildings may be interconnected with a common cockloft that permits rapid fire spread.

Boston also has a higher percentage of three-story wood frame buildings with wooden exterior walls than any other city. These "three-deckers," as they are called, contain from fourteen to twenty rooms in a single structure but they are often joined in rows of four with no fire walls between them. The exterior walls are frequently covered with aluminum or vinyl siding or with asphalt shingles which firefighters call gasoline shingles because they ignite rapidly and burn with great intensity. These unusual dwellings were built during the great immigrations in the last part of the nineteenth century, when there was very little public or private transportation and people had to live within walking distance of their jobs. The last three-deckers were built in 1917 and fire codes do not permit the construction of this type of structure any more.

The city is a major seaport, and has the oldest subway system in the country, a large international airport and numerous high rise buildings. These factors also contribute to the fire problem.

While the Fire Department divides the various districts by numerical designations, each section has its own name so that whatever district is indicated, whether it be East Boston, South Boston, North End, South End, Beacon Hill, Back Bay, Charlestown, Jamaica Plain, Dorchester, Mattapan, Allston-Brighton, Roxbury, Hyde Park, West Roxbury, Readville, Roslindale or Downtown, it's all Boston, and each area has peculiarities from a fire fighting perspective.

To protect the city from fire, the department has 1,600 fire fighters, fifty-six fire companies, including thirty-three engine companies, twenty-one ladder companies, one rescue company, a two-section marine unit, and special Squrt and Aerial Tower Units. The companies are fairly well distributed throughout the eleven fire districts that comprise two fire divisions. The department also has a mutual aid arrangement with thirty-one surrounding cities and towns and it is not unusual to have as many as fifteen or twenty companies from outside communities working in the city when simultaneous fires are in progress. Boston fire companies frequently operate in the suburbs when they are requested under the arrangement. In recent years Boston and all of these communities have experienced reductions in manpower under austerity programs. These reductions have made these mutual aid pacts a vital part of fire protection for the entire metropolitan area.

Fire fighting is recognized as the most hazardous profession in the country. The national injury rate among fire fighters is 42%. In Boston, the rate is often double that average because of the workload.

The author has attempted to produce a book that is enlightening and entertaining to the average reader. It is also his intent to try to provide information to those who have chosen the profession as a career.

Many books have been published about the theoretical methods of controlling fires. This book attempts to relate actual events that take place under fire conditions and the methods employed may differ dramatically from the text books.

LEO D. STAPLETON

Glossary

Commissioner The Fire Commissioner of the department, appointed by the Mayor of the city. Usually a civilian.

Chief of Department The Chief Executive Officer of the department, appointed by the Mayor, usually from the Deputy Fire Chief rank.

Commissioner/Chief The existing head of the department. A former Deputy Fire Chief who holds both mayoral appointments.

Deputy Fire Chief Highest Civil Service rank in the department.

Division Commander A Deputy Fire Chief who commands a division, either in the field or at Headquarters.

District Fire Chief Commander of a fire district or assistant to a Headquarters division commander. All Chief officers above are addressed by the title "Chief."

Fire Captain Commander of a fire company. Usually called "Cap."

Fire Lieutenant Commander of an on duty shift of a fire company. Usually called "Loo" or "Luft."

Fire Fighter A member of a fire company. Boston fire fighters are usually called "jakes".

Good Jake An exceptional fire fighter, regardless of rank.

On the line A reference to fire duty.

Line A stretch of hose, regardless of size or length.

Big line a two and a half inch diameter line of hose.

Inch and a half a one and a half inch diameter hose.

Booster line hard rubber hose on a reel, used primarily for nuisance fires.

Pipe the nozzle attached to the end of the hose, equipped with a shutoff.

Pipeman the jake operating the nozzle.

Hosie jake assigned to an engine company.

Truckie jake assigned to a ladder company.

Engine an engine company, equipped with a pumping engine.

Truck A ladder company, equipped with an aerial ladder and other ladders.

Stick The one hundred foot aerial itself. The term originated when aerials were made of wood, although all are now steel or aluminum alloy.

Bucket An aerial tower. A ladder device with a bucket on the top. Used for delivering water at heights, rescue purposes and many other duties.

Ground Ladder A ladder raised by hand that rests on the ground. These ladders range from sixteen to fifty feet.

Donut Roll A fifty foot length of big line, rolled for easy carrying and use. Designed for work off standpipes in high rise buildings.

Standpipe A six to eight inch diameter pipe, usually filled with water, that rises from the basement to the roof in stairways of high rise buildings. It has two and a half inch outlets on each floor for fire department use and is connected to an automatic fire pump in the basement.

Flexicot A body wrapper.

Hitch A combination of boots and pants, arranged so a member responding to an alarm can jump from bed into gear without loss of time.

Rake, adz, axe, Halligan, K12 Tools which are used for forcible entry, cutting floors, pulling ceilings, opening roofs, etc. The tools of the trade.

Deck Gun Deluge set. A heavy stream appliance operated from outside buildings.

Pentagon, Enchanted Kingdom Fire Headquarters.

Radio Terms:

Box The fire alarm box on the corner of a street. An assignment of apparatus is provided for every box in the city.

Strike An order to transmit whatever alarm is indicated. Example: Strike second alarm Box 1234.

First Alarm Response Provides three engines, two trucks, and one district chief to a building fire.

Working Fire A call for extra assistance at a fire. Increases the help at the scene but not considered a multiple alarm.

Multiple Alarm Request for additional assistance ranging from a second to a ninth alarm response.

Identifying Calls Radio identification. Deputies are C6 and C7, with aides identified as C600 or C700. District chiefs use car I.D.s such as Car 4 for District Four; the aide is Car 400. Fire companies use company numbers for radio I.D., such as: "Engine 33 to Fire Alarm." Fire Alarm is the central receiving and dispatching station.

THIRTY YEARS
ON THE
LINE

Qualifications: "Jeez, Was I Ever Really That Smart?"

The deputy was leaning back, feet up on the desk, reading the bulletin from the State Division of Personnel. It was an announcement about a pending examination for the position of Deputy Fire Chief, Boston Fire department. It listed the duties as follows:

> Under supervision, to perform administrative and technical fire fighting work, assisting the Fire Chief in the direction of a municipal Fire Department; to act for the Fire Chief in his absence or as delegated; to assist the Fire Chief in co-ordinating and directing the activities of a municipal Fire Department; to direct personnel and maintain departmental efficiency, order, discipline and other personnel matters; to respond to fire alarms and direct fire fighting operations; to direct or perform inspection of buildings for fire hazards; and to perform related work as required.
>
> **Eligibility:** This examination is open to the permanent District Fire Chiefs in the Boston Fire Department who have been employed in this grade after certification, for at least one year prior to the date of the examination.
>
> **Examination Subjects:** The written examination will test the following knowledges, abilities and skills that have been established for the position;

1. General Laws applying to the fire department.

2. Approved methods and procedures, theory, principles and practices of Fire Administration and Supervision

and ability to apply such knowledges in exercising full
authority over all members of the department.

3. Fire Fighting and life saving methods, equipment, tech-
   niques and ability to impart such knowledge.

4. Ability to have full responsibility for the efficient administration of the department.

5. Ability to maintain and obtain obedience to all rules,
   regulations and orders governing the department.

6. Accountability and a sense of obligation, responsibility
   and discipline.

He caught himself dozing off as he finished reviewing the
form. Thank god he never had to do all that crap again. His heart
went out to every poor district chief who was up to his ears in
NFPA handbooks, management practices and all the other nonsense that had to be learned to get ready for that two days of
misery. He knew just what they were going through.

It required a one year commitment of studying at least four
hours a day, every day if you were to have any chance at all. The
competition is fierce and the exams are very difficult but the system is reasonably fair. If you put the time in the books, have an
average intellect and keep the rosary beads and rabbit's foot handy
to cover all bases, you might make it.

Of course, it helps a lot if the existing deputies are thoughtful
enough to get pensioned or die when you are high on the list. In
his own case, hey, he just might be one of those thoughtful guys
pretty soon, hopefully by the pension route. Thirty years is a long
time at this racket and those winters seem to get longer and
longer.

If he did decide to wrap it up soon, no doubt one of those
district chief students would be glad to see him go. And some
captain, some lieutenant, and some fire fighter too, 'cause when a
deputy leaves, four guys move up and there's always someone better coming along. Well, good luck to them, whoever they were. He

wouldn't trade it for any other job and he hoped they'd enjoy it as much as he had.

Probably the most exciting time for fire fighters has been the last three decades. This old town has seen riots, sit ins, strikes, civil disorders, bombings, forced busing as well as hurricanes, blizzards and hundreds of thousands of fires.

But it looks like things might start to change in the eighties. Congress has created the Federal Emergency Management Agency, and while it is fumbling and stumbling with growing pains and underfunding, it is taking the first serious look at the national fire problem. If the right course is pursued, a hundred years from now people will be talking about that cretin who lived in the nineteenth and twentieth centuries and actually fought fires for a living. What was it they called the poor jerk? Oh, yes, a fire fighter. It sounds exciting but it also sounds a little stupid.

Well, he guessed they'd be right on both counts. As a matter of fact, sometimes he felt kinda stupid about some of his decisions. As he threw the pamphlet aside he thought, did I ever really know all that stuff they require? He hadn't opened a book in the fourteen years since he made deputy. Boy, imagine the writer's cramp he'd get if he tried to take that test. Oh, he realized how important the studying is for the exam, primarily because the competition is so tough and ya gotta beat all those other guys. But once you make it, from a practical point of view, you can throw all the books away. Oh, you keep reading all the trade journals to see if any magic has arrived, and you might write a coupla things yourself, but there are really only a few things that are important in doing the job, none of which are listed in the pamphlet. Hm, maybe he'd make up his own pamphlet. Here's how it would read:

1. Knowledge of fires and fire fighting is the prime requirement. Applicant will obtain this only by practical experience. Ya gotta keep goin' to them, baby.

2. Ability to pass the knowledge on to subordinates. Ya gotta teach them to keep them alive.

3. Knowledge of men and how to handle them. Sure, ya

gotta take care of them, treat them impartially and do the other stuff that's written down. But you also have to treat them with respect and humanity as individuals. They don't want to be babied, but they don't want an unfeeling martinet who cranks out orders like a machine. There's a narrow line between the two extremes that is essential to good leadership.

4. Above all, be decisive. Men would rather get direction and orders that they disagree with than nothing. An old sea captain once said, "When they come to you with a problem, remember one thing. They want a decision. They have already discussed the issue among themselves and couldn't resolve it. Now it's up to you, you are the final say. It does not really matter whether the decision you make in a particular instance is right or wrong, as long as you make it." While this may not always apply to fire fighting decisions, it is good advice for handling men.

Well, that's enough of that nonsense, he thought. Wonder what kinda night this will be. They're all different. He got up, stretched, yawned and headed for his bed in the other room. It was a little after midnight and he hadn't had a run all night. Maybe they'd have an all night in. Naw, whaddya dreamin'? When was the last time? He arranged his boots and pants into a night hitch beside the bed and crawled in.

If you do leave, pal, you're really gonna miss it; well, most of it anyway. The memories flooded over him as he dozed fitfully and he was transported back through the years . . .

The Day
The Boredom
Ended

The young fire fighter was bored. He was sitting in the front seat of the massive crash truck. It was the newest and most sophisticated fire engine in the country. It carried 3500 gallons of water and could throw a stream over 300 feet. It could produce enough foam to last eight minutes at full flow. It was designed to be operated by one man using controls that resembled a computer. The unit was built in England and cost a quarter million dollars. But like everything new, it still had a few bugs in it and that was the reason he was in the front seat. A Scottish mechanic had been flown into work on the controls and the monitor nozzle on the roof. He was up there now with another fire fighter and instructions were being relayed down to the cab so the young fire fighter could hit the switches as they were called for.

He was bored for a couple of reasons. First of all, the fog had rolled in this morning and a lot of flights had been cancelled so there was very little activity, although the airport was still operating. He never tired of watching the planes take off and land. They really fascinated him.

The other reason he was bored was the job itself. There was just not as much action on the crash crew as he thought there'd be. He'd been here over two years now and had never been to a serious fire or incident on the airport grounds. Oh, sure, they kept ya busy with rubbish fires, fuel leaks, inhalator cases, runway checks and inspections, and yeah, they sure drilled you enough with the foam and everything, but it wasn't like he expected.

He wanted to get on the Boston Department but he was overseas on a sub when they had the exam so by the time he got home and found out about it, he was out. He had taken the exam for the

Logan Crash Crew instead and did good enough to get the appointment.

It was a good job and the guys were the same as he supposed the jakes in Boston were. Most of them had been on crash crews in the service and really knew their stuff, but no action. Once in awhile they would be sent into Boston or to other towns they had a mutual aid arrangement with and that was great. He had been to the Chelsea conflagration and to Salem, Peabody and Lynn as well as the big town, but it wasn't often enough.

There was another exam coming up for Boston soon and he was studying like hell for it. His old man was still a jake in Boston and he was always telling him, don't get itchy. If you stay in this business long enough, you'll get all ya want. Well, maybe so, but it takes a long time coming.

He was startled out of his daydream when the side door of the station was yanked open by a workman with a contractor who was doing some repairs to the field. "There's a plane down on Four R!"

The fire fighter at the patrol desk hit the alarm and the automatic doors started to rise. As the rest of the fire fighters on duty headed for their apparatus, the chief yelled to the young jake in the big truck, "Take off and bring him with ya," pointing to the Scotsman on the roof. He drove out the door and swung to the right on the taxiway toward Four R.

It was really foggy and he had to go slow, but they trained all the time on the layout and everyone knew how to get anyplace on the field blindfolded. For some reason, maybe because he hadn't heard any noise, he thought it was a small plane, a Piper Cub or something. Boy, I hope I can find it. He turned right on Four R and started down the runway.

Suddenly, directly in front of him, he saw four bodies. At first he thought they were mannequins. They were not making a sound and there was not a mark on them. As a matter of fact, there was hardly any noise anywhere, although he thought he could hear a scream way off in the distance.

It dawned on him that they were people and he started shivering. The fire fighter on the roof yelled down, "Keep goin'. They're dead. I think I can see fire glowing through the fog."

He kept driving along and they came to the entire wheel assembly of a plane and it was blazing furiously. The Scotsman and the jake on the roof swung the nozzle around manually and he started the water and foam and they smothered the fire immediately.

The chief had arrived and ordered Box 612 to be struck. This was a prearranged signal that indicated a crash had taken place. Help would be dispatched from all the surrounding hospitals as well as from the Boston Department.

The chief directed that they make a complete tour of the site to see if anyone was alive. As they moved along one young soldier was found alive, strapped in his seat and horribly burned. He was the one who was screaming. Everyone else was dead.

This was Delta Airlines Flight 723, a DC-9, en route to Boston from Manchester, New Hampshire. It had come in too low and had hit the sea wall just in front of the runway. The crash apparently flipped the plane end over end and as it turned it split open, throwing the first victims they found a considerable distance beyond the wreckage.

When they came to the main part of the fuselage, it was really gruesome. It had telescoped and compressed and so had the people inside. Arms, legs, heads and bodies were all jammed together inside. Even little infants were caught in the pile. God, he thought he'd vomit. No, no, you can't. This is what they pay you for. You're the one always bitchin' about no work. You wanna be a jake, this is part of it. No deals. No backing away when it gets tough, get in there and start pulling. Yeah, but look at them. Look at those little kids. What's that on the ground? Jeez, it's a shoe with half a leg in it! There's some ears, hair. What's that other stuff? Teeth! There's hundreds of teeth everywhere and jawbones! Alright, alright, stop looking and start working.

By now there was a lot of help around: ambulances were pulling in, two Boston rescue companies, and some engines and trucks. He was really impressed with the way the rescue companies dug right in so businesslike. It was exhausting work, trying to pull the mounds of flesh apart, but it was done. It had to be.

He learned a lot about himself that day as well as about a lot of other guys. He found out that a couple of guys he never thought were much good, really did a terrific job at the scene, and a few others disappointed him. About himself, he found out that while he was horrified by the incident, he could do the job. He didn't enjoy it but he did it. He could make it in this business.

He also saw a few really ghoulish characters at the site. Photographers who seemed to relish carnage, while most of their peers looked at them in disgust. The pictures could never be published, even in the worst newspaper rags, but the ghouls kept snapping away, the worse the better. There was no work for the doctors and nurses once the poor soldier was removed, but they stayed and helped remove the victims.

At last it was over. Every body and piece they could find was gone. The FAA and National Transportation Safety Board took over to try to find the cause. Several months later it was ruled that the pilot had made an error in his approach. He came in twenty feet too low, forty feet to the right of the runway and three hundred feet short of the touchdown point.

When the young fire fighter got home that night, he was surprised to see his father waiting on his front steps, a case of beer in his arms. "I guess you had a long day; thought ya might like to talk a little."

When they got inside and sat down they each had a coupla beers in silence. Finally, the kid started to talk. He talked and talked and he never stopped until he was worn out. His father never said a word until he was finished.

When he spoke he said, "You know, the first dead guy I saw on the job was a young man that got caught in a freight elevator. It was my first day. He was crushed with his head between the edge of the elevator and the landing. It took three hours to get him out. The officer had us tie a rope around him while the rescue company did a lot of cutting with torches and saws. I was helping to hold the rope. The poor guy had one eye above the landing and it was staring straight at me all morning, getting duller and duller. The same thoughts went through my head that you said went through yours. This is the job, can I do it? You have to decide right then. There are no compromises if you want to be a good jake. Oh yeah, you'll see plenty who'll duck when it comes time to pick up a meat job, but most of them won't. I think you really started to learn today that, yeah, bad as it is, you can do it. The dead ones will never hurt you. We had an Eastern Airlines go in the drink years ago with about the same number killed as you had today and it was tough too.

"But, listen, it doesn't happen every day. You'll be pretty jiggy the next few runs you go on over there, but it will fade away. Oh, not all of it. There's always a little residue that stays with you and that's part of the price you pay for taking the job.

"You take the next exam for Boston and you'll get on eventually. When you do, remember, you'll have one big advantage."

"What's that, Pop?"

"Well, you saw more people killed in one shot today than the average fire fighter will see throughout his career. You got through it O.K. You'll never see anything worse in the city."

Everything
Was O.K.
Tuesday

The First National Bank Building on Federal Street looks like it is knocked up. Most high rise office buildings have straight sides with a smooth unbroken flow to the top. When they are under construction, building materials are transported up the outside of the structure by way of service elevators. If any of this material or the elevator itself catches fire, at least the fire isn't in the main building.

Whoever conceived (in the architectural sense) the First National, made it look pregnant (in the medical sense). It's not a bad looking joint, it just juts out from the fifth to the ninth floor. This design prevented the use of external service elevators to bring up materials during construction. Hence, two large shafts rose inside the structure for this purpose.

Whenever new buildings are under construction, especially high rises, the fire department visits periodically to keep abreast of the rapidly changing conditions that will affect fire fighting. These big buildings have standpipes for fire department use. There are six or eight inch pipes that extend the entire height of the building. A standpipe contains water, has outlets for the fire department hose on each floor, and is connected to a fire pump in the basement.

When a fire occurs, the department brings its own hose, connects it to an outlet near the fire and puts out the fire. In case the fire pump fails to operate, on the outside of the building is a connection that the fire department can connect into to provide water.

Simple, huh? Sure, as long as everything goes as planned. When the building is being built, though, at different times during the construction, different conditions exist. The standpipe is extended floor to floor as the structure rises, but it is kept dry to prevent freezing. The fire pump may not be installed until late in the game, so fire department inlets are essential at the street level to provide water in case of fire. Also, a lot of vandalism takes place during construction, with outlet valves missing or damaged. Guys get careless too, and often use the dry standpipe to yell down orders for lunch, beer or whatever, leaving the valves open. It's also a tempting place to throw empty cans, wrappers and other debris.

On a pleasant Tuesday morning in December, 1970, the deputy, the local district chief and several fire companies visited the First National for a periodic check. The building had reached its full forty-story height, had been topped off and the standpipe had reached the fortieth floor. The fire pump was not connected yet so the department conducted an operational drill.

A department pump was connected to a hydrant in the street, hose was stretched into the standpipe inlets and fire company members took donut rolls into the building. The service elevators in the twin shaft were checked out and one of the passenger elevators in the lobby was also found to be operating. A discussion took place about the operation of this elevator in case of fire. The Laborers' Union official declared that it was a rule that this elevator must be operated by a member of his union, while the fire department insisted it have control. It was resolved by the Union declaring its operator would work the elevator, but would take orders from the department.

Members checked the standpipe outlets on each floor, closed some open valves and then connected fire department hoses at a few floors, including the top. When everything was ready, water was pumped into the system from the street, pump pressure was increased and the lines were operated at the various floors while nozzle pressures were measured. The pressure at the nozzle on the top floor was fifty PSI, excellent for fire fighting. The drill was completed, an amiable and satisfactory exercise. The chiefs found the building engineers to be cooperative and very knowledgeable.

At 1106 hours, December 28th, Box 12-1423 was struck. Fire Alarm announced on the department radio, "Box 12-1423 was struck for a report of a fire in the service elevator, fourteenth floor, O.K. Car 3?"

"Car 3 has it," answered the district chief.

"C-6?" queried the Fire Alarm operator.

"C-6 has it," answered the deputy. He and his aide were returning to downtown from headquarters.

"That's the First National where we drilled last week," said the deputy.

"Yeah," said Moe, "I think we got sumthin', isn't that smoke pushing around the middle?"

They could see the building from their vantage point on the expressway and it did look like smoke drifting lazily outward.

"Yeah, well at least we know everythin' works in the place."

The first ladder truck at the scene reported smoke showing and the members headed into the lobby with the rescue company and their gear. They were met by a group of workmen coming down the stairs. "It's goin' like a bastid in the service shaft," said one guy as he ran by them heading for the door.

Another worker grabbed the engine company as it came in with its hose. "The fourth floor is all fire. This stairway will take you right to it," he pointed over his shoulder.

The lieutenant on the engine said, "They gave us the fourteenth, we better hit the fourth first." He took his company up the steps. When they started up it seemed every one of the nine hundred workers in the building was coming down, but the fire fighters wriggled upward past them.

Meanwhile, in the lobby, the truck and rescue men got on the passenger elevator. The operator wasn't around, so they started to work the manual controls.

"Hey, leave that fuckin' thing alone," they heard someone shout, and they saw a short little laborer running toward them. "I'm the only guy can operate that elevator, we made a deal last week."

"O.K.," said the captain of the truck, "let's go, take us to the twelfth."

As they started upward, they could hear workmen yelling and running as they passed each floor. A little smoke started coming in, but not too bad.

The elevator stopped and they figured they had reached the twelfth, the point two floors below the fire, which is a standard department procedure. As they waited for the doors to open, the elevator suddenly started to descend.

"Hey," said the captain, "let us off. Whaddya doin'?"

The operator wouldn't answer and they kept dropping. They tried to grab the controls from him, but the elevator hit the lobby and the door sprang open. The operator ran across the floor.

"Where the hell are ya goin'?"

"Outside, you asshole. Don't cha know this fuckin' place is burnin'?"

"Yeah, but you're the operator. What about our deal?"

"Stick the deal and the elevator up your ass," he cried.

So much for inter-union cooperation.

They headed back up and got off at the twelfth. The smoke condition was not too severe and they headed for the stairway up. But as they looked over toward the service shafts, they could see fire roaring up and they knew it was down below them. The captain grabbed his portable. "Ladder 8 to Car 3, we're at the twelfth and there's heavy fire coming from below in the service shafts. It's not extending out onto the floor. We'll keep goin' up and see how high it's gone."

Car 3 acknowledged and the ladder officer and his men went back to the elevator, leaving the rescue company to stretch the donut rolls on the twelfth and start operating on the fire.

As the deputy's car swung off the expressway and headed for the fire, he could hear the exchange of information between the portables. Engine 25 reporting fire on the fourth, Ladder 8 on the twelfth and heading up, Rescue 1 operating at the twelfth, Car 3 reporting a working fire. If it stays in the shafts, we should catch it O.K, he thought. I wonder how far it's gone?

As he was pulling up he heard, "Ladder 8 to Car 3, I'm at the twenty-fifth floor and the fire is extending up to here."

Car 3 acknowledged and the deputy did also as he walked toward the building and tapped the district chief on the shoulder.

"O.K. Frank, go 'head inside, I'm gonna get a lot more help."

"Yeah, we're gonna need it. Take a look at the inlets."

The deputy ordered a second alarm and turned to look at the connections to the building. A line was stretched from the street and the fire engine, but it wasn't into the system. He ran over and couldn't believe his eyes! The inlet connections were gone! There was nothing sticking out but pieces of pipe with no threads on them or anything else. "Shit, I'm gonna burn down a forty-story building."

"C-6 to all companies in the building, we have a water problem, be ready to back down if ya hafta. C-6 to Fire Alarm, strike third alarm, Box 1423." He was going to have to try to get a line through the lobby and try to pump into the standpipe at the first or second floor level, a most unsatisfactory arrangement, but the only thing he could think of right now. He was getting more calls from upstairs. The fire was starting to get out of the shaft on a few floors as it ignited combustibles that were close to it.

He knew he already had a fire that had gone twenty-one floors in the shaft; now it was starting to move outward and he had a lot of jakes and still plenty of construction workers in the building. "C-6 to Fire Alarm, strike fourth alarm, Box 1423. Tell incoming engines to bring donut rolls to the Federal Street side." He directed two arriving engines to start the stretch into the lobby for the connection he must make if he was to get any water at all.

A guy grabbed him by the arm and he tried to shake him off.

"Chief, Chief."

He looked around and there was one of the engineers from last week. "What the fuck happened to the inlets, we're gonna burn down this joint if we don't get water quick."

"Someone stole them last night. When I came in this morning and saw it I almost had a heart attack. But listen, will ya? I went to work on the fire pump and got it connected in the basement just now. I think you'll get water O.K."

"Jeez, I hope you're right. Wait a minute, I'll see what I can find out. C-6 to Engine 25, do you have water yet?"

"Engine 25 answering. Yeah, we got a good stream and we're working our way over to the shaft. A coupla windows just blew out too, so it's not too juicy."

Thank God. "C-6 to Rescue One, do you have water?"

The answer from the twelfth was also affirmative. Great! "Maybe we'll be O.K. yet," he said to the engineer. "If we are, I'll kiss ya, but I'm gonna get a line in the system anyway.

"O.K. Chief. Meantime, I'll get a plumber to put on new connections."

As more and more companies arrived on the extra alarms, they were sent up the commandeered elevator with their hose. The fire did extend out from the shaft on eight different levels and many windows blew out due to the combination of the heat of the fire and the water from hose streams that would hit them as the men were killing the fire. It is not a good practice to knock windows out of a high rise building, as the glass is deadly when it falls from such heights, but you can't help the accidental breakage that must occur from the fire itself. You just keep your fingers crossed and hope no one gets hit.

He had told the police to rope off a four block area but that's much easier said than done, especially downtown. The high rise buildings create wind tunnels in the area and the glass travels a long way, so you must clear a big section of both people and cars.

Shortly after the water problem was solved, the chief of department arrived and assumed command in the street, so the deputy entered the building to direct operations inside. It was a long battle throughout the afternoon, particularly on the floors the fire had spread out of the shaft. Sixteen big lines were used before it was over, but they did the job.

The shafts and elevators were badly damaged, some of the concrete in the structure itself was spalled and a lot of construction materials were destroyed. The opening of the building had to be delayed, but all in all, it was a very good job and a lot was learned about high rise structures. A coupla things were also learned about the courage, or lack of it, of little elevator operators with union rule books in their pockets.

The pregnant building has been open for years now and is very well run. The department seldom responds to fires there because of the efficient staff still directed by the same engineer. The building is still pregnant in what has to be the longest gestation period in history.

Ya Gotta
Breathe,
Don't Cha?

On Thanksgiving Day, 1967, a Boston Fire lieutenant died in an attic during a fire in a two-and-a-half-story dwelling in Dorchester. He died because his gas mask didn't protect him properly from the carbon monoxide in the room. The mask he was wearing was plainly marked that it could not be used where there was more than two percent CO present. What it didn't say was how the hell you found out what percent of CO was present. The way the fire lieutenant found out was by dying.

This death caused an intensive investigation into respiratory protective equipment in Boston. The first thing that was learned was that ten guys had died in the previous two decades while wearing the same type of mask. The evidence was inconclusive in most of the cases examined because inadequate investigations were made at the time. Fire fighters have always accepted death as one of the risks you assume when you take the job and each of the ten cases were shrugged off as just one of those things.

The chief of department at the time of the Thanksgiving Day tragedy did not just shrug it off. As soon as he got a look at the record he realized that the equipment was killing his men because it was taking them into a hazardous environment and then not protecting them properly. He ordered the filter type masks removed from service in early 1968. This was an extremely difficult but courageous and correct decision.

The greatest opposition to the move came from the fire fighting force itself. You might get flattened once in a while with the filter, and once in a great while someone got killed, but most of the time it was terrific. It only weighed seven pounds, you could sling it around your neck and it was there when you wanted it. Besides, whaddya gonna replace it with?

This was the most difficult part of the problem. The department had one type of self-contained breathing apparatus in service. This was the Chemox Mask, a unit designed for the Navy in World War II. It was probably safer because you carried your own supply and it lasted about an hour, but jeez, you can't expect to use a Chemox for everyday stuff, do ya? Ya got those big bulky breathing bags in front, it weighs twice as much as the filter and it's a bitch to get started in the winter. We only got it for ships and the subways, now are we gonna hafta use it in buildings?

But the chief was adamant: the filters were out. He had not slept since he found out the masks were inadequate and that was it, period. He called in the three major manufacturers to demonstrate their latest self-contained masks. All three had thirty-minute approved units which carried a supply of compressed air in a steel cylinder worn on the back.

One of the three was chosen and an order placed for a prompt delivery. During the interim, the Chemox was used and it was obvious it was not designed for everyday use. At every fire that took place in the next few weeks, problems regarding the mask were reported. It was a very difficult period for the men and for the chief.

At last, though, the new stuff arrived and training commenced immediately. As each company completed its orientation, the air masks went into service. There was no question that the air coming from the units was better. The new compressor system provided a supply that was actually fresher than the air in the street.

But it wasn't long before trouble developed. The first complaint was that the supply didn't last thirty minutes as advertised. It was more like fifteen or twenty. The unit was also pretty bulky, making it difficult to climb through windows or operate in cellars, and there was no way you could sling someone over your shoulder with it on. The weight now, how about that? Thirty-three pounds! Jeesus. Let's see, the filter was seven, the Chemox thirteen and now, through a miracle of modern science, we're up to thirty-three, pisser!

Next came the cold weather problems. If water got down into the breathing tube and froze, it cut off your air supply, nice. So, you opened your emergency supply valve, the air hit the ice in the tube and blew the shit out of your regulator. It sounded like a bomb going off and if the regulator cover hit anyone it cut about a five-stitch gash in his flesh.

The chief got all these complaints and he was badly disappointed but there was nothing much he could do. The manufacturers made it clear to him that the existing masks were the best that the state of the art could produce and anything better was a long way off. There was no way he could put back the filters with the evidence he had and he knew that the ones he had purchased, while they were far from perfect, did protect a man properly because they were self-contained.

Several months later he suffered a severe heart attack and was pensioned — frustrated that he couldn't solve the problem, but still convinced he had made the only move he could have under the circumstances. Future events proved he was right, but his vindication was a long time coming and he wasn't around anymore when it did.

For the present though, things went from bad to worse. The mechanical problems with the units multiplied and men lost confidence in them. Once that happens with fire fighters, look out. Men stopped wearing masks at all at fires and you really couldn't blame them. They felt they'd be able to perform better without the weight and bulk and were willing to accept the risks in order to do the job. The chiefs in the field were in sympathy with them because they were constantly witnessing the problems with the masks. As mask use went down, smoke inhalation injuries went up and a dangerous job became more so. It was a bad scene that went on for a long time.

The new deputy in charge of training fell heir to the problem as soon as he received his new assignment. He had spent all of his career in the field up till now and was thoroughly familiar with what was going on. His new assistant had also just arrived from a fire company. He had asked for the assignment because he had just been widowed and had to be home nights to take care of his kids. They both had a thorough understanding of fire fighting and fire fighters, but neither one felt like a white knight, riding to the rescue with a little gas mask in hand.

They first wrote down all the problems with breathing apparatus they could think of and it was a lengthy list. Next they wrote down what they thought was necessary for a fire fighter to protect him properly, but still allow him to do his job without interference. It didn't look that hard once you wrote it down.

Next the deputy composed a letter that briefly described the problem and the solution, as they had determined it. Now, what the hell do we do with it, he thought. He started composing a list of people that might be interested and might be able to help. Harvard School of Public Health? Yeah. MIT? Yeah. American Industrial Hygiene Association? Yeah. International Association of Fire Fighters? Yeah. International Association of Fire Chiefs? Yeah. How about the local Senators and Congressmen, Kennedy and them other guys? Yeah. Hey, how about NASA, those guys in space gotta breathe too, yeah.

O.K., let's mail all this shit and see what happens.

Out it went and in a short while, he started getting replies. Both Internationals confirmed what the old chief of department had determined. The filters were not protecting men properly and several fire fighters had been killed around the country. That information put the kiss of death on any possible return to that mask which the deputy had been toying with as an option.

He had a long interview with a professor from Harvard who seemed to know more about breathing apparatus than anyone. The professor candidly told him that everything on the market was unsuitable for fire fighting, but he also told him that the solution was going to take a lot of time and a lot of money.

The deputy also contacted the manufacturers and their answer was much the same. At least he found out they were human though. One guy who sympathized with their plight explained the problem to him from the manufacturers' point of view: "Listen, you want a new mask, well a lot of guys do too. But what's happening all around the country right now is that most fire departments are doing away with the filters for the same reason you guys did. What's available to them? Why, the air masks we are selling. Business is great. There's a six month backlog of orders.

Now, you want me to tell my boss, hey, some guy up in Boston ain't happy. How about we spend a couple of million bucks in research, make him what he wants, O.K.? He's gonna tell me to get lost. If we spend the dough and make you what you want, how many ya gonna buy, maybe four hundred? Big deal. Then some guy in Texas will say, 'Hey, I don't like the one you made for Boston, how about a shorter one, or a longer one or a green one or a blue one?' You see the problem. The first thing you gotta do is try to get everyone else complaining and then decide together what you want. Until then, what you got is the best there is."

It was pretty discouraging, but at least the guy was honest.

One day the deputy got a call from NASA Headquarters in Washington telling him a NASA representative was arriving the next day. When the guy came in, the deputy took him up to the chief and the commissioner and the man said, "The NASA has decided they are going to respond to your needs. We have been using taxpayers' money to put men in space and on the moon. In doing so, we have learned an awful lot and produced some dramatic scientific improvements. We now want to share this knowledge with you, the public, for your generosity to us. What would be a better way than to create a new breathing system for the fire service?"

Great!

He then went on to describe a unit that would answer all their needs: small, lightweight, one hour duration, everything. "Er, how can you do this, Mr. Smith?" asked the deputy. "Everything I've learned recently makes it look like a pretty tough job."

"Well, we have some new space age materials that we're going to use to make the pressure vessels and it will be quite an advancement, you'll see."

"O.K., we're in. When can we get this stuff?"

"Well, let's see. It's April, 1969, how about July?"

"You mean this July? Well, all right!"

"Yes, we already have an arrangement with a company in Denver, Colorado, but we have to wait until the new fiscal year starts in July." (This was before the start of the Federal Fiscal Year changed to October.)

When Mr. Smith left, the deputy raced for his office and called in his assistant. "Mike, Mike, we're all set." He described what had taken place and Mike looked at him.

"Well, I hate to be skeptical, but it sounds impossible to me.

"Yeah, well you wait and see. Keep looking out Southampton Street in July and you'll see a big truck with 'NASA' on the side, loaded with masks."

But July came and went, no truck and no masks. In August, the deputy could wait no longer and he called Mr. Smith.

"Er, Chief, I'm glad you called. I'm afraid we have a little disappointing news. The NASA can definitely build you that mask; the only problem is, no one can afford it. The materials we were going to use, when we figured the cost, made it impractical. I guess we forgot that when we build a mask for space, we don't care how much it costs as long as it works. And it only has to work once on one guy. Your needs are a lot different."

The deputy's heart sank, but Mr. Smith went on.

"Listen, though, I'm coming up next week; we're going to try something else."

When he arrived the following week, he was a lot less formal and it was nice to see he was human. He told the deputy quite frankly why the NASA was interested — no more of that crap about paying back the taxpayers. His boss had gotten a letter from Kennedy saying, "Hey, go find out what the fire fighters in Boston are bitching about." This time he brought the professor from Harvard and a scientist from MIT and told the group that NASA was prepared to fund a project through the Cambridge office. The project would have MIT produce a mask by means of a mathematical computation if Harvard and the fire department would undergo studies to produce the necessary information. The program was going to take a few years, but it was a more realistic approach.

All the parties agreed and a contract was issued to Harvard and MIT with the fire department providing a cost free participation. The first thing the professor from Harvard told the deputy was that if they were to make a mask for a fire fighter they must find out what kind of person he was physically and what he actually did for a living, the environment he worked in, etc.

This started a series of seven studies that went on for the next eight years, long after the program to build this particular mask failed. The knowledge gained in the studies has produced really valuable information about the fire service which is constantly quoted today.

But the program failed within a year because Nixon closed NASA in Cambridge and moved the funding to Ames in California, so everything dried up. It was another disappointment, but ya gotta keep punching.

The deputy and his assistant went to Washington and tried to get some funding with the help of the Fire Fighters' International Union but the attempt failed. On the plane going home they saw an article that stated Congress had just awarded a grant for the study of migratory birds. "Hey, pretty good, huh?" "Fifteen million bucks for migratory birds and shit for fire fighters. Nice priorities."

The professor at Harvard was great, though. He kept getting little seeding grants and swiping from other projects to keep the study of fire fighters going.

The guy from NASA kept in touch too and in 1971 he told them NASA was really going to build a mask but the approach was to be different. They were getting a group of NASA scientists, a mask manufacturer and a users committee to find a solution. The deputy was one of the men on the committee.

The program operated out of Johnson Space Center in Houston and the optimists felt the mask would be ready for production in a year. It took five long years due to budget problems and bureaucratic hurdles. The prototypes were produced in 1975 and field test sites were selected. The process was done regionally so that Houston, LA and New York, were chosen.

If you wanted to see a pissed off deputy you should have been there the day he found out Boston was not selected. But the tests went on and the mask looked pretty promising.

It was announced that the commercial mask would be available in mid-1976. The deputy called the manufacturer and said, "Listen, we got shot down on the field tests, but we want the first masks on the market. We been waiting a long, long time. We want to buy fifty as soon as they come out and then we'll do our own field tests, whaddya say?"

The manufacturer agreed and the order was placed. The deputy had only stayed in training one year and had returned to the field several years ago so he was still going through the frustrations of watching men drop from smoke inhalation. He had remained in charge of the gas mask research and Harvard Study Programs, but his primary job was fire fighting.

In July the new stuff arrived and it looked pretty good although kinda fragile. Would it stand up to the abuse it would get at fires? The only way to find out was to put them in service, and in they went on the rescue companies and the busiest engine companies in the city.

The deputy was on duty the first night and it was a real sweat job. There were several fires around the city but none in his area so by midnight he was getting a little jiggy. The phone rang and he almost jumped out of his boots. "Division One," he answered.

"Hey, Deputy, I used that new mask three times so far," said a fire fighter from an engine in Dorchester.

"Er, howja make out?" he was almost afraid to ask.

"Fucking thing's beautiful, we knocked the shit outta the fire and went right by a Southie company."

He exhaled in relief. "O.K., that's great. Use it as much as you can."

"Don't worry, we will."

It was beautiful, at least by comparison. It weighed ten pounds less and provided a tremendous flow of air. It really was the start of a dramatic turnaround in the department.

Of course, it wasn't perfect. During the next six months they broke every part of it. It was a little fragile at first, but the manufacturer kept abreast of any defects, and made changes as much as was possible. Boston reported eight different things that had to be altered. Hm, the deputy thought, if NASA had let us do the field tests we'd have fixed this stuff before it came on the market. Well, maybe.

When six months had passed, it was time to make a decision, and the commissioner elected to change the whole department to the new masks. It took another six months to get the money and make the purchase, but by the fall of 1977 it was done. Every company had four units. The first change was in smoke inhalation injuries. By the end of one year they had dropped from five hundred to eighty.

Oh, they're still not perfect, but what is? It would be nice if you could make a one-hour mask that weighed five pounds and you could tuck it in your pocket, and maybe someday, someone will, but the new one's a pretty good start.

The deputy got a couple of awards for the program, but he really could not care less. His assistant died of lung cancer before the masks arrived and never got to see the results of his contribution. Besides, people were starting to say he invented the mask and he thought that was pretty funny. He had trouble making a knot in his shoelaces, now he was an inventor. A few guys knew better, though. As he stepped down from the podium after receiving one prestigious award, an old pal from his drill class whispered, "Hey big shot, don't let it go to your head. Ya know what they say. Awards are like hemorrhoids; every asshole gets one eventually."

He never forgot it.

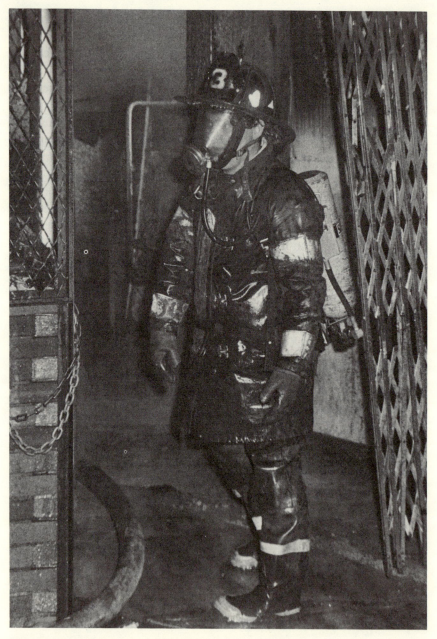

You'll go much further with it on. Box WF-2219, Feb. 9, 1980 Roxbury District

The People
Ride In A Hole
In The Ground

Boston has the oldest subway system in the country. It was started in the 1890's and opened shortly after the turn of the century. It's a complex system that fans out in a spoke from downtown and radiates to various sections of the city underground and under the harbor through four different tunnels. It then rises above ground into several districts and surrounding communities. It uses subway trains and street cars and both have caused serious fire problems inside the tunnels.

In the last few years, great progress has been made in the fire protection equipment in the system. Federal money has poured in and has been wisely used for this purpose. The reasons for the increased protection date back to several serious train fires that took place in 1972-1973. The fires caused the death of one passenger, injured many more and injured a large number of fire fighters and MBTA personnel. The fires were due to a defect in the train's electrical contact equipment and the problem has since been corrected.

At 0650 hours, January 4, 1973, Box 1412 was transmitted for a fire in the front car of a two-car train. It was located over a quarter of a mile inside the tunnel that runs under the harbor from South Boston to South Station on the downtown side. From the South Boston or Broadway Station end it was over a mile to the site.

There is a wind that blows continuously in the tunnel and on this day it was blowing toward the city. When the deputy arrived on the in-town side, he knew which side of the tracks the train was on but he had no idea how far in it was. He ordered a box transmitted on the South Boston side and directed the chief in that district to start a line from that end.

At his own end, he ordered all the companies to get on one line and start it down the stairs and into the tunnel, having been assured that all the power in the system was killed. Heavy black smoke was pushing up through all the ventilation grates in the Dewey Square-South Station area.

The companies on the line stretched it down to the subway platform and were met by heavy smoke pouring out of the left hand tube. They put on the long duration masks that the department required for this type of use and started forward. They had no idea how far they had to go. They described the advance as trying to wade through a wall of black shit, it was so thick. With a line of hose over your shoulder and dragging between your legs to the next guy, you moved along. The hose kept catching on every other railroad tie and you had to keep clearing it off.

The line kept getting longer and longer. In the street, the deputy now realized it could be much further in than he thought and he ordered a second alarm struck. All of the responding companies on this alarm were added to the same line and it kept getting longer and longer. The portable radios were ineffective because of the location of the fire and not much information was getting up to the street.

On the opposite side, the chief in South Boston had his line going in too, but since all the smoke was blowing away from his men, he sent the officers ahead to find out how far they had to go. Soon, he saw them coming and a throng of people were with them.

"It's over a mile away, Chief, it's much closer to in-town. It's the front train and it's fully involved. It must be a bitch coming from the other side."

"How many people?" he asked.

"The cars were loaded, but most of them came this way away from the smoke. A lot of them are coughing and probably need some oxygen, but they're all walking out. If anyone went the other way though, they're screwed. You couldn't live in there."

The chief got up to the street, directed that ambulances be sent to South Boston and relayed the information to the deputy in-town. "We're keeping our line coming, but it's over a mile and will take a long time. I'll need a lot more companies over here to get it in. Most of the people seem to be O.K. but there's plenty of them. There's no cars on the other side of the tube. The train that's burning so far is the front car nearest to your side. If any passengers went towards you they'll never make it."

Down in the tube, the line was moving along. One of the first men on the hose tripped over something and fell. Jeez, I think it's a body. He reached down and felt around. I can't tell if he's breathing or not. He picked him up and slung him over his shoulders and shouted to the officer that he was heading back.

"O.K., go ahead. Take another guy with ya. Boy, I hope there's only one."

Jackie was the pipe man and he had the nozzle over his shoulder going in further and further. For cripes sake, how long is this goddamn thing? Boy, is it black. Hope this mask keeps workin'. Keep listening for the alarm. If that bell starts to go, I'll be screwed. Probably never make it back before it runs out. Keep goin' and shut up. It's juicy all right, but I can feel a breeze blowin', too. If I do run out of air, I bet if I get down low I'll be O.K. Just shut up and keep goin' willya. Oops, I can feel some heat. Must be gettin' near it, keep it up. Is that a glow? Yeah. "Hey, Luft," to the officer, "I can see fire, we're almost there."

"O.K., I can see it too." He turned to the man behind him. "Pass the word, fill the line." He could hear the muffled shouts passing back.

Up on the street, the deputy was pacing back and forth nervously across the mouth of the subway entrance. Nothing yet, nothing yet. It seemed like an hour. The guy from Ladder 17 had stumbled out with a man over his shoulder a little while ago and he was dead. Wonder how many more. The word from the other side was that all those people were O.K., although several had gone to the hospital. Back and forth, back and forth.

"Hey, Deputy," came the shout from below.

"Yeah."

"Start the water on the line."

He wheeled around and pointed to the pump operator. "Fill it. Remember now, it's downhill, not too much pressure." He watched as the flat line bulged and disappeared down the stairs. Now more walking, back and forth, back and forth; boy, one line better be enough. Well, the one from Southie was still coming. Hope we don't need it though.

Jackie had the nozzle opened and he was listening. Couldn't hear a thing, keep listening. The air started trickling out the open pipe, then it started coming with a rush. It was gonna take awhile before the water got here but at least it's on the way. He and the lieutenant knelt astride the track, watching the fire roar through the first car. Well, we'll kick the shit outta it in a few minutes. There was a spurt of water and then a solid stream. They started hitting the roof of the tunnel and moving the line back and forth. When the water hit the roof it bounced off as a spray and dropped down on the fire and the smoke became dense once again.

"Keep it movin', Jack, old kid, that's the boy, back and forth."

As the fire got pushed back they moved along the side between the train and the wall of the tunnel, hitting the fire as they went. They reached the end of the first car and the smoke lifted completely. They had made it! The second car was not burning, yahoo!

They passed the line back to the next guys in the tunnel and ran forward, pulling off their masks. Looking back, they had a clear view. The fire was really being killed. They went beyond the unburned car and met some guys from Southie. "Dr. Livingstone I presume?" said Jackie.

"Up yours, Stanley, our line's almost here," came the answer.

"Well, you can make it up. The In-town jakes put the fire out as usual."

The line from Southie was almost there. They had made great progress because they had had good visibility, but it wasn't used.

"Hey, Deputy," came the shout again.

"Yes."

"They got it! They're knocking it down now. The line from Southie's there too."

Whew. He turned around to see a pretty young woman standing there with a mike in her hand. He recognized her. She was from one of the TV stations. Might as well get it over with.

He gave her all the information he had, emphasizing how difficult the job was, but it didn't seem to register with her. She was wondering why there were so many fire engines here; they had filled the Square and rush hour traffic was all backed up. The commuters were late and it was a mess.

"Hey lady," he finally said, "Ya see all those gleaming fire engines?"

"Yes, they have everything blocked."

"Do you know why there's so many of them?"

"Well, it seemed like a lot."

"Yeah, it is. That's because of one little guy," he said.

"One man, who's that?"

"Do you see that line of hose going down the stairs? Well, it goes all the way down there into the subway pit. Then it goes along those tracks, way, way back in a long dark tunnel. At the end of that line, there's a subway train burning and giving off smoke that will kill ya. But also at the end of that line is a little shitass fire fighter with the biggest pair of balls you'll ever see. If he doesn't have guts enough to fight his way through that tunnel and stay there when he gets to the fire, all this stuff you see in the Square don't mean shit. But he stayed there and put out the fire and now, pretty soon, all these beautiful engines will be leaving and everyone can go to those jobs."

The girl had been desperately giving the cut sign to the cameraman, but he kept it going. What the hell, it's on tape anyway, it'll never make the air. But it will make it to the back room. They'll love seeing that snotty little gal get eaten out.

Fires are funny. It depends a lot where they are as well as what's burning. The next MBTA train fire the deputy had was also very serious. It was a two-car train loaded with homeward bound commuters and one car was fully involved in fire as well. But this time the train was not in the tunnel, it was on the elevated structure opposite the Cathedral in the South End. All the commuters rushed out of the burning car onto the tracks and were picked off by aerial towers and aerial ladders. Three lines were run up over ground ladders in no time and the fire was quickly under control. The TV and news pictures were spectacular and everyone was happy. It was written up as though it were really a tough job, but he'd take ten of them to one in the tunnel, every time.

Whaddya Mean,
Dead Fish?

Fire fighters wear funny looking clothes to protect them from fire and the elements. A leather hat with ear flaps, long, black fisherman-type boots, a long black rubber coat and finger gloves or mittens, depending on the time of year. This stuff is called protective gear because that is its function, to protect.

In the late sixties, a fire fighter entered a room over a ladder and through a window during a building fire in Roxbury. While he was waiting for water in the line, the fire dropped out of the ceiling, enveloping him. As he headed for the window, his fire coat ignited and he dove for the ladder. Another fire fighter grabbed him, pulled him down to the ground and kept beating on him to put out the flames. He suffered severe burns to his hands, neck, head and torso, but he managed to survive the experience. His coat did not, however; it was burned to a crisp.

The deputy in charge of training was given the task of finding out what was going on, so the first thing he did was call the department chemist.

The department has had a chemist ever since the disastrous Cocoanut Grove Fire in 1942. This Boston night club was jammed with almost two thousand people on that November night and nearly five hundred of them died when a fire spread rapidly through the mass of flammable decorations that lined the ceiling and walls. The main exit was a revolving door and it became jammed with victims, cutting off the escape of scores of people. Legislation to prohibit such materials and exits was enacted following the fire, and the department employed a chemist to test all decorations to be used in places of public assembly.

The job has since expanded into many other areas relating to the fire business, including development of protective clothing, and the expansion is related to the incident involving the fire fighter's coat. The chemist said they'd have to perform some fire tests on the coat to determine the cause of the rapid spread of fire. So he and the deputy went to the Training Academy with a photographer and an armload of the latest coats purchased by the department.

The Academy is a sprawling complex with classrooms, fire buildings, drill yard, oil tank cars, tank trucks and everything else necessary to train recruits and keep the modern fire department up to snuff.

It has a couple of big drawbacks, however. It is located on Moon Island, which is used for sewage disposal, and the smell in midsummer is mind boggling. It is also over the hill from the police pistol range and an occasional errant round hits the drill yard. These risks go along with the job and the new recruit is fully covered if the smell knocks him out or a cop gets him.

One new jake brought a pistol down with him once and started lobbing shots back over the hill and the police instructors were a little perturbed.

The biggest drawback to the Island though, is its distance from the city. It's about ten miles from in-town and you have to go through the city of Quincy to get there. Consequently, you can't bring a large number of fire companies down there at one time, because the city would be unprotected. So, unless there's some special training of companies that has to be done at the Island, most drilling is done at each individual fire house and the training officers rotate around the city, except when there's a recruit class going through their twelve week indoctrination. With no classes in session, it's a pretty quiet, isolated spot, particularly in the winter with only a watchman in attendance.

"The Weasel" was the watchman on this particular day and he was doing what he does best: fishing for flounder off the dock. The Weasel is one of a small number of guys who came on the job, went to a few fires, and came to the conclusion that a guy could get killed here if he wasn't careful. He soon came down with an illness known as fire fighter's triple disease. It happens to guys who really like the job except for three things: heat, smoke and fire. These characters migrate rapidly to less hazardous duty and live charmed lives by selecting the right horses in the political wars that are fought every four years in the city. The Weasel was a topnotch political warrior and a great fisherman and he kept the Academy spotless, 'cause that's one of the requirements and there ain't no way he's gonna screw up and go back to a fire company.

As he was baiting his hook, he looked up and saw the small red car coming down the driveway. "Holy shit, it's the deputy, what the hell's he doin' here?" There was no class in session and all the officers were in the city training the companies. His first thought was that he had done something wrong. Jeez, maybe it's the fishing.

He hid his pole behind the wall and walked to the car, saluting as he approached. "Er, good morning, Deputy, Doctor," he nodded to the chemist, "I was just checking to see if any ice was forming around the dock. It seems to be clear."

"Yeah, I know you are, Weasel," said the deputy, "How they bitin'?

"Lissen, I want you to go down to the fire building and light a couple of fires in the barrels. There should be enough shit lying around down there to make good hot fires."

"Yessir, we have plenty of stuff for the next class coming down in a coupla weeks."

"O.K., get it ready and we'll be down soon.

"Oh, yeah, we need a volunteer. There's sumthin' wrong with our fire coats, we think they burn so we gotta find out. You can put one on when we light the fire." He could see the Weasel blanch a little.

"Er, is that the kind of coat that jake in Roxbury got burned with?"

"Yeah. that's right. we gotta find out."

"Ah, don't ya think that's a little dangerous, sir?"

"C'mon, you'll be participating in research for your brother fire fighters. It's really an honor."

"Uh, yessir," the Weasel said as he reluctantly headed down the drill yard.

The chemist turned to the deputy and said, "I never realized what a cruel man you are. You are totally lacking in the milk of human kindness."

"Lissen, Ph.D., stay with your test tubes. There's no way we could get him into one of those coats if we tried. The Weasel is a survivor, first and foremost. His biggest worry now is whether one of those cops will shoot him some day."

They set up a mannequin with coat, fire hat, boots, and gloves and got in position with a camera at a window. Taking a small hose along with him, the deputy pushed the mannequin toward two barrels filled with wood and paper that was burning intensively. It was a crude experiment but it proved quite effective as first the lower part of the sleeve, then the collar, and finally the whole coat burst into flames when it got within a few feet of the fire.

"My God," said the chemist, "No wonder that jake got burned. We're giving them less protection with that nylon coat than they get in their street clothes."

This simple test involved the department in a research program relative to all fire fighters' personal protective equipment that is still going on, but the coat had to be done first. During the next few months, the chemist tested every coat on the market and found that not one was suitable. He finally ended up designing one that he thought would suit the department's needs for fire protection and he developed a specification.

It's a pretty difficult task to develop something that won't burn but will keep you warm and dry and still stand up to the abuse a fire fighter will give it during fire fighting, but he did the best he could. When he was ready, he told the deputy in training he had a spec, and an order was put out for five hundred coats.

The manufacturer who got the bid was a local guy and was very cooperative. He had been making coats for years and he thought the new one was going to be a big improvement over what was on the market.

By the time the first fifty were ready, the deputy was desperate for coats. None had been brought in for so long that men were wearing old football jackets, sweaters or anything to fires. They not only were getting drowned all the time, they looked lousy. He put the fifty in service as soon as they arrived, giving them to guys who had been without coats the longest. Boy, he hoped they worked out. If not, what the hell was he gonna do with five hundred?

The day after they went in service he arrived at his office at nine o'clock. "Did they work last night, Mike?" he asked his assistant.

"Yeah, plenty. Three multiples, one in Dorchester, one in the South End and one in Jamaica Plain."

"Jeez, I wonder how the coats worked out."

It didn't take long to find out. His phone rang and it was a captain from a Dorchester company. "Yeah, Jack, howja do with the new coat?"

"That's what I'm callin' you about. It was pretty good I guess. Nice and warm and I didn't get wet or anything but when I got back I kinda smelled like dead fish."

"Whaddya mean, dead fish?"

"That's the only way I can describe it, dead fish."

"What kind of fire was it, what was burning?"

"Gee, I dunno, just an apartment house."

"Well, O.K., I'll get back to ya later."

He wasn't too concerned because Jack was such a conscientious guy he'd report any little thing. It's probably nuthin'. The phone rang again.

"Hello, Chief, this is a fire fighter from Engine 28. I just used the new coat last night and it was great. I've been freezin' my ass off all winter but the new coat is very warm. I didn't get wet either. But, er, the reason I'm calling ya is my wife is really pissed off. She says my underwear smells of dead fish and she refuses to wash it."

"Oh, you must have been at the same fire as Engine Thirteen, they're complaining too."

"No sir, we didn't see Thirteen last night. I was at a fire in J.P."

Oh, oh, we got troubles. As soon as he hung up the phone it rang again. Another call, another dead fish.

"Mike, get in here and get the doctor down here, right away. Notify the companies not to let them respond with them on."

"O.K., pal," said Mike, "I told you not to order five hundred at once."

By the time they got all the coats in, the manufacturer had arrived. As soon as he had gotten the call he had stopped the production line. They all headed for the Fire Academy.

The coats that hadn't been used didn't smell so they started with them and wet a few down. No smell. Then they lit a fire and left them in the room with the smoke and fire. No smell. Finally, Mike said, "Maybe it's a combination of things. Maybe the smoke, water and somethin' else."

"Like what?"

"I dunno, maybe guys sweating or sumthin'."

"O.K., what if we have a few guys wear them and make them sweat," said the chemist. "We'll see what happens."

"Yeah, O.K." said the deputy, "and since you're so smart, Mike, you can be one of the guys."

The next fires were set and three training officers, including Mike, put on coats and breathing apparatus and went inside. They stayed until their air supply was exhausted and they had sweat so much that perspiration was running out of their exhalation valves.

When they came out, what a stink. Yahoo, dead fish! Now they knew the cause anyway. The chemist turned to the manufacturer, "I've been giving this a lot of thought since I heard about it. Tell me something, did you wash the treated cotton inner liner before you assembled the coats?"

"Jeez, I dunno, Doctor, I'll have to check with the vendor. Why do you ask?"

"I don't remember anything in the specs about it, do you? "

"No, there wasn't, mainly because I never thought of it. Let's find out."

A call to the vendor revealed the material had been treated but not washed afterwards. The cotton was washed in bulk at a number of laundromats. The coats that had been delivered were washed in washing machines at the Fire Academy. Numerous tests were made over the next couple of weeks. The smell of dead fish never returned. The rest of the order was assembled and delivered and was a great success.

The department has bought thousands of coats since then and the specifications have been altered and updated. But one statement remains in every new spec and every new order: "The treated cotton liner on the inner garment shall be prewashed so as to be odor-free."

Another lesson the deputy learned from this incident: if something looks good to you, don't run out and buy a big order. Get a small quantity and field test the shit out of it. After anything is used by fire fighters at fires several times, it will either be destroyed or badly damaged or it will survive. If it survives, buy it.

This one stayed afloat. Fishing trawler *Ocean.* Box 7128, July 29, 1979, Boston Fish Pier, South Boston District.

Fire confined to superstructure, nothing below decks.

I'm Pretty Sure
It's Out Now; Or,
Some Nights Ya
Shudda Stood In Bed

The department has a rule that has been in effect for several years and has worked out quite well. When a fire has been knocked down, the rule permits the officer in charge to call for a detail. The detail consists of fire companies that have not been engaged at the fire to come in and relieve members who have controlled the fire and who are wet and exhausted. The size of the detail depends on the judgment of the officer in charge relative to how much work is left to be done.

Records are kept to make sure that details are given in rotating order so that a company that has already been to one serious fire on the tour will not be used for the detail. The detail also guards against rekindling of the fire and this fact alone has saved the nervous systems of several chiefs. It's a pretty good system, all in all.

Another rule requires the Fire Alarm office to make an announcement over the department radio whenever a serious fire is in progress and the temperature is below freezing. The purpose of this rule is to remind companies at the scene to drain any equipment that contains water and is not being used in order to prevent it from freezing. Another pretty good rule.

At 1911 hours on January 11, 1981, Box 7128 was struck for a fire on a fishing trawler at the Boston Fish Pier. The deputy arrived with the first alarm response that included the fire boat, three engines, two ladders and the rescue company. The fire originated in the engine room of a ninety foot trawler with a wooden hull. The first-in engine ran a line from the fire boat and attempted to penetrate the engine room via the only entrance, a ladder that descended from the main deck into the superstructure. The heat was intense and progress was difficult.

The fire boat reported they could see fire in the water side portholes. A scuttle was removed on the main deck forward and an attempt made to work back toward the fire but it failed because of lack of access and extreme heat. Ventilation was difficult because of the heavy plastic windows used in the pilot house and upper structure. The windows had to be cut with power saws.

About twenty minutes after arrival a violent explosion took place in the engine room when a tank containing hydraulic fluid ignited. This drove the men back up the ladder and increased the intensity of the fire tremendously. It now became a battle to prevent the spread up into the pilot house and after hold.

At this time, the Fire Alarm office announced, "The temperature is now 8 degrees with a wind chill of minus 20 degrees. Precautions should be taken to guard against the freezing of booster equipment and air masks. O.K., C-6?"

"Yeah, O.K., C-6 has it."

Up until then, he hadn't been thinking about how cold it was, although everyone knew it was pretty bitter out. The announcement of the wind chill factor was new. It made everyone feel much colder than they were. What asshole dreamed that up? No doubt some genius at the Pentagon who was home watching Walt Disney World on TV.

The battle was not going well on the trawler and the fire was extending upward. He kept watching the water line of the vessel and could see it was a little lower than when they arrived. The fire boat informed him that the fire had broken through the hull on the water side opposite the engine room. O.K., that's it, he thought. "C-6 to Car 6."

"Go ahead," the district chief on the trawler answered.

"Get everyone off and report to me when they're all clear, acknowledge."

"Yeah, I got it, everyone off the boat."

In a few minutes the report came back. "All personnel are off the trawler. Engine 1 is on our fire boat and the rest are on the dock."

The deputy then had hand lines from the dock and deluge guns from the boat pour water into the openings in the deck that had burned through. It was a lost cause; the fire had gotten too far ahead of them.

The trawler, which was worth about a half million, was going to be badly damaged. After about fifteen minutes of hitting it, the fire was pretty well knocked down. The boat was riding low in the water but was still upright.

It now became pretty obvious as to just how cold it really was. Everyone and everything was covered with ice. Better get them back to quarters quick. "C-6 to Fire Alarm."

"Answering C-6."

"The fire at Box 7128 is knocked down. Send a fire detail of one engine and one truck and we'll be holding the fire boat at the scene."

The message was acknowledged and he started dismissing all companies but the boat and the first two arriving companies who would be relieved by the detail.

Suddenly, he heard a creaking sound coming from the trawler and as he watched, it settled a little lower, the decks became awash and it started capsizing outward. In a few minutes it filled completely and sank, disappearing from sight. "Er, ah, C-6 to Fire Alarm."

"Go ahead."

"Cancel the fire detail at Box 7128."

"C-6, your message is broken up. Would you repeat. Did you say cancel the fire detail at Box 7128?"

"Yes, dammit, cancel the detail, the goddam boat sank, ya understand?"

"O.K. C-6, we have that message, thank you." The operator could tell he was a bit perturbed.

When they got back to quarters and managed to warm up with a change of clothes and some coffee, the captain of the ladder truck, who was a longtime friend of the deputy, said, "You know, that's the third one of them I've been to with you and you sank everyone of them. If you had been a Uboat commander during the war the Germans would have won easily."

No comment.

The tour wasn't over yet on this night. Far from it. The temperature kept dropping and every run they went on they got frozen.

The fire house wasn't all that warm either because of a problem with the heating system. They stayed in the kitchen between the runs because it was the warmest room. The captain made sure he gave the deputy the message he received from the Coast Guard that they had placed markers around the sunken trawler so no vessel would crash into the submerged hull. He received a suitable growl in reply.

At 0336 hours, Box 7234 was struck for a fire in the Andrew Square section of South Boston. The district chief reported on arrival, "Fire showing, three-story duplex."

"Oh, oh, saddle up boys, sounds like business," said the captain.

"At least it's inland," shouted someone else and the sensitive deputy turned around but couldn't see who it was. "Car 6 to Fire Alarm, strike second alarm, 7234." This order required the response of the deputy and everyone else in the house and they sped off on the expressway toward the fire.

As they emerged from the underpass, they could see the fire in the distance and it looked like a beauty. They heard the district chief call again. "Car 6 to companies responding to second alarm, we are having problems with defective and frozen hydrants. Get on individual hydrants as you come in but make sure they're not frozen before you connect." A very intelligent instruction.

As the deputy pulled in he could see they had another problem too. The building was a three-decker duplex that faced the square, and the first floor of the front was occupied by a barroom. On the roof of this section was an enormous billboard that covered the width of the building.

The fire was on the second and third floors of both sides of the duplex and the flames were shooting up around the sign. Oh, shit, another one, he thought.

These signs were usually securely bolted and fastened into the main timbers of the structures they were erected on. They would usually survive hurricanes, blizzards and every other kind of element. But fire was a different story. If the building itself was sound, the weight of the sign wouldn't bother its stability, but if the timbers it was locked into started to burn, the weight could have a disastrous effect and bring down the sign and possibly the building. The way the fire was breaking through around the sign made this a distinct possibility at this fire. Besides, no one had any water yet.

When the first engine had arrived at the fire and connected to a hydrant, the pump operator attempted to turn the main stem, but the hydrant fell over. This was a breakaway hydrant that is a fairly recent development. When a hydrant of this type is hit by a car or truck, it breaks off in such a way that no water is released. This eliminates those scenes you have seen in movies where W.C. Fields or someone crashes the hydrant and the water goes sky high. Not with a breakaway. This is a great achievement but it has one drawback. A lot of civilian drivers will hit hydrants and break them off. If no one is looking, they stand them back up and drive away. No one knows it's broken until the next time it's tested or used. When the pump operator hooks up, it falls over.

The deputy could think of at least three multiples he had gone to that occurred solely because of this phenomenon but he couldn't dwell on it now. In addition, the other two hydrants the first alarm engines took were frozen and the fire was extending rapidly. "C-6 to fire alarm, strike third alarm Box 7234, and send an aerial tower."

He directed the district chief to pull out the companies on the inside who were waiting for water and set up heavy stream appliances. When the tower arrived it was placed in the front, but before it received any water it was necessary to strike a fourth alarm.

More and more hydrants were frozen. But finally, the thawing equipment started to clear the ice from the barrels of the hydrants and water came in quantity. Deck guns were used from the tops of the engines and both guns were used from the bucket of the tower.

"Fire Alarm to C-6."

"Go ahead."

"The temperature is now minus two degrees . . ."

"I hope they don't give that factor again."

" . . .with a wind chill factor of minus thirty degrees, precau . . .

The deputy turned his volume down before he could hear the rest. "I'm gonna kill someone who's driving a desk up the street."

By 0730 hours the fire was under control, but it was obvious the building was so badly damaged it would have to come down.

The deputy requested a Building Department inspector in order to produce a crane to help remove the sign and the upper floors. As his relief arrived at the scene, he passed on the information he had and showed him around the perimeter.

He handed him his light and portable radio and headed for his car, covered with ice from top to bottom and shivering, thinking, I didn't save much of anything tonight. They'd have done just as well with that asshole from headquarters.

His relief could see how dejected he was and shouted after him, "Don't feel too bad about this building, pal, at least you didn't sink it!"

Shit, it doesn't take long for the word to get out.

Snow Is For Skiing; Keep It In New Hampshire

Winter in New England is beautiful. The sun shining on snow covered mountains with skiers gliding gracefully down the slopes, the ice covered trees and frozen ponds. God, it's glorious. At Christmas time, the thought of riding on a horse drawn sleigh with bells tinkling, passing down icy roads through rolling white farmlands, makes life worth living. Poets and postcard makers are inspired by such wonders.

In Boston, snow is a lot of shit and so is the winter. The town is so old that it was laid out centuries before the invention of the automobile. The streets are narrow and winding, and yes, quite picturesque. Tourists flock in constantly to travel the Freedom Trail and see how different it is from their modern, clean, spacious and thoroughly boring environments. Traffic is horrendous downtown and a constant battle is waged between the illegal parkers and the army of ticket wielding meter maids.

In the residential areas, parking is also a problem. When the thousands of three-deckers were built in the last century, there were no cars, just horse and buggies. Now that everyone has wheels and is more affluent, there are at least three cars to every building and there's not enough room on the streets to take them all. Constant jockeying for position is the norm. It's not unusual to see a father standing in front of his house, looking up and down the street, scratching his head, wondering where the hell his kid left the car last night. Garages are nonexistent, except in the outlying, newer sections.

The constant moving of cars takes place in the good weather, but when the snows come, it's a little different. As soon as the storm ends and the snow plows have thoroughly buried your car and probably removed a fender in the process, you get out your shovel and start throwing the snow off your car and back in the middle of the street, thus requiring additional plowing. Once your car is clear, you pull out and then have last year's beach chair close at hand. You stand it in the middle of your spot and that's it. It's yours, you shoveled it. No one will violate it.

If the snow keeps piling up all winter and you keep shoveling and marking your spot, you got it made. People unlucky enough not to have a spot can be seen constantly patrolling, looking for a chairless space they can jump into.

From the fire fighter's point of view, this constant shovelling and piling of snow keeps making the already narrow street narrower. Each storm sees the cars just a little further away from the curb, making passage of apparatus a little tighter. The same plows that bury the cars also bury the thirteen thousand hydrants in the city and when the snow stops, every fire company must clear all the hydrants in its area.

When a fire takes place, the whole job is complicated by the snow. Not only getting to the scene, but dragging lines over snow banks, raising ladders on top of the piles and every other task is more difficult. Delays in getting into operation allow fires to grow and spread. But, what the hell, spring may start in March this year, so ya stagger through.

Each winter the city averages about four big storms, with about eight to twelve inches of snow each storm. If the weather gets mild between them, some of the piles will shrink, and if you're lucky enough, you might be able to put your beach chair away for awhile.

1978 was a bit different. In late January, the city was hit with a twenty inch blizzard, more than twice the size of the usual storms. The weather stayed very cold and the streets were down to one travel lane because of the great accumulation. Piles of snow were up to four feet high on both sides of the street. For the next week or so, the city was digging out. The struggle between the plows and the fire fighters was endless, one plowing the hydrants in, the other digging them out. But progress was made.

On February 6th, the worst blizzard in the history of the city struck. Winds of over one hundred miles an hour blew in from the ocean, dumping an additional twenty-seven inches of snow, and the temperature was bitterly cold. Thousands and thousands of cars were abandoned in the middle of the streets, making them impassable. Hundreds of MBTA buses were caught in the jams, increasing the congestion. The entire city was a disaster.

The rest of the state, particularly along the sea shore, was devastated also. Four thousand cars and their occupants were trapped in a section of Route 128 and several people died before help could reach them.

But in the city, drastic action had to be taken. The governor declared a state of emergency, called out the National Guard and forbade the use of motor vehicles, except for emergency purposes, for the next six days.

In the fire department, those men who were on duty when it started were screwed. There was no way your relief was gonna get in, baby, so tell your wife you'll see her in the spring. Every guy that did eventually make it in was used to beef up the force, so you couldn't be released anyway. The normal on duty force doubled over the next few days as more and more finally made it.

The department had to take extraordinary and unprecedented measures during this emergency. First of all, every side street in the city was impassable. The city plows and National Guard had to concentrate on getting the main drags clear first, and this involved not only removing the snow, but all the cars that had been left in the middle of the streets. It took several days.

But meanwhile, the fires didn't stop and had to be put out. Since no apparatus could get in a side street a system was set up so that engines would travel the main street as close to the location as possible. Then, engine men would each carry a fifty foot length of hose and start plowing up the side street toward the fire, getting a hydrant as close to the building that they could find and connecting lengths together until there was enough. Ladder men would carry thirty-five or forty foot ladders through the drifts, hoping they'd be able to reach the roofs or any trapped occupants with them. It was exhausting and frustrating work and several buildings were lost because of the delays. During the period thousands of responses were made and there were about thirty extra-alarm fires.

Inhalator responses were extremely difficult. If heart patients had to be removed to the hospital, fire fighters would improvise sleds and drag the victims for blocks, keeping the resuscitator on them, trying to get to a main street and an ambulance.

When they were not at alarms of fire or other incidents, they were digging out hydrants. Many times it was necessary to dig down four feet just to reach the top of the bonnet. Then to dig to the street and open a pathway for a connection was even more difficult. After finding a hydrant, it could take a half hour or more to clear it, but it had to be done.

The deputy and his aide were riding up Mass. Ave. one morning, two days after the storm. They had just taken a dialysis patient to a hospital. The poor guy had been waiting two days for help and he was really sick. He was very grateful for the lift. "Jeez, howdja like to be in his shoes. Every few days get on that machine. I wonder if it's worth it. I guess it is to him, he sure was glad to see us. Boy, count your blessings."

As they rode northward, the deputy thought he saw smoke over to the left, toward Northampton Street. "That looks like it might be an auto fire or sumthin'. We better head over that way."

They turned at the next corner and then took a right on Northampton.

As they neared the end of the street, they could see fire roaring out the first floor windows in the rear of a building on Columbus Ave., with heavy smoke pushing from all the upper stories. "Oops, that's no auto. C-6 to Fire Alarm; strike a box for a fire on Columbus near Northampton."

"O.K., C-6, we'll strike Box 2212. We just sent 37 and 26 to investigate smoke in that area."

As he got out of the car at Columbus, he could see it was a serious fire. People were at the windows on the upper floors, with their escape cut off by the smoke. He could also see an engine and truck coming down the street and he directed them into position.

"C-6 to Fire Alarm, this fire is in a four-story brick, people trapped on upper floors, strike second alarm."

The truck company raised its aerial to the top floor and occupants started climbing onto the stick to be led down by the ladder men. The deputy directed another truck to the front and two more to the rear to raise ladders. Lines were run in the front from engine

companies as they arrived and ground ladders were placed to occupants on the second and third floor. The deputy had a pretty
good view of the operation because he was standing on a pile of
snow over seven feet high. He could see right into the second
floor. As occupants came down ladders, fire fighters raced up the
stairs to see if anyone else was trapped. Things were starting to
look a little better.

"C-600 to C-6," his aide called from out back.

"Go ahead."

"We can't get any ladders into the rear, the snow's too deep,
but we can't see anyone hanging out either."

"O.K., have the truckies report to me out front."

"C-600 to C-6! "

Hm, he's kinda excited. "Go ahead."

"A guy just fell out the fourth floor window, we need an ambulance!"

He called Fire Alarm and told them an occupant had fallen, but
in a few minutes his aide called back, "Chief, the ambulance is
here. This isn't an occupant. It's a guy from Ladder 26."

Oh, shit, he thought as he raced for the corner, just in time to
see the ambulance speeding away with the victim.

"How'd he look, is he alive?" Kinda stupid question after a guy
goes four floors.

"I dunno, Chief, he was unconscious, but I know he was breathing."

As soon as the fire was knocked down, the deputy turned it
over to the district chief and headed for the hospital. All he could
think of on the way was the poor fire fighter that he had helped to
pick up after he had fallen off a roof years ago. The poor kid was
unconscious for weeks and when he finally woke up, he was never
right again. His brain was damaged and he was a pathetic case.

He ran into the emergency ward and was met by the department chaplain and the doctor. "This your guy in here, Chief?"

"Yeah, he's mine."

"Well, he's pretty lucky. The only thing we've found so far is a
couple of broken ribs. He has no head injuries and his vital signs
are good."

"Can I see him?"

"Yes, he's in the second room down."

He recognized the kid when he stepped in the room. "Hi, Jimmy, howya doin'?"

"O.K., Chief, my side is really sore but they said I'm alright."

"What the hell happened to ya?"

"Well, it's kinda funny in a way. I took a guy down a ladder from the third floor, front. He told me his friend was still in there in the back. So, I went up the ladder and in. It was a little juicy, so I kept holding my face piece on my face and taking breaths as I went along. I got to the back room and there was no one there. So, I figured maybe he was upstairs. I went up the stairs and into the back room. There were a lot of boxes piled in the room, it must have been for storage. As I got over towards the window, I heard the door slam behind me. Oh, oh, I thought, I hope I can get out.

"The smoke was really starting to build up and I'm lookin' around for this guy but he isn't there. I broke out the window, figuring they'd be a truck out back with a ladder, but there was none."

"Whatcha do then?"

"Well, I said to myself, don't panic Jim, go back out the door. I started back across the room and I kept bumping into boxes, I couldn't find my way out. I went back to the window and as I looked out, the smoke really banked down and the front of my hair went on fire! Panic, Jim, panic, I thought, and I jumped right out the window. I hit the deep snow and fell over and my mask bottle crashed into the fence. I was so scared I hadn't even dropped it off before I jumped. I guess I did panic alright. The next thing I knew I was in here."

"Jim, you're a lucky guy. I don't know whether to kiss you or kill you, but I'm awful glad you made it. I'm not gonna go over the litany of things you did wrong now, you just take it easy."

"No, Deputy, you don't have to tell me anything. I'm gonna make my own list when I get outta here, and it's gonna be pretty long. It's pretty scary to be in the dark, in the smoke and all alone and hear that door slam behind you."

By the end of the week the state of emergency was over and traffic started to move again. But the snow stayed around till spring and every fire they had for the rest of the season was complicated by it. Of course, there were a few advantages. The deputy actually got to like standing on the big piles, directing fires. The view was really much better and it made you feel like a tall general. He had no regrets, though, when it all melted away and disappeared in the sewers. That's the end of that shit till next year. Now we can get back to some serious jockeying for a parking place near home.

Yeah, it comes every year without fail. Box 2-2445, Feb. 13 1983, Jamaica Plain District.

His Holiness Is Coming; Or, It Ain't Stealing If It's Blessed

In mid-1979, the Holy See announced that Pope John Paul II was going to visit the United States in October. This would be the first time a reigning Pontiff was to come to America.[1] To non-catholics this was an interesting event and was well received particularly because of the worldwide popularity of the new Pope.

But to American Catholics, it was truly a momentous event. The Church is two thousand years old and has been ruled by a Pope ever since St. Peter was elevated to the position by Christ himself.

The Pope has a tremendous influence on the life of a practicing Catholic. Every edict that is issued from Rome can affect one's mode of living. But Rome and the Pope are a long way off, and throughout its history, the Catholics of the United States have felt a little left out of things, because no Pope ever came here. After all, there's only a handful of cardinals in the country, and Rome's loaded with them. And they all seem to be Italians just like all the Popes. Now, though, things were changing. Not only was the Church paying more attention to us and the Pope himself was coming; he's not even Italian, he's Polish! It was really mind boggling.

The question now came as to where the Pope was to stop during his visit, and the political and ecclesiastical maneuvering was something to see. But at last the itinerary was announced. Sure, he

---

1 Pope Paul the Sixth actually was in the United States in the early seventies. He said Mass in Yankee Stadium, but his visit was to the United Nations and it was physically necessary for him to touch land in the United States, although it was not an official visit.

was gonna visit New York, Philly, Chicago, L.A. and a few other of those hick towns, but where was he coming first? Where would he get his first view of the United States? Why, Boston, of course. What other city had such an ethnic mix of Poles (of course), Lithuanians, Italians, devout (sometimes) Irish, blacks, Puerto Ricans, Jews and every other nationality you could imagine? Why there's even a bunch of those Protestant Yankees here for the true ecumenical spirit. The fact that it's also the closest major city to Europe had absolutely nothing to do with it, at least that's what the Bostonians say.

Now that the selections had been made, the preparations got started. He was gonna be here twenty-four hours so let's do it right. It was decided that a massive altar would be erected on Boston Common near Charles Street and over the underground garage. The site was chosen because the Common could accommodate up to a million of the faithful, and not so faithful, for an outdoor Mass. But it also was selected for security reasons. Next to the altar was an entrance to the garage, and underground rooms could be set aside for the Pope and all the American cardinals that were coming to greet him and participate in his first Mass on American soil.

The selection was made following a meeting of all those responsible for the Pope's safety during his stay. There were Boston, M.D.C., State and Capitol Police, members of the Mayor's and Governor's staffs, the Boston Fire Department, and above all, the Secret Service.

President Carter had assigned the Service the duty of protecting the Pope throughout his stay. This was a very wise decision when you consider what happened to the Pope in St. Peter's Square in 1981.

When the Secret Service comes to town, baby, they really take over. They are a no nonsense outfit with the authority to back up what they say. They are constantly guarding the highest officials and they know what they're doing. They don't know too much about fire fighting, but they know what they want done.

The fire department's task was to be relatively simple. A big line was to be connected to a standpipe in the garage and flaked out with enough hose to reach the altar or any other area with smaller lines to protect the visitors in the rooms. The big line was to be used in case of fire and also in case of an attack by any group of radicals who might try to reach the Pontiff. Although a few technical disagreements arose with the Secret Service, they had the final say and the plan was put into operation. Several fire fighters were selected for the detail at the scene. They had to be investigated by the FBI before being accepted and they knew well in advance where they were to be stationed, what their duties would be and who they were to report to. They were also instructed to wear their best dress uniforms but this was an unnecessary order because, after all, they were all Catholics and this is the Pope, man, the Pope.

October 1, 1979, was the big day, and the weather was horrendous. A driving rainstorm started before the Pope arrived and continued through most of the event. It was really pouring. But it didn't seem to deter either the Pontiff or the millions who lined the street. While the procession of cars passed by rather swiftly, it was more for security than for the weather. The Pope was great!

He is a handsome, rugged, stocky man with fair skin and a wonderful smile. His affection for the crowds was obvious and he stood, exposed to the elements, waving and bestowing blessings as he passed by. When he arrived at the Common and was taken downstairs he was greeted by the cardinals and started preparing for Mass. The cardinals and the police and fire details had been waiting there for some time.

Everyone was pretty excited and a little nervous because they wanted everything to go all right and according to plan. But nobody was more excited and nervous than Richie, the fire fighter from Rescue One who was part of the detail. Richie was concerned because his plan was slightly different from anyone else's. He understood the tremendous impact of the Pope's visit and how much it would mean to the average Catholic even to catch a glimpse of this great spiritual leader in person. And if you were lucky enough to squeeze onto the Common and witness the Mass first hand, it would be really sumthin'.

But supposin', just supposin', that ya received Holy Communion directly from the Pope! Why it would be almost like a miracle. If a guy could pull that off, he'd not only become a respected member of the community, he'd probably go right to heaven when he died. In Richie's case, these two achievements would be a real miracle.

The Pope was going to give out Communion, but in Boston, as in every other place during his visit, it would only be to a small number of people. They'd be some politicians, no way around that, and some of the military and some nuns and some retarded kids. Nobody complained about the nuns and kids, everybody complained about the pols, but what could ya do?

Richie was stationed down below throughout the long afternoon waiting for the Pope but he was to move up to the altar with the big line during the Mass. He was gonna be right near the Communion line when it formed and he figured he could jump right in, but he was gonna need an edge. If he could get friendly with one of the cardinals maybe he could figure out a deal.

He spent the afternoon talking to them along with the other guys and found out they were pretty friendly. One in particular, Cardinal Krol from Philly, was a great guy. He was interested in Boston and the fire department and spent a lot of time discussing both with Richie. Shortly before the Pope arrived, Richie asked him for a favor and he agreed to the request.

Richie was moved up to his position at the altar, and finally the dignitaries started coming up the stairway. As the cardinals came up, they passed by the line of those who had been chosen to receive Communion. Cardinal Krol was near the end of the line and as he came abreast of Richie he said in a loud voice, "Why Richie, how are you, are you still on Rescue One?" He crossed over and shook Richie's hand and returned to the line with Richie trailing behind him.

Zing, right into the Communion line he went between a soldier and a sailor. He figured the Secret Service guys would know he was a friend of Cardinal Krol, and besides, they could see he was in uniform. He stayed in the line throughout the Mass, head bent and deep in prayer. Actually, no one looked better or more pious than Richie.

Finally, it was time to receive Communion and the line started moving forward. Richie clasped his gloved hands together and kept pace, eyes now raised to Heaven. As he started to ascend the stairs, he felt two huge hands grab his shoulders and he was pulled out of line. He turned to see a very perturbed Secret Service man staring into his eyes. "Hey, fireman, you're the guy we've been looking for."

"What's the matter? My friend Cardinal Krol from Philly fixed me up."

"Listen, you jerk, you screwed up the count. There's only so many in each city get Communion and we were one over. We've been checking the line all during Mass, and I gotta admit, you almost fooled us with that Mickey Mouse suit you got on. Now get back where you belong and shut up or I'll charge you with violation of a federal law, ya got that?"

"Yessir," said Richie and he moved back to his post and was quiet for the rest of the Mass.

He was really crestfallen. He had told everyone on the company he was gonna get Communion and he had failed. He knew they were all watching on TV so he couldn't even lie about it. Well, he had come close. He had his head hung down for quite awhile, but as he was looking down, he got an idea. Hm, wait till it's all over, then try plan number two. It was sure to work. Yeah. If you couldn't get Communion from the Pope, what was the next best thing? Why, a piece of the carpet from the altar. After all, it was blessed and the Pope himself walked right on it, didn't he?

When the Mass was over and the crowds were dispersing, Richie made his move while the rest of the detailed guys were making up the line. He cut off several pieces of the rug and tucked them inside his coat. When everything was made up, they were dismissed and Richie returned to the station.

As soon as he came in the kitchen, everyone started yelling at him, "Hey Richie, big deal, ya were gonna get Communion. We watched the whole thing on TV and ya never made it.

"Of course I didn't, ya dummies. I had it all set up with my pal, Cardinal Krol from Philly. I was right in line and everything. But, did ya see those beautiful little retarded kids? "

"Yeah, what about them?"

"Well, one of them got pushed aside by the crowd and I saw him standing there. He couldn't tell no one, so I gave him my place."

They looked at him suspiciously.

"Besides, I got something just as good, and I brought you each a piece."

He showed them the carpet. "The Pope actually walked on this carpet. This is right off the altar he said Mass on."

"Jeez, Richie, that's pretty good, howja get them?"

"I cut it right off the altar after everyone left."

"Ya mean no one gave it to ya? That's stealing, Richie. Ya stole right from the Pope."

"No I didn't. Don't ya know it's blessed. It ain't stealin' if you're a Catholic and it's blessed, don'cha know that?"

"Richie," said one guy, "with that kind of logic, it's a good thing ya didn't get Communion. If ya did the Pope's hand would have fallen off."

"Naw it wouldn't," said Richie, "he gave it to the Mayor and all those other pols and nothin' happened to him, did it?"

Richie was not the only one to get a piece of the red carpet. As a matter of fact, it all disappeared. Not only from the altar, but from the airport, the Cardinal's residence in Brighton and any place else it was spread. A rather brisk business developed selling pieces of the sacred rug. It did so well that even some non-catholic businessmen had it for sale.

If the truth were to be known, not all of it was present on the day the Pope was here, and of course, that stuff wasn't even blessed. Richie was really shocked. He never sold one piece of the carpet he had appropriated. After all you have to draw the line somewhere. Most Catholic homes in Boston now have a piece of red carpet tucked away. It spread almost like the loaves and the fishes in the Gospel. It is extremely difficult to tell by looking whether a piece is blessed or not. As someone said, "If the Pope had actually walked on all that carpet, he'd have qualified for the Boston Marathon."

Yeah,
The Roof
Still Leaks

In June, 1960 a new fire house was opened at 700 Tremont Street in the South End. Its purpose was to centralize protection in the area and close two ancient stations, eliminating one fire company and moving another one to Dorchester. Engine 22 and Ladder 13 were the new occupants, and the combining of two houses into one in such an active fire area made them the busiest companies in the city.

The South End is densely populated and lined with multi-storied apartment houses. The move helped increase protection in the increasingly active three-decker Dorchester section.

The fire house itself is a one-story structure erected by the low bid contractor in the best city hall tradition. It started at the same time as the Traveler's Insurance Building, a fourteen-story high rise, downtown. But the Travelers was occupied long before the fire house, which took over three years to build. When they finally got in, the first time it rained, water could be heard running from the roof down inside the walls. The heater was cranky and the first winter the main floor remained a nice, chill thirty-eight degrees for weeks at a time. The automatic generator never was automatic, the stove and refrigerator never worked right and the plumbing always leaked. The best that money could buy. These types of things can be adjusted to, but during that first week, three guys' cars were stolen from the back yard and ya can't put up with that. The only thing a guy has of value with him in work, other than himself, is his car, and the city ain't gonna pay if it's stolen. The captain wisely, he thought, had flood lights erected in the yard so the thieves would be thwarted. But when they returned from a fire one night, everyone's batteries were gone and the crooks were grateful for the good light to work by. Finally, permission was received from headquarters to move the apparatus over and let the on-duty members park in the house and it's been that way ever since.

The conclusion may be drawn that it was not the best neighborhood in the city and that is correct. Across the street from the station were the three toughest joints in town, the State Cafe, the Handy Cafe and the Universal. The drug store on the corner sold booze on Sundays and anything else illegal that was available. The druggist was a cheerful guy who only got pissed off if you asked him to fill a prescription: he couldn't be bothered with that shit, he was too busy. Next door to the fire house was a block of five-story apartment houses. The first one was a whore house and the hookers were all black. The next joint was all winos and the corner was filled with black gays, or fags as they were called before the closets started emptying out in the seventies.

On the other side of the fire house was Concord Street and the city erected a nice flagpole on the corner with a little patch of grass around it, to satisfy the esthetic and patriotic tastes. The whores, being art lovers as well as great Americans, loved it. The pole was a nice place to hang out and sell your wares and it was a fine mark of identification for the "white hunters" who cruised the area every night. "Yeah, if you wanna get your pipes cleaned, go up Tremont till ya see the flagpole and turn left." Across Concord Street was a beautiful Protestant church and that poor minister had his work cut out for him. He had a missionary's zeal, though, and kept tryin'. There were enough prodigal sons and daughters in the area to fill the church but not many returned to the fold.

While most of the gang that frequented the joints across the street were about as low a class of poor blacks as you could find, there were several hardworking black families that were trying to make a go of things and raise the kids right, but it was pretty tough around there. The kids never harassed the jakes in those days but in the mid-sixties everything changed and it's never been the same since. When they moved in the first day, the captain was in the kitchen. He could see two little black kids peeking in the window and he could hear them talking.

"Who's that dude in the white shirt?"

"He's the cook."

"Cook? No, yo shittin' me."

"No, I'm tellin' ya, the ones in the white is the cooks, the other guys is the fire fighters."

"Man, thass what I gonna be when I grows up. The cops ain't got no cooks."

Later in the day, he was out near the patrol desk and he saw a middle-aged black guy filling up a bucket full of water inside the front door. Oh, oh, I better nip this in the bud or the whole neighborhood will be in and out all the time. "Hey, mister, whatcha doin', you're not allowed in here, this is a fire house."

"Sheet, man, I'se the Mayor 'round here. I run this place. Besides, I just got done sweepin' you gutter," and he pointed to the pile of broken bottles at the curb.

"He's right, Cap," said the guy on patrol, "I watched him do it."

"Sure, I'se just protectin' ya. See them animals, across the street, they always put bottles along the gutter. When the fight start, they break 'em and start cuttin' each other up. I'm keepin' your side clean."

As time went on, the Mayor and the Captain became great friends. He really did run the area. At least in the day. He got some reflective belt straps from the cops and crossed the school kids every day, long before the city hired school crossing guards. He was a disabled vet and lived on his pension, although his wife Mildred worked in a department store in town. In the summer time, he and his gang of pensioners used to make up some kind of punch with cheap booze and sell it in the vacant lot across the street. If business was good, the Mayor would be coming over for more water all day long to make the punch go a little further. They also used to cook ribs and sell them. One day they got caught swiping some sides of beef off a truck making a delivery to the Handy Cafe and they ran like hell up Concord Square with the driver in hot pursuit.

The captain was always grateful for the announcement the Mayor made to the men on the first day the House opened. "Boys," he said, "I know you whities may be tempted by those beautiful black chicks next door, but let me tell ya, every one of them got that bad ass disease. If ya touch them, your dick will drop off." The captain figured this one warning had saved him a lot of trouble through the years, and anything the Mayor wanted he could have.

While the Mayor was in charge in the day, a different element took over at night. It was really wild. The first summer there were three murders across the street and a number of stabbings and muggings. The fire house became a beacon for help if you got hurt. So many victims staggered in that someone put a sign on the patrol desk that said, "Doctors' Office Hours, 2 to 4 a.m., stabbings and shootings a specialty. For abortions, visit Engine 3 on Harrison Avenue."

The hookers on the corner were a pain in the ass until you got used to them. They were right outside the Captain's window and he could hear the dickering going on every night. After a while you could ignore it, but at first it used to drive him nuts. He was trying to study for chief and they'd be yelling and screaming at the white hunters. One night he had enough. The going rate at the time was twenty bucks, but Lizbeth was asking twenty-five, 'cause she knew this dude was not a regular customer. He was only offering fifteen and it looked like they'd be arguing all night. She was saying, "If that's all yo payin', go down to the alley and see Twinkletoes; he a fag and he take good care of ya, but yo wan' Lizabeth, it gonna cost ya twentyfi', ya hear?"

"C'mon, baby, no one gets twenty-five around here; besides, I'm the best hump you'll ever have."

"Sheet, you only a white ass, you muthas don't even know where to put it. You think I'm some cheap whore?"

Finally, the captain raised the blind. "Lizbeth, will you for cripes sake shut up, I'm trying to study. If you can't make a deal with that asshole, I'll pay the difference. Just take him next door and roll him or do whatever the fuck you do and leave me alone."

"O.K., O.K., Cap'n. But you ain't shittin' me. You firemens is all cheap muthas, you won't give me nuthin."

He reached in his pocket and said, "Here, take this." He handed her a fin and off she went.

As the years passed, the stuff that went on became like old hat so you hardly noticed it. But not to Bill, though. He was the lieutenant on the engine and he worked the same shifts with the captain, all the time. He knew everything that went on and enjoyed every minute of it. He got to learn all the hookers' names and was always questioning them about the performance of their marks. He had names for every fag in the corner house and was an expert on the white hunters. He claimed that no one had ever lasted in the house next door more than nine minutes. He'd sit on the bench out front in the summer and if a hooker he knew came by he'd ask for an in depth report. Once he saw an Oriental guy coming out of the house followed by Agnes. As she came by he said, "Hey Agnes, how was that guy?"

"Whaddya mean how was he, just another dude is all."

"Yeah but he was Chinese. Was he any different?"

"Chink? No shit. I never even looks at they face, long as they pays, baby."

One night when business was really brisk, the whore house was so busy that there was no room at the inn. So, the hookers were hustling the johns into the alley behind the fire house and taking care of them in their cars. When Bill saw that, he couldn't wait. He copied down the license plate of one guy as he drove into the yard. Bill then called the Registry of Motor Vehicles and gave the special code word that the department uses for identification purposes at auto fires. When he got what he wanted, he raced for the kitchen which was in darkness. He peered out through the blinds and at the moment of truth, so to speak, he yelled, "Hey, Fred, how's everything in Peabody?" Poor Fred must have ruptured himself, jumping up, pushing the girl out and starting the car. He careened out the other side of the alley, crunching one of his fenders on a light pole.

Bill was also a great favorite with the kids. He looked a lot like a popular TV character called Uncle Martin on the show, "My Favorite Martian." When the kids asked if he was him, he never denied it, and it was pretty cute to see all the little guys staring at him while he stood there, arms folded, looking like he came from Mars. He also became a bit of a marriage counselor and would give advice to the lovelorn or anyone else who sought help. His most perplexing case was with the Mayor and his charming missus, Mildred. They had a bitch of an argument one day and it continued as they were passing the fire house. As they passed Bill, he held out his hands in supplication, "Wait a minute, wait a minute, what's going on here?"

"You mind yo business, Bill," said Mildred.

"She really pissed at me, man," said the Mayor.

"Yeah, he spen' all his pension check and I got nuffin. I'm all through, I ain't workin', I ain't cookin', and I ain't fuckin' no more!"

"Mildred, Mildred dear, you can't do that. You're destroying the three most basic principles of a happy marriage," said the peacemaker. "How can you expect the Mayor to survive under such conditions?"

"You shut you mouff, Bill, you just as big a asshole as my man. I hope your wife shut you off too," and she stormed up the street.

There was a great lady in the neighborhood named Gladys. She was a middle aged black who lived with her husband and daughter on Mass. Ave. From the first day, she befriended everyone in the house and she knew whose wife was expecting, who was getting married, etc. Every New Year's Eve she'd stop by at midnight and kiss everyone she could catch. She used to go to the Firemen's Ball every year and someone always made sure she got home all right. She'd also show up at every wake when someone died. Really a great lady.

But things change, and the mid-sixties were a turning point. The Watts riots started a period that saw trouble in all the major cities across the country with a deterioration in the relationship between the black communities and the establishment. The books have all been written analyzing why it happened but the fire fighters never figured it out. In June, 1967 the Six Day War took place in Israel, but Boston had its own little war going on at the same time. Riots took place in Dorchester and Roxbury and the department had a tough time with one officer shot and several fire fighters injured. The trouble that took place the following year when Martin Luther King was assassinated added to the problem, and things have never really been the same. Fire fighters have been the target of a lot of abuse since then and it still continues. But you just do the job and accept it, like so many things in life. The change resulted in some big losses though. When the busing started in 1974, the alienation of the two groups was complete.

One of the saddest days for the captain was when his father died. At the wake he received a telephone call at the funeral parlor. When he answered, it was Gladys. "Er, Captain, I'm very sorry to learn about your father. I'd like to come to the wake, but I'm all tied up this week. But I wanted to express my condolences."

After he got done thanking her and hung up, he turned to his wife. "That was Gladys, she says she can't make it because she's tied up." He knew, though, that the reason she couldn't come was because his part of town was not safe for blacks, just as her part wasn't safe for him.

The house provided a charmed life for the fire fighters for its first decade or so. Fire fighters get killed in Boston unfortunately, but none came from the house, although they went to thousands and thousands of fires. It was always a guy from 3 or 15 or some other house who paid the penalty. But on June 17,1972, the luck finally ran out. Nine Boston fire fighters were killed at the Hotel Vendome on that day, in the most tragic fire the department had ever had. Five of them were from the house on Tremont Street.

Oh, it's still a busy place, and they go to plenty of fires, but the neighborhood has changed dramatically. The joints across the street are gone and so is the whore house and the gays' place. Yes, and the Mayor and Mildred disappeared too. All in all, kinda dull, except when they go to fires. The new young officers probably wouldn't know how to fix a gunshot wound or settle a dispute for the hookers, and they get no advice from anyone like the Mayor, but they're just as good as fire fighters and they're a lot more adept at ducking rocks. Oh, yeah, you can still hear water running in the walls.

...And
Justice
For
All

The district chief's aide was all smiles. Their regular chief's car was back in service. It had been gone for a month getting repaired after some idiot had plowed into it at a fire. The jerk had driven right through the fire lines, hit the car, bounced off a ladder truck and kept going.

It wasn't so much that it was a great car or anythin'. It was the piece of shit they had been given as a replacement that he was glad to see gone. It had an oil leak that was continuous. Every day, you added a coupla quarts and then cleaned the floor of the garage. But the regular car was back. I'm gonna pull it out on the street and scrub the shit outta the floor with sulpha naphthol. He pulled the car out onto the apron and went to work with the disinfectant, a hose and a scrubbing brush, whistling all the time.

Pete had just been through a difficult night. He had gone paycheck in hand, to the Combat Zone, downtown, which is lined with joints featuring nude reviews and real college girl strippers and hostesses, or at least that's what the ads say. He figured he'd hoist a few, watch a skin show and then see if he could get lucky with one of the charming professionals that tour La Grange Street.

But it hadn't gone according to plan. Oh, he saw the show, and he had a few too. Then he had a few more and a few more and by the time he staggered along Washington Street and started his hunt, he was pretty well gone. He vaguely remembered being asked if he "Wanna go out, baby" and slipping his arm around one of the girls, but the next thing he knew he was waking up in the parking lot off La Grange, and he was lying between two parked cars. He could feel a lump on his head and dried blood over one eye and he felt like a shithouse. His skull was throbbing. He checked his pants and yeah, he knew it, his wallet and dough were gone. He checked his underwear and felt certain his sexual needs hadn't been satisfied but he no longer cared about that.

God, Pete, you're an asshole. He pulled himself up and stumbled down to Washington and went in a joint for some coffee. He shudda known better, he thought. This wasn't the first time he got rolled down here. Now he's wiped out for the week. What the hell time is it? Jeez, eight o'clock. Well, at least it's Sattiday, no work. He's sick of the goddamn job anyway, but his parole officer insists he keep at it or he goes back to the joint.

He finished the coffee and started toward the South End, stopping to throw up as he got near Broadway. Boy, I'm still bombed, he thought, turning the corner. I'd grab a cab but I got nuthin'. Hey, they's a car on the damn sidewalk with the motor runnin'. Hm, nobody 'round. Think I'll just sneak into it and get home quick. He quietly opened the door of the chief's car and put it in drive. The aide heard the sound of the car moving and spun around.

"Hey, hey, where the hell ya goin'? Come back." He could see the guy behind the wheel was a civilian and he raced for the patrol desk. "Call Fire Alarm, someone just stole the fucking car!"

About two miles away, the chief in District Four was starting to type his morning report when the phone rang. "Yeah, District Four," he answered.

"Chief, this is Fire Alarm. Someone just stole Car Twelve and we think he's headed your way. Will you see if you can find him and follow him?"

"Sure, I'm on my way." He ran for his car, shouting for his aide.

As they drove out the doorway, the aide said, "Which way? "

Good question. "Jeez, I don't really know. Let's head over towards Columbus Ave. and keep our eyes open."

They went up Concord Square and just as they reached Columbus, the department radio squeaked, "Hello, hello, fire department. This is a police officer. I have a fire department vehicle at Mass. Ave. and Columbus."

Great. Car Four swung left and sped toward the intersection. When they arrived, they could see Car Twelve, the police officer seated in the front seat. He was starting to pull it over because it had traffic blocked. He pointed west toward the continuation of Columbus. "The guy ran up that way."

"O.K.," shouted the chief, "Let's go."

Wait a minute, he thought. What is this? A role reversal deal. He's the cop ain't he? But they kept going along Columbus, creeping along, looking at both sides of the street, but no one was in sight.

Pete was crouched down beside a parked car, scared shitless.

As he had driven off in the car, everything was goin' along O.K. when he suddenly hears some talking on the radio. Jeez, what kinda radio is that? Holy Jeesus, I think I stole a fire car. He sped up the street, turned left and tore along Columbus Ave. As he was moving his head started to clear. Hey, I gotta dump this thing, they'll shoot me for crissakes. He jumped out at Columbus and ran. But he couldn't run far, he was really dizzy, so he dropped down behind a car.

Oh, shit, here comes another fire car. I think they see me. He got up and started running again.

"There he goes, stop the car." The chief jumped out and started running after Pete and his aide pulled over and followed him. As he was puffing down the street, the chief was thinking, what the fuck am I doin' now? This guy looks like a big bastid. He'll kick the shit outta me if I catch him.

Suddenly, Pete ran up a long flight of stairs leading into an apartment house. The chief got to the bottom and started up gingerly.

Pete tried to open the door but it was locked. He turned around, raised his hands up and clenched them into fists. God, he looks like a monster, thought the chief. Where the hell is Moe? He looked back and could see his aide coming a half block away. Oh well, at least he's comin', and the chief continued up the stairs. As he neared the thief, ready for a kick in the face or anything else and scared to death, Pete bent over, threw his hands over his head and shouted, "Please, don't hit me, I surrender."

Whew, what a relief. I thought the sumbitch was gonna eat me. "Don't move, don't move now, you're under arrest." Can I arrest him? Who knows. "Get the cop," he yelled back to his aide, "and get on the air for more cops."

Since it was Saturday morning and the courts were open, Pete was taken right in by the cops. Do you want a lawyer? No sir. A positive identification was made by the aide who was in the garage. How do you plead? This judge is real law and order. Guilty, your honor. Do you realize what you have done? You stole a fire car. What if there was a fire and someone died because the chief wasn't there? What then, huh? I'm sorry, your honor. Well, you're gonna be a lot sorrier. Six months, Deer Island House of Correction. This is based on the seriousness of the offense and your past record. We will also contact your parole officer. Take him away.

November 5, 1971. Ladder 30 responded to the box down Columbus Avenue from the Egleston Square Station. It was 1900 hours. This box was quite often a false alarm, one of the 15,000 pulled every year in the city at that time. False alarms represented 25% of the total alarms. They were pulled by all types, ranging from little kids who had to be raised up to the fire box by their brothers to half-baked nitwits of all ages: whites, blacks, blues, greens. It was something that was done, period.

Whenever a puller was apprehended, the reasons given were interesting and showed real intelligence: "I dunno, I always pull it," or, "My brother told me to do it," or, "Gotta get whitey," or "Aw, them assholes is jus sleepin' anyhow."

The eighties look a little more promising, at least as far as false alarms are concerned. The department has removed a lot of the most frequently pulled boxes, but also society seems to be changing a little. No, not improving, just changing. Kids who used to pull false alarms are now involved in different activities such as sex orgies, sniffin' coke, mugging, raping and killing each other. It's a hell of a lot more sophisticated.

But as Ladder 30 turned into Heath Street on that night, Fire Fighter James Doneghey reached up to grab the helmet which was slipping from his head, and as the truck swung he was catapulted into the street from the running board. He landed with a sickening crunch. He was rushed to the hospital but his injuries were very severe and his prognosis was poor. By the next day, it was obvious he wasn't going to make it and everyone was bullshit. He was not the first jake in Boston who would die from a false alarm and he wasn't going to be the last, either. What a waste. Nobody wanted to get killed on the job, but at least if it's at a fire, it's accepted as part of the business. You're just as dead either way, but for a shitty false alarm, ugh.

When the chief in District Four arrived in for the next night tour, he was just as pissed off as everyone else. Damn it! Another good guy gonna die. Well, he couldn't help him now but maybe he could do something for the guys in his own district. They had their share of false alarms, sure. But the two worst boxes were always pulled about three or four in the morning. They were a coupla blocks apart and were on the line between the South End and Downtown. Everyone figured it was probably some baker who hated jakes. Who the hell else was going to work at that hour?

Well, we'll catch the sumbitch. He circled his district, looking for volunteers in each station and he was overwhelmed by the response. He called the deputy and got permission to implement his plan. He would hide a guy near each of the boxes and give each a portable radio. If someone pulled one, just call it in and follow the guy. Don't try to grab him, he may punch your head in. Keep following and reporting and we'll be on the way. He alerted the cops to the plan too, and they agreed to cooperate. The men at the boxes would be relieved every hour by other volunteers. Great. Hope the sumbitch pulls one tonight. The only snag that developed was that only one portable was available. Well, give it to the guy at Box 1482, that's the one he usually pulls. Tell the other kid at 1516 that if he sees it pulled, run down and get the guy with the portable, O.K.? Yeah.

The volunteers started at midnight, just in case. It was really a busy night in the district. Box after box. A coupla building fires, three autos, rubbish fires, accidents and even some false alarms, but not from the boxes being watched. Aw, shit, thought the chief. It's after four now, the bastid is probably startin' to bake jelly doughnuts by now. He was returning down Tremont Street from an auto accident, figuring, well, it might take a few nights, but we got plenty of guys to do the job.

Fire Alarm called on the radio. "Car Four, he just hit 1516."

Great. "Strike it, strike it." Better have plenty of help there, he thought as his aide jammed the accelerator to the floor. They pulled up at the box and there was no one there. He switched to channel two on the radio and called the kid at Box 1482. "Where's Eddie?"

"He's at 1516, Chief."

"No, I'm at 1516, didn't he come and get ya?"

"I ain't seen him yet."

Where the hell is he? He's probably followin' that baker. Let's see, where's the closest bakery? Yeah, down Washington; we'll go that way.

Eddie was indeed following the guy, but he was really moving. He couldn't go get the man with the portable or he'd have lost this nut. And he looked like a nut. Filthy, bearded, clothes all disheveled. And big. About six three. Better not get too close.

Jeez, there's another fire alarm box up the street. Wonder if he'll hit it. Yeah, he's heading right for it. Gotta try and grab him. The chief said not to but he's gonna get away if I don't give it a try. He just pulled the hook!

Eddie ran up and shouted, "Stay right there, you're under arrest."

Just then a police car, blue lights flashing, pulled up. The chief got another call from Fire Alarm. "He just pulled 1622."

"O.K., we're on the way." Shit, wrong direction. When he arrived at the box, the police had the guy in cuffs and Eddie explained why he hadda keep following him. "Well, you did a great job, but he could a shot you or anything. It ain't worth getting hurt over."

When his relief arrived in the morning, the chief told him they finally got the guy who was pulling 1482 and 1516 all the time and no, it wasn't a baker. "We probably should apologize to all those bakers we been blamin' the last coupla years.

"Yeah, those poor guys got it tough enough gettin' in so early," said his relief.

"Lissen, I just heard some bad news. Jimmy Doneghey of Ladder 30 died last night. There was just no way they could save him, I guess."

Boy, I hope the judge reads the paper when we get this clown up there.

The next morning the chief went into court with Eddie and the arresting officer. The news about Fire Fighter Doneghey had been on the front page. A tall, nice looking man in his late twenties, clean shaven and dressed in a new blue suit, sat in the front row on the bench with an elderly woman seated beside him.

"Who's that guy?" said the chief to the assistant D.A.

"That's the guy you bagged at the false alarm."

"You gotta be shittin'."

"No, that's him all right and that's his mother with him."

When the judge called the case, the arresting officer went on first, then Eddie and then the chief with the Fire Alarm records. He had seen the man's arrest sheet and this was his third time in court for false alarms. He mentioned the fact that the fire fighter had just died from a false alarm but the judge cut him off. "That is inadmissible here and has no bearing on this case."

"But your honor, he's not the first man we lost — "

"Chief, you are dismissed."

"But I just — "

"If you don't step down, I'll hold you in contempt."

The guy's mother was on next and she related what a nice son he was and how well he took care of her, and the judge listened with a sympathetic ear.

"Lissen," the chief said to the assistant D.A., "This bum has been pullin' those boxes for two years. I know he's not to blame for the guy we had killed, but dammit, he's liable to kill someone else."

"Yeah, I know it, chief, but that sweet little old lady is charming the pants off His Honor."

Finally, the judge made his ruling. He gave the guy a stern talking to and placed his case on file. One more time and he'd be in serious trouble.

As the chief stormed out of court, he said over his shoulder to the D.A., "That's the last fucking time you'll see us up here. Next time we'll take care of it ourselves." The judge took his glasses off and looked down the aisle.

"Order in this court room. This is not a circus. This is the house of the law where justice is served. Silence."

Yeah.

Stay In The City, Boys, The Santa Ana's In California

S pectacle Island is one of the many islands that dot Boston Harbor. It is uninhabited now, but in the fifties it was populated by the custodian of the city dump and his family, and an army of rats, mice, flies, cockroaches, water bugs and fleas. The custodian and his missus and kids lived in a nice house near the dock; the rest of the gang lived in the garbage that was delivered daily in the barges. The garbage piles were the same height as the hill on the Island. On top of the hill, at one end, were two lighthouses, one that worked automatically and one that was inoperative. Dumps have been eliminated in recent years in the city but in those days, pre-environmentalist times, Boston had a few, including the Island.

Dumps were always burning. Fires are started deep in the piles by spontaneous ignition. There was always a haze of smoke over dumps but no one ever minded as long as it wasn't too bad. Occasionally though, the fire would break out of the pile and spread, creating foul smelling clouds of dense black smoke. In the case of Spectacle Island, or "Speckie," as it's called, if the fire broke out, the smoke would go toward Long Island in one direction. Long Island is the site of a city operated hospital for elderly poor people. In the other direction was Logan International Airport. When the smoke got bad enough, the fire department was called, either by the hospital staff or the control tower. The department would dispatch fire companies and they would be transported by fire boat. When they arrived, the boat would pump into a standpipe that extended up the hill for the purpose. The companies would carry donut rolls up the hill, make connections and play into the piles of garbage. The purpose was to quiet the fire down as much as possible to dissipate the smoke, so the patients and the pilots would be happy. It was not expected that the fire could be put out.

July 4th, 1955 was a beautiful day: the temperature in the mid-eighties, the humidity low and the beaches already starting to get crowded with families. Castle Island is a favorite spot in the city on such a day. It is connected to the eastern end of South Boston by a filled in road and is separated from Speckie by a half mile wide channel. There are barbecue pits, playgrounds and beaches. You can drive out there with the kids, bring a lunch, stake a claim on a barbecue pit and picnic bench — if you're early enough — point the kids toward the beach and stretch out in your beach chair, can of beer in hand. You've got it made and it costs you zero. Ah, utopia! On this day, though, the arriving citizens could see that heavy smoke was coming from Speckie and since the breeze was from the southeast, all kinds of shit was falling out of the sky on the tables, pits and beaches.

"Hey, what the fuck is this?"

"Don't they know this is a holiday?"

"This is my only day off."

"Where's them asshole firemen, they gonna ruin our picanick if they don' put out the fire."

The firemen, minus the descriptive adjective, were on the way. Fire Alarm had already been called by the Logan Tower and the hospital, and now by an increasing number of irate taxpayers who were attempting to celebrate the country's one hundred seventy-ninth birthday in the American way.

The two jakes from the nearest truck company jumped off at the fire boat dock and lugged their masks, boots, coats, hats and tools over to the edge of the wharf and handed them down to the crew.

"How come he wants us to take all this shit?" said one.

"Well, he's been a lieutenant so long he's gettin' real crotchety, but he insisted on the boots."

"Yeah, but for cripes sake, it's on an island, ain't it?"

"Hey, you guys," yelled the lieutenant, "knock off the bull and get aboard. This isn't a pleasure cruise."

As they chugged down the harbor, though, it was almost as nice as a cruise. God, it was beautiful out. Sunshine, nice breeze.

Glad I'm not down duck like those no supper guys. "Duck" is the Deer Island House of Correction off to the left in the harbor where most of the nonsupport guys are sent by the dear woman till normal payments are forthcoming.

"Boy, lookit all the cars parked at Castle Island already, gonna be mobbed. If the guys down duck hadda taken the family to Cassie more often, maybe they wouldn't be doin' time."

"Yeah, maybe some of them would rather do the time, dja think? "

"Jeez, take a look where we're goin'. Gonna be a long day."

They could now see Speckie and it was pretty discouraging. The heavy smoke was pierced by long tongues of flame, leaping skyward.

"What time is it, anyway?"

"Oh, oh, only nine-thirty. Hope my relief gets in early, cause we'll still be here whatever time he gets in."

As they pulled into the dock, the lieutenant gave them their instructions. "Get a sixteen foot ladder from the boat. Pile three donut rolls on it and take a pipe. Four guys on the ladder. Carry it up the hill and I'll show you where to connect the line. Pull your boots up. Bring your coats and hats with ya, but ya don't have to put them on yet."

When they were ready, they started the long climb, keeping beside the standpipe all the way up. They could see water weeping from the joints in the pipe and they knew the fire boat was pumping into it. The lieutenant had them drop the ladder and connect the hose, just below the worst part of the fire in the garbage. They started hitting it with the heavy stream and they were followed by two other companies who made the same kind of connections.

They knew now why he wanted them to have their boots on. On the way up they had waded through rats that were gathered below the fire, squealing and screaming. One had even got in the top of one guy's boot and the guy almost shit. He kept whacking it until it was dead. After that, boy, everyone had the boots up as high as they'd go. There weren't too many up near the fire, but there were plenty of bugs. They'd keep crawling up your boot and you kept brushing them off.

They started to knock a lot of the fire down and one company started advancing toward the center of the pile.

"Ya want us to start movin' in too, Luft?"

"No, stay here and keep that ladder handy. I told that captain not to walk on that shit."

He no sooner got done talking than they heard a yell. A coupla guys were starting to sink into the pile.

"Hey! Hey! give us a lift! There's fire underneath us!"

The lieutenant had them slide the straight ladder across to the two men and pull them out and they all returned to the hill.

"See," he told his own crew, "This stuff is very treacherous. Couple guys got really hurt out in West Roxbury years ago. One guy lost his foot from the burns. The fire is burning continuously underneath, undermining the pile. The only way to really put one out is to get a crane, pull it apart, put it out and then use solid fill to mix it with. But that ain't gonna happen here, so do what I tell ya."

"Yessir, Luft."

The battle went on until the late morning. They could see a small Coast Guard boat pull into the dock. It carried the district chief of their district. He hadn't responded with them because he was at a building fire downtown, but here he came now with rapid strides, up the hill.

"Oh, oh, here comes 'wonder boy,' prepare to do hand stands."

The chief coming toward them was brand new. He had just been transferred downtown after his promotion. He came from a fire company out in Hyde Park, or out in the woods as it was called. He was pretty young for the rank, but he had been near the top of each promotional exam. But God, he was so eager. He gave orders with machine gun rapidity and always seemed to know what he was doing, although he hadn't been around long enough yet for people to see just how sharp he was.

The chief took a brief look at the fire and nodded to the lieutenant, "Come with me Luft," and he headed up past the fire, following the standpipe to the top of the hill. At the top, the hill was overgrown with yellowish grass about three feet high. It extended across the top and over to the two lighthouses about five hundred yards away. "Lute, I want you to move two lines up to the top outlets below the hill. This fire is going to extend up and catch the grass. The way the wind is blowing it will endanger the light-houses. I'm going to set a backfire up here and make a fire break. We've gotta protect the lighthouses."

"Jeez, Chief, a backfire? I never seen one of them."

"Yes, we used them a few times out in District Ten during the grass fire season. They use them in California during the Santa Ana every year."

"What's a Santa Ana?"

"Why, don't ya ever read about them? That's a wind that blows out from the desert that's very dry. They have bad brush fires out there that destroy homes and thousands of acres.

"Yeah, but, wouldn't it be better to just bring up a line and keep soaking down the grass?"

"No, no, get the lines up."

When the lines were in position about a hundred yards away from the pile and below the top of the hill, the order was given to start soaking the grass opposite them. The backfire would be set and as it worked toward them, the area they were soaking down would help them to cut it off. Theoretically, this would then give a hundred yard burned out area as a break to stop the fire from trav-eling toward the lighthouses.

"Whaddya think, Luft?" the lieutenant was asked.

"Well, I dunno. I never saw this before. If it works, it's great. I just hope we have enough of a punch with these lines to cut it off. Pay attention, though. This guy's quite a student and you guys are studying yourselves. We might all learn somethin'." As the fire crept toward them, it seemed to be going well; the break was get-ting wider and wider. When it was about twenty-five yards away, the wind suddenly picked up. The fire started speeding rapidly across the top. "Keep the line goin', keep wettin' it down," shouted the lieutenant, but it was really going like a freight train now. It roared up to the soaked area and leaped across, racing through the dry grass and straight toward the lighthouses. In a few minutes, they were both fully involved and in about a half hour, one of them fell over. It kinda looked like an Indian village after the cavalry got through with it. No wonder they were pissed off at Custer if their teepees ended up looking like the two lighthouses.

They returned to the garbage piles with the lines and kept hitting the fire all afternoon. About four o'clock, black clouds moved in from the west, the wind shifted and a big thunderstorm struck. It rained about a half inch in the next hour. So much so that the fire was knocked down to a point where they could be dismissed. The district chief had been pretty subdued since the incident at the top, particularly when the house fell over. As they reached the fire boat with all their gear, one of the Coast Guardsmen on the little cutter hollered over, "Chief, the Commandant is on the radio. He wants to know what happened to his lighthouses."

"Er, tell him I'll call him when I get back, willya?"

When the two jakes got back to their station, their reliefs were waiting for them. "Hey, howja make out? You two students learn anything fighting fires in piles of shit?"

"Yeah, funny ya should ask," one of them replied. "First of all, that old lieutenant ain't as dumb as we thought. On the other hand, we're gonna keep in the books. We're gonna be district chiefs. At least we could burn down two lighthouses as good as 'wonder boy' can."

Castle Island was abandoned. The smoke had kept coming all day and ashes and other debris kept falling in the potato salad and yeah, the kids were in swimming all right, but every time they came lookin' for somethin' to eat, here came more shit from the sky. At last, though, it started to clear up and back to the grill with the burgers and dogs. Before they were cooked though, it started rainin' like a sumbitch and ruined everything. Those fucking firemen really screwed up this holiday. Wait 'till they're on the ballot for a raise or sumpthin', I'll lean on that "No" lever till I break it.

Tragedy On Pembroke Street: Ya Gotta Have Fire Engines

The house gong sounded at 0235 hours and the district chief rolled out of bed and into his hitch. As he moved toward the door, pulling up his pants, he heard the announcement over the PA system, "22 and 13 to a church fire, Northampton and Tremont." The chief slowed down. The alarm was for the engine and the truck, but it was over the district line in Five and he wouldn't respond. He could hear the box being struck over the tapper system as the two companies went out the doors and swung left. Hm, church. Well, I hope they haven't got much there. Churches are great for praying, but they're a bitch for fires.

As he started back toward the bed, another alarm started striking on the tapper. He counted, one-five-five-six. That's mine, he thought, and he walked out of the door toward his car. His aide said, "Warren Ave. and West Brookline, Chief, " and they climbed in and drove out, turning right and heading down Tremont Street toward the location.

"Fire Alarm to Car Four," called the operator on the radio, "We're receiving calls for a fire on Pembroke Street."

"O.K., Pembroke, we have it," he answered.

Just then the chief at the church fire reported a working fire.

"Shit, all my first due companies are at the church, wonder who I'm getting," thought the chief.

Fire Alarm notified him that his companies would be coming from a downtown station, at least a couple of miles away. His car turned onto Pembroke, which is lined with five-story apartment houses. They're mostly rooming houses with a mixed bag of occupants: poor, elderly, white, black, winos, hookers, etc. He could see heavy fire shooting out a second floor front window. He notified Fire Alarm he was at the scene and had a fire and he turned to his aide: "Charlie, we're gonna have to wait for help; I'm goin' up the front to take a peek, you get around in the alley." He started up the long flight of outside front stairs and he was met by a woman in her sixties, obviously drunk, and she screamed at him, "I set it, I set it, they're all burning up there."

He grabbed her arms, "Who, who's burning?"

"Everyone," she shouted as she ran by him.

He started up the stairway to the second floor and could see flames reflecting off the wall ahead of him. When he got to the second floor landing and turned toward the front he saw flames coming out of the front room, into the hall and going up the stairway toward the third floor. He could hear screams and shouts for help up above. He knew he couldn't get up past the fire and he knew they couldn't get down. He grabbed his portable and called, "Car Four to Fire Alarm, strike a second alarm Box 1556. People trapped in the building." He ran down the hallway to the back looking for a rear stairway, but there was none. He opened a window and looked up. Heavy smoke was pushing out each floor and a few people were on the balcony fire escape yelling for help. He could see Charlie in the back yard, waving his light up at them and telling them help was coming. "Tell them to cross over to the next building, Charlie, it's going like a bastard in here."

Engine 7 swung in from Tremont Street, following Ladder 17. They could see the fire halfway up the block and they stopped at a hydrant and dropped a line. It snaked out behind the pump as it sped toward the fire. The chief yelled to the officer, "Big line, right up the front, see if ya can catch it. There's still plenty of people in the building." Another engine was coming down from Warren Avenue, following Ladder 26. The chief told the truck officer to get ground ladders to the rear and try to pick off the occupants trapped above the fire. He ordered the engine company to run a line into the fourth floor, over Ladder 26's aerial, which was already coming out of its bed. The chief could see Ladder 17's stick dropping in to the edge of the roof and the tiller-man racing up to get the skylights. Good. If he can open it up quick, we might save some of them.

It was Frank's first night tour since he was appointed. He had just completed drill school last Wednesday and this was his first actual run. He jumped off with Manny as the engine stopped behind Ladder 26, with its hose trailing out behind toward the hydrant they had hooked near Warren Avenue. Boy, it's really goin', he thought, he's not really gonna send us up there. He and Manny kept pulling off hose and the lieutenant said, "O.K., that's enough, break it there and get the pipe on." The lieutenant seemed like a pretty sharp guy and he'd been showing Frank all the gear earlier in the night. "Frank, grab the pipe and start up the stick," might as well break him in right, "I'll be with ya and so will Manny, get goin'." He slung the nozzle over his right shoulder and let the line drop between his legs and reached for the rungs on the aerial. He looked up, boy that's a lot of smoke comin' out. As he passed the second floor, fire was still comin' out the windows but he could see water slamming out through the fire from the inside.

"What's that, Luft?" he shouted back to the lieutenant.

"That's 7, and they're starting to hit it, keep goin', everything's O.K."

The lieutenant could see two more lines being run up the front stairs and he knew they'd be protecting his company from below. When they were about halfway up, the fire blew out the window that they were climbing toward. Frank stopped and froze on the ladder.

"Keep goin', keep goin', you're down below it," said the officer.

"Jeesus," thought Frank, "these guys are nuts."

But it was true. The fire was coming out but it was going up the front of the building, not down. He got near the top and locked his knee over a rung, like they taught him in school, and the officer yelled down to the chief, "Water in Engine 26's line," and the chief waved at him in acknowledgement.

"O.K. now Frank, here it comes. Play the line in the window and hit the ceiling. Keep moving it back and forth."

Frank braced himself as he heard the air escaping from the open nozzle. With a rush the water poured out the end in a solid stream. He did as he was told and in only a minute or so, the fire started turning to smoke.

"Now, move up, put your face piece on and get in the room."

He slipped his mask on and started in. "What's that, Luft?" He recoiled in horror. Standing just inside the window, which was recessed, was the figure of a man. It was badly burned with the flesh hanging off of it. "It's a guy and he's dead, he's dead," he screamed at the lieutenant who climbed up beside him.

"Yeah, you're right, Frank, now calm down." He shouted down to the chief, "We got one up here, chief, we'll need a flexicot."

The chief knew from the request that it was a victim and that he was dead. "O.K., Luft, we're getting the fire on the second and third, see if ya can move into the hallways up there."

The lieutenant stepped down into the room and pulled the line past the victim, dragging in enough to move across the room and into the hall. "O.K. now, Frank, Manny, grab this guy, nice and easy and lay him down on the bed." He could see Frank hesitate. "Come on, kid, he won't hurt ya, just put your hands right on him, that's it," he said gently. He knew it was a tough way to start, but ya gotta learn it sometime.

After they put the victim down, the lieutenant pulled back the half opened door to the hall. "Shit," he thought, "here's a couple more." A middle aged man and woman were lying in the hall and as he bent over them, he could see they were both dead. They were covered with soot but neither were burned. They were close to the front stairway, but they never made it down. The smoke had killed them. He could see fire in the ceiling over his head and he yelled down the stairway. "Hey, on the stairs."

"Yeah," came the reply.

"Tell the chief we got fire in the ceiling up here, but I think we can handle it if we get a coupla rakes right away. Send a truck up here. And, er, tell him we could use a couple more flexies, too."

When the chief heard that, he was dismayed. Jeez, he thought there was maybe only one, now there were at least four, 'cause they had found one burnt to shit on the third floor too. He knew they had taken about eight over ladders in the back and they were all O.K., and they had picked off three more in the front, but there might still be quite a few more in there.

As the fire was gradually brought under control, the chief directed a thorough search of all the upper floors. He walked along, speaking to each company, "Look everywhere, in the beds, under

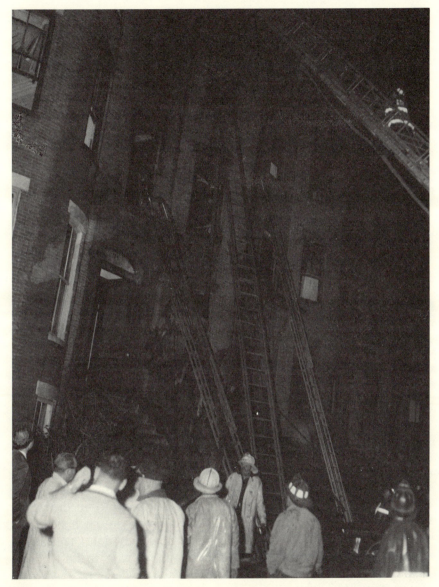

Four dead, several rescued over ladders. Box 2-1556, Sept. 25, 1966, South End District.

them, in all the closets, the bathrooms, behind the doors, every-where, ya understand?" He made sure they poked every pile of debris. Sometimes, if they're burned badly enough, they don't even look like bodies, just piles of unrecognizable stuff. But there were no more.

Up on the fourth, the three bodies were placed into the flexicot body wrappers. The stairway between the third and fourth was burned out and the lieutenant was tying a rope on the end of the wrapper, through the ring. "Er, whaddya gonna do, lower them down through the window, Luft?" asked Frank.

"Naw, we'll send them down through the stairway. We never take them down a ladder when they're dead, unless there's no other way."

"Why not?"

"Well, you might drop one, and if you do, the relatives will claim you killed them when they get to court. If ya drop one in-side, no one knows the difference."

When they reached the front door with one victim, the chief had them stand inside until the ambulance was pulled up near the fire. "See, Frank, he's waitin' 'till everything's ready," said Manny. "If there's no ambulance there, you're standing around in the street with a body and all the neighbors are there. If there's any relatives, they go nuts. As soon as he gives us the word, rush right down the stairs and get him in the meat wagon." As the companies were making up, the chief came over to Engine 26. "How'd the new kid do, Luft?"

"He did very good, I think he's gonna make it. Kinda tough fire to start with though, huh, Frank?"

"Jeez, I hope so. I liked the fire part, but that guy in the win-dow really shook me up. I don't think I'm gonna do much sleepin' when I get home. But at least I realize now they don't feel any-thing once they're gone. It's a pretty tough way to hafta die, though."

The chief headed back to the station. The church fire had also turned into a multiple alarm. He was lucky to get any help at all. If he had only had 22 and 13 with him when he got there, he knew he could have held the fire and cut it off on the stairway up to the third. If he did, he'd have saved them all. Well, buster, you been doin' this long enough so you shouldn't be speculating on maybes or if wes; what happens, happens, period. At least we got a lot of them. Howja like to be that crazy broad when she sobers up. She sure did kill them all. Her hot plate went on fire, so she tried to smother it with a pillow. Nice. When the pillow started going, she ran out and left the door wide open. There it went, right up the stairs. Aw, she probably won't know the difference. The papers will write her up as a hero and she'll get an award, if they can keep her on the bright long enough.

The Great American Melting Pot: You Ethnic Mutha!

Albert was pretty happy as he leaned over the banister and watched the princess start up the five flights of stairs. This could be a big night. He had been tryin' to get her alone ever since she started work in the shoe plant on Harrison Ave. a coupla months ago. She's from Haiti and they say her daddy is a king or sumpthin' back home, which is why she's so uppity. He'd been workin' on her and workin' on her without no luck until now, but here she come! Oh, he knew it was onny cause he had this new 'partment and she curious, but if things go right, she gonna find out what a 'merican prince is like tonight.

Albert had recently moved into the top floor of a five-story apartment house on the corner of St. George and Brookline Street. He had been painting and fixing his two rooms and it really looked cool. The last place he was in was crummy with roaches, rats and everythin' else, but this place is nice. The other dive he was always gettin' ripped off and the neighbors were tough, but here is pretty good. The fourth floor was two Puerto Rican families and the kids was little babies so they don't bother you. The next floor had that weird big fat guy, a Greek or sumpthin'. He was always sneaking in young white broads and doin' funny stuff, but that don't bother Albert none. Sumtimes he's kinda noisy, but maybe they all hear sumthin' tonight from the princess and old Al, yahoo!

Shortly after midnight, the Greek Svengali two floors below had the three young white girls where he wanted them. They were almost comatose from the hash he had been nursing them with and he was removing the last of his clothes in the bathroom. He thought he smelled something burning and he walked naked toward the bedroom. There was a small hole with burned edges on the mattress. "What you do, what you do that for?" he yelled at the little redhead.

"Din do nuthin'," she slurred in her deep Southern accent.

He ran back in the bathroom and filled a glass with water, pushed the girls off the bed and poured it in the hole but a little smoke started creeping up from inside. He grabbed a pan and filled that, but when he came back, the smoke was a little thicker and the girls were starting to cough.

On the second floor, Mrs. LeClair was wide awake. That evil guy upstairs was at it again and the music he was playing was thumping and thumping. When she smelled the smoke at first she didn't pay attention, but when it got a little worse, she called the fire department.

The house gong went off at the fire house on Harrison Avenue. The man on patrol announced, "3 and 3 to a building fire, Brookline and St. George." The engine and truck sped out the door, turned into Brookline Street and stopped on the side of the building. Tommy Flannery was tillering the back end of the truck, which meant he was the roof man. As he jumped off the seat and headed for the turntable to begin his climb, he strapped on his mask harness and his belt and tucked his axe in his waist. He could see the Polog raising the stick and he knew he'd drop it into the roof perfectly. As he started up, he kept looking in the windows to see if he could see the fire. As he passed the third floor, he could smell a mattress and see smoke pushing from the rear room. Just a mattress, Sal oughta knock the shit outta it with the booster.

Sal D'Amico was Tommy's pal. They'd been working together for eight years now. Sal was usually the pipe man on Engine 3 and Tommy knew he'd be racing up the front stairs right now with the line. He looked down and could see Julio connecting to the hydrant on the corner. Julio was a Rican and had only been on a couple of years, but he was a pretty good worker and he learned fast. As he stepped on the roof, he saw two skylights, one over the front stairs and one over the back. It's just a mattress; I'll just see if I can open the back without breaking it, just vent the stairs a little.

Out at the front, District Chief Standish got out of his car and yelled to the truck officer who was following the engine company up the stairs, "Whaddya got, Jock?"

Lieutenant Jock MacIntyre shouted back, "It smells like a mattress, Chief, third floor, I'll let ya know."

As Sal turned from the second floor landing and headed up the stairs, he looked up and saw the biggest pair of balls he had ever seen. They were attached to the huge Greek who was standing naked on the third floor landing. "Who called you? Nothin' wrong here. You no come in."

"C'mon pal, I can smell it, we gotta put the fire out."

"No, no, you get outta here."

Oh, shit, thought Sal, another one. Two weeks ago they almost got killed when a big black guy held a shotgun over the banister in a joint on Tremont Street and threatened to blow their heads off. They all dove off the stairway into a room and yelled out the window to the chief. Boy, that big cop from Four really saved the day. He came rushing in with his gun out, pointed it up at the screwball and said, "Drop it or I'll shoot your prick off," and the guy dropped it. That took some guts. They can have that cop job.

But as Sal moved up to try to get by, the guy actually swung at him. His fist hit Sal's helmet and drove him back. "Hey, Luft, I can't get by this guy," and he started up again, only to have the Greek try to kick him back down. There was no way he was gonna let anyone see those girls, or he'd end up in jail again.

The chief could see the smoke starting to push out the side windows. "Hey, how you making out up there?" The chief turned to Engine 22's officer who was standing by waiting for orders. "Ya better start a line up the back stairs," and as he glanced up again, "make it a big line, I don't like the look of this." The officer and his crew ran to their engine and started pulling off the two-and-a-half inch hose, getting enough to take them to the third floor rear. By now the second ladder truck had arrived and the chief ordered them to throw their stick to the top floor on St. George Street and start evacuating the building.

The fire had now caught onto the headboard of the bed and the flames were catching the curtains and starting up the wall. The three girls staggered out, coughing and retching, and went toward the back stairway, still naked. Flannery had lifted the skylight and light smoke was drifting up the stairway. He better go down and get a couple windows on the top floor and see if anyone's there, just in case. He went down the ladder and knocked on the door of an apartment, no answer. He turned the knob and it was open, no one home. He walked along to the next flat and knocked.

Inside, Albert had finally reached his goal. The princess had succumbed and they were locked in a passionate embrace on the bed, bouncing rhythmically up and down. Man, this is it, he thought. This gal is what I been dreamin' about. Albert never heard the knock. The next thing he knew there's this big Irish mutha standing beside the bed, watchin'. "What chew want, what chew doin' here? Can't you see we's busy?"

"Yeah, well I'm sorry pal, but the building's on fire, ya gonna have to leave."

"Fire, I don't smell nuthin'," and he kept moving vigorously.

"I'm not kiddin', it's on the third floor."

"Oh, the third floor, well then, is they any 'mediate danger up here?"

"C'mon, we gotta get out," said Flannery. As he looked back toward the door, he could see the smoke was really building up. Jeez, Three should be eating it by now, what the hell happened? Albert was pulling on his pants and the princess putting on her dress.

Sheet, I knowed it was too good to be true, thought Albert.

Flannery got to the door and he knew they'd never make it down the back stairs, maybe down the front. He ran out and took a look: not too bad. He grabbed them both by the hand and pulled them toward the stairs. "The smoke gonna kill me man," said Al.

"No, I'm gonna put my mask on ya. Keep comin'." He took his face piece and said, "This got air in it. I'm gonna keep passing it back and forth to each of ya," and he clamped it on the princess' face and she grabbed it eagerly.

Down below, the problem was finally resolved. Sal kept trying, but the Greek kept pushing him back. Lieutenant MacIntyre, a tall rangy ex-cop, pushed by Sal and said, "This is your last chance, get outta the way." When the Greek refused, he punched him as hard as he could in the center of those huge testicles, knocking him backwards onto the landing, and Sal scooted by with the line and started toward the back room.

Out front, the chief could see people starting to appear at the fourth floor windows and smoke was starting to push out around them, although not too heavily. "Fuego, Fuego, come down, get out," he yelled, but they didn't seem to comprehend. "Get some ladders up to them, they don't understand me," he said to the lieutenant of Ladder 13. We oughta be able to get them down the front stairs, he thought, but I better get ladders up, just in case. Oh, wait a minute, Julio's working tonight. He saw the little guy standing by the pump, waiting to fill the lines when he was ordered to. "Hey, Julio, come here for a minute," said Standish, "see those people, they're Spanish. Tell them to get the fuck outta there."

"O.K. Chief," said Julio, eager to please, and he ran underneath the windows and started yelling up, "Hey, hey, get the fuck outta here!"

"No, no, Julio, in Spanish, in Spanish."

As Sal moved down the hall he could feel a lot of heat pushing him down. "Big line, we need a big line," he shouted back to the men on the stairs and the word was passed to the chief. He turned to the officer on Engine 7, who had a dry line coiled in the street. "O.K. Luft, follow Three's line, right up the front, Twenty-two's going up the back." He didn't like the way it was going. "Car 4 to Fire Alarm, we have a working fire."

"O.K. Car 4, working fire Box 1651, operator K."

This would get him another ladder, engine and the rescue, just in case. Engine 22 was in position on the rear stairway near the third and the fire was coming out the hallway and spreading up the rear stairs, when they called for water.

Sal was starting to hit the fire, which was now coming out into the hall and he knew he couldn't hold it with a small line. He started backing up, but he could hear feet pounding down the front stairs. He hadta hold it till they got by. He could hear Tommy's voice shouting encouragement, "Keep goin', keep goin'," and a parade of people including Albert and the princess and a gang jabbering in Spanish made it to the stairs and stumbled down toward the second floor. He kept swishing the booster back and forth, back and forth, but the fire was going over his head and he finally backed down to the landing. It went roaring by and up the front stairs, jeez I hope they're all down. Here came Seven up the stairs with their big line, boy do we need it.

The chief could see the people coming out the front and a few others coming down a ladder on the side. "Well, it's gone now," he thought, "Car 4 to Fire Alarm, strike second alarm, Box 1651." The second alarm companies were not long in arriving because the alert Fire Alarm operator could tell by the messages that things weren't going great. But by now the fire had reached the top floor by both the front and rear stairways. Lines now had to be run over ladders into the top two floors and it became a long and difficult battle.

At last, though, it was knocked down, but Albert's love nest was a disaster. As the second alarm apparatus and the deputy chief were leaving the scene, the chief headed for the car to put his light away. In the front seat was a naked woman, half stunned and covered with soot. "Hey, lady, what the hell ya doin'?" He jumped back in alarm. "Were you in that fire?"

She looked at him with unfocused eyes and said with a smile, "Why no, I wasn't, I'm a close friend of the chief."

"Whaddya mean," he sputtered, "I'm the chief, you get the fuck outta there or I'll have ya arrested." He turned to his aide, "Where'd she come from? Who put her in the car?"

"Well, Twenty-two got three of them bolicky broads comin' down the back stairs. The other two were only kids and took off. This one's a little older."

"Yeah, but who put her in the car?"

"Well, er, the deputy did. He thought it was a big joke."

Hm, I'll get that sum bitch.

The chief started back toward the fire building and now here came the goddamn Greek, wrapped in a blanket. "Lissen you asshole, you know you were the cause of the fire spreading, I'm gonna have you pinched."

"Good, good, get cops. I have a complaint. One of your men punched me, what chew gonna do about it?"

Hm, what next? "One of my men, I can't believe that. But, O.K. get all your witnesses together and we'll make out a complaint."

"What witnesses. They was none. It happen on stairs, no one else see."

"Jeez, that's a shame, I guess there's nuthin' we can do. Ya gotta have witnesses, that's the American way." He waved to the Arson Squad inspector, "Take this guy down to Four, we're gonna charge him with interferin'."

This time when he started into the building, all the Spaniards were jabbering at him in Spanish and he didn't know what they were bitching about so he brushed them off, but when Albert told him his tale of woe, he really sympathized with him. The shoe plant was in his district and he had seen the princess the last time he inspected. "Well, Albert, I'm sorry, but lookit, you're a good lookin' guy, you'll get another shot at her."

"Well, maybe, but if that big mick hadda gimme another two minutes, I'da been all set."

About two weeks later, his girl friend from the car was rescued from another fire on Newton Street and a month later she was caught setting a fire on Canton Street. When he heard it, the chief was a bit perturbed. He'd put in the cause of the fire as careless disposal of cigarette. Now they bag this dame and she tells everyone she's been settin' fires all over the South End. I better write that job off as a bad scene all around. And I'll tell that wise ass deputy too; he approved the cause I gave, so he's not so goddamn bright either.

Burn,
Baby,
Burn

Moshe Dayan's picture was on the front page of every paper and periodical in the country. The brave Israeli soldiers were knocking the shit out of the Arab world with their Hertz rent-a-tanks. They had captured the imagination of the entire country and were getting all the ink. It was June, 1967.

If you skipped by the front pages and looked inside, you would have seen that Boston was having its own little war, which became known as the Welfare Riot if you were on one side, or the Police Riot if you were on the other. If you were a Boston fire fighter, it didn't matter whose riot it was, you got the shit anyway. As riots went, it didn't rival Detroit with the 82nd Airborne in attendance, or Washington, Chicago or Bedford Stuyvesant, but there was more trouble than in Philly where Frank Rizzo said any riot in his town would only last one day.

It started with a sit-in at a welfare office on Blue Hill Avenue one afternoon for reasons that have since become blurred. That night, several fires were set in the area and some looting and vandalism took place. It was a new experience for fire fighters. People were cursing them and throwing rocks and bottles. For a chief officer directing a fire it was weird. He'd be trying to watch the building to formulate decisions and run the fire, but his mind was on the crowd standing behind him and throwing stuff at him and his men. In a couple of instances, the men and apparatus had to be pulled out until enough cops could protect them.

The next day started off quietly, but the chief of department brought in all the deputies to formulate a course of action. They had been working on a riot plan ever since the trouble in Watts but it wasn't complete yet. They had to finalize it now and get an order out before tonight. The plan wasn't bad considering the rush job. If a full scale riot developed, a rapid determination was to be made of the area involved so a perimeter could be set up. Each fire station inside the designated section was to be locked and secured and the men and apparatus were to report either to fire headquarters or a station on the opposite side of the trouble spot and both would be designated as command posts. Fire companies would be set up in task forces of two engine companies and one ladder company. No apparatus would be dispatched inside the area. A district chief and his aide, with two police officers in the car, would be sent to any alarm and the chief would determine when he arrived if he needed assistance. Whatever he called for, one or two task forces, would be sent in with a police escort.

As soon as the plan was finished, it was cut, printed and shipped to each company with instructions to learn the plan immediately. The day had become increasingly busy, with several fires and incidents but not a full scale riot. If the chief of the department determined it was a riot, a new signal, number ten seventeen, would be struck and the plan would be implemented.

The night tour reported for duty and soon after six o'clock, things started heating up. The district chief in District Four responded to box after box with rubbish fires, autos, false alarms and fights. It was gonna be a long night.

Shortly after it got dark he was returning from an alarm on Tremont Street. He knew there was a fire in progress in the next district over, Five, but no report had been given for awhile. Suddenly, the radio started blaring, "Ladder Four to Fire Alarm, urgent."

"Go ahead, Ladder Four."

"The lieutenant has been shot, he's been shot. Send the police."

"Right Ladder Four, you're reporting that the lieutenant has been shot and you want the police. Can you give us any more information, Ladder Four?"

"We're taking him to the City Hospital, we're clearing out of the area. Tell the cops some guy is firing from the rooftop."

Oh, oh, thought the district chief, that does it. I wonder how bad he's hit. He could hear Fire Alarm calling for information on the type of wound.

"He got hit in the wrist and hand and he's losing a lot of blood."

Thank God, that doesn't sound too bad.

In a few minutes a beep sounded on the radio followed by the new signal 10-17. Boy, I never thought we'd be hearing it so soon. We just got done reading the order. "O.K.," he said to his aide, "we gotta go to headquarters." They took off down Tremont to Mass. Ave. and sped down the street, passing roving gangs of kids on the way.

As they pulled up on Southampton Street, they could see all the lights blazing on the second floor. He must have held all the egg-heads on duty. Bet you don't see any of them out on the street tonight. As he entered the office on the second floor, he saw the chief of department sitting on the edge of his desk.

"Well, ya made great time getting here, Chief, nice going. That gives you the right to be the first one to respond without apparatus as soon as I get you a coupla cops. It's a real honor."

"If I knew that, I'dve got a flat tire and given the privilege to some other asshole."

A contingent of helmeted police arrived and two were assigned to each chief's car. The chief and his aide knew the two guys they got because they were from Four so they put their gear in the car and waited for a call. It wasn't long in coming.

First run, Northampton and Washington Streets, in the middle of the worst area. It had been decided that if no fire was visible, they would just slow down, look around, see if anyone needed assistance and leave without winding the box. It was a really strange feeling to go up Northampton without apparatus. They could see hundreds of people at the intersection. Oh, boy, here it comes. As they got closer it looked like they'd never get through and the car would be swarmed over with the gang. But the crowd parted as they got near and they could see the flashing blue lights of two police cars, a wagon and a couple of motorcycles in the middle of the street. Thank God.

There was no fire and they were given another run. When they left that one they got another and another. They had about a dozen before they got back. No fires but a lot of big crowds and they were starting to open the hydrants. They returned to

Southampton Street, had a cup of coffee and waited for their next turn.

The rest of the night followed the same pattern, although they called in a task force a few times for large rubbish fires and autos. The other command post was having a tougher time with several building fires, including one that killed two women. About three o'clock, it quieted down, all over the area. "They must be getting tired. Yeah. They're calling this the Welfare Riot on the radio. They say they're not getting enough food and they're hungry."

"Hungry my ass, I think they're thirsty. They broke into all the liquor stores. I seen them all drinkin' but I didn't see a soul eatin'."

It stayed quiet for about three quarters of an hour. The chief of department said, "If we get past four o'clock and it stays the same, I'll reduce the force. We gotta get help back to the rest of the city." So far, the other districts had been pretty quiet all night.

At a few minutes to four, the district chief was sent to a call from Tremont and Camden Street in Roxbury, the area of the worst disturbances. As they passed up Mass. Ave., on every street he looked down, every hydrant was open. Jeez, they must all have hydrant wrenches by now. If he had anything, he'd have a real water problem. They turned left on Tremont and now they could see it. Two buildings on Camden Street were roaring. There goes the plan to reduce things to normal. "Car Four to Fire Alarm, we have a fire on Camden Street, near Tremont, send two task forces." He could see the flames shooting directly across the street and the other side was lined with five-story tenements with people at all the windows it seemed.

He turned to the cops and his aide. "O.K., we're gonna have to wait for help. Run along the street and tell them to clear out of those buildings. Try to get them to go out the back." He ran past the fire buildings which were both two-story and vacant and he could see an empty lot on the other side. Good, no exposure on this side. But lookit all the hydrants. "Car Four to Fire Alarm, send two more task forces. Have them come in Shawmut Avenue and start closing hydrants. They're open all over the area. Bring plenty of police, there's gangs of kids roaming the streets."

Hope the jakes get here before the tar and feathers. Riot, June, 1967, Roxbury District. Photo   courtesy of BFD.

The tenements across the street were emptying out, but the fire was starting to ignite the window sills. Boy, it was a long wait when you're all alone. His aide's head appeared at a top floor window.

"This buildings clear of people, Chief, but we need a line on the second floor, the fire's comin' in two rooms."

"Yeah, yeah, as soon as they get here. They must be comin' by way of Brookline. You better come down till we get some help."

A group of black kids were chanting, "Burn, baby, burn, we gonna burn the town, whitey."

Shit, they must all be readin' the same books. Next they'll be singin' "We Shall Overcome." Where the fuck are those companies? If they don't get here soon, we may burn the town ourselves without any more help from these guys.

He was gonna tell them to shut up but thought better of it. Things had changed a lot in the last coupla days, better keep quiet. For cripes sake, I can't even hear a siren and now the fire's really gettin' in across the street. Hope they ain't got any tar and feathers. They might start thinkin' they owe us one and try to do it to a chief.

At last he could hear them comin' and boy they never looked so good! "Twenty-Five, get a line in the building on the right, Twenty-Two, try to knock down the fire on the left." As more companies arrived, he assigned them to different positions with lines to bring it under control.

At first, the pressure was lousy but it improved as the extra task forces started closing all the hydrants in the area. More police arrived too, and the crowd started to disperse. As they headed up a side street, one kid turned around and yelled, "Dis here's just the start, whitey. Yo gonna hear a lot more from us."

It was pretty prophetic. Oh, this riot ended after a few more days and the following year there were a couple of days of trouble when Martin Luther King, Jr. was assassinated, but that's not the worst part. When there is big trouble, everything is well organized after a few tense hours. Task forces are formed, police forces are mobilized and men are protected the best that is possible. What's more difficult are the day-to-day incidents where tempers flair over minor things and there is no protection at the scene, because it's not big enough to strike any special signals or take extra precautions. It's too bad relations declined so badly and there really hasn't been much improvement but ya gotta keep hopin'. For the present, though, if you're a jake in the big city, keep the left hand high and the riot shield handy. You'll need it eventually.

Get 'em all out across the street.

On The Line Photographs

Engine Company 18, Boston, 1920

Unless otherwise credited, all photos in the photograph section were taken by Boston Fire Department Photographer, Bill Noonan.

Photograph Identification: Photos have a caption, number of alarms, Box number, date and section of the city by district name. Example: a fourth alarm Box 1234 is identified as Box 4-1234, Jan. 1, 1983, North End District. A working fire is identified as Box WF-1234.

The Three-Decker Problem in Boston

Photos on this page and the next three are from the Bellflower Street Fire and are courtesy Boston Fire Department. (See "I wonder who put out the grass fire?") Box 5-7251, May 22, 1964, Dorchester District.

Rapid fire spread due to closely built combustible construction and open, highly flammable rear porches. Box 5-7251, May 22, 1964, Dorchester District.

Wind velocity in excess of 40 MPH, temperature of 70 degrees F, and low humidity further added to the problem. Box 5-7251, May 22, 1964, Dorchester District.

Aerial view of the Bellflower Street fire showing a typical Boston three-decker and its conflagration potential. Box 5-7251, May 22, 1964, Dorchester District.

Does a Ghost Burn?

Trans World Airways, L1011, Logan International Airport Box WF-612, April 20, 1974.

Boston Fire Department assists Massport (Logan) Fire Department under mutual aid plan — concealed ceiling spaces and undivided areas contribute to $17 million loss. Box WF-612, April 20, 1974. Logan International Airport.

Churches Are Great For Praying

Front view of church fire during worst phase of arson fires in 1982. Box 9-
1526, July 21, 1982, South End District.

But Tough For Fire Fighting

A side view of the church.

The fireball through the circular stained glass window is typical when fire has engulfed church interiors, but this photo is unique. Box 9-1526, July 21, 1982, South End District.

Formula for 5 alarm fire: Excessive height, inaccessible areas, concealed spaces, unprotected vertical openings, combustible construction, delayed alarm. Box 5-1539, March 29, 1968, Back Bay District.

Hot air explosion blew out side wall and extended church fire to ten other buildings. Fastest five alarm in history of department. Box 5-1539, March 29, 1968. Back Bay District.

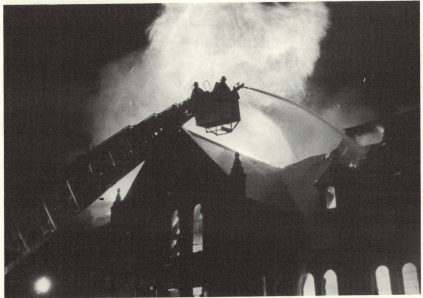

This church fire occurred while another five alarm fire was in progress next to the Old North Church and it taxed the department and the Mutual Aid Plan. Box 5-1585, July 20 1978, Back Bay District.

Start the water. Box 9-5352, Jan. 7, 1981, Brighton District.

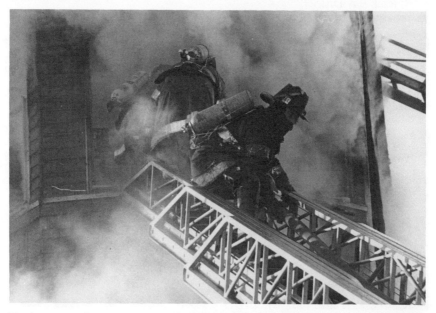

Feed up more line and move it in. Box 2-1744, Jan. 30, 1981, Roxbury District.

Boston Jakes
Using The Tools Of The Trade

Clean it all out, frame included. Box 3-3332, Feb. 2 1978. Dorchester District.

Get your facepiece on — it's kinda juicy. Box WF-1772, Feb. 6 1980, Dorchester District.

Great silhouette — but a tough job. Box 8-1223, March 13, 1980, North End District.

At least we'll be warmer inside. Box 3-186, Jan. 19, 1979, Dorchester District. Two dead.

We're ready — light up on the line. Box 2-2445, Feb. 13, 1983, Jamaica Plain District.

It's starting to vent itself. Box 3-1211, Feb. 2, 1983, Downtown-North End District.

An adz is a multi-purpose tool. Box 2-1744, Jan. 30, 1981, Roxbury District.

This is as high as I go. Box 2-1224, June 20, 1979, North End District.

Stay down below it. Box 2-1841, March 11, 1980, Dorchester District.

Steam rolling off the jake's helmet as the line is filled. Box 8-1539, Jan. 6, 1981, Back Bay District. Two jakes killed in collapse.

Peel it all off. Box 2-2414, Nov. 26, 1981, Jamaica Plain District.

Come on in, the floor's solid. Box 3-1471, Feb. 17, 1983, Downtown District.

The ridge line is open — now get the dormer Nov. 4, 1981, Roxbury District.

Cut the hole — then push down through the ceiling 'till it vents properly. Box 2-3364, Feb. 3, 1981, Dorchester District.

Snow Is For Skiing

Twenty inch storm. Box 5-3648, Jan. 15, 1978, Dorchester District.

Convenient place to lean. The blizzard of '78 came on top of this pile. Box 5-3648, Jan. 15, 1978, Dorchester District.

Keep It In New Hampshire.

Forty-seven inches on the ground. Two lengths of suction hose due to snow piles. Box 2-2367, March 2, 1978, Roxbury District.

Ladder truck blocked by snow in rear alley. Box 2-2212, Feb. 9, 1978, Roxbury District.

A jake jumped from fourth floor rear into snow when trapped by fire. Box 2-2212, Feb. 9, 1978, Roxbury District.

Twelve rescued over ladders following blizzard — the only truck to get in the street. Box 4-1361, March 1, 1978, Beacon Hill District. One dead.

Warm Weather Is A Tit

No cream pal — just as hot as you can make it. Box 5-1545, Jan. 4, 1981, South End District.

Spring is due in seven weeks. Engine 7 should thaw out by then. Plant Shoe Fire. Box 5-2411, Feb. 1, 1976, Jamaica Plain District.

Clench your fists inside the mittens. Box 4-6173, Jan. 4, 1980, East Boston
District.

This is gonna be a long night, baby. Box 3-1514, Jan. 29, 1980, Park Square District.

What time's my relief get in? Box 3-6173, Feb. 20, 1979, East Boston District.

. . . Some nights ya shudda stood in bed. Box 4-7234, Jan. 12, 1981, South Boston District.

Photo   courtesy Ed Fowler

Hotel Fires: A Lot Of Guys Named Smith Got Rescued . . .

Paramount Hotel. Gas main exploded in street. Box 5-1471. Jan. 28, 1966, Combat Zone District. Ten dead, thirty injured.

A Lot Didn't

Sherry Biltmore Hotel. One hundred rescued over ladders. Box 5-2321, March 29, 1963, Back Bay District. Four dead.

Hotel Vendome. Vacant, being renovated. After fire was knocked down, rear section collapsed, killing 9 jakes. Box 4-1571, June 17, 1972, Back Bay District.

Copley Square Hotel. Fifty rescued over ladders. Photo shows six aerial ladders in position. Four more and two aerial towers in rear of building. Box 4-1562, Jan. 29 1976, Back Bay District.

Copley Plaza Hotel. Fire overlapped from 4th to 5th floor. Five hundred evacuated, many over ladders. Box 5-1561, Mar. 29, 1979, Back Bay District. Two dead.

Arson: Boston Style

Keep moving the ladder pipe — there's plenty to go around. Box 7-255, July 21, 1982, Jamaica Plain District.

258 Extra Alarm Fires — 1982

The bucket lets you put the stream in the right place. Box 7-7115, May 16, 1982, South Boston District.

Yeah, let's have it, it's getting in next door. Box 4-7251, June 3, 1982, South Boston District.

Hope the Mutual Aid guys get here soon — we're the last Boston company left. Box 3-1848, June 11, 1982, Savin Hill District.

Gonna be a much bigger crowd here shortly. Box 9-254, June 11, 1982, Jamaica Plain District.

This district chief use to have an aide, now he can't even find a fire engine. Box 3-3336, July 2, 1982, Dorchester District.

The overhead wires hamper ladder placement. Box 5-2428, June 11, 1982, Jamaica Plain District.

Fill The Line Quick — We Gotta Hold It

First nine alarm fire in department history. Box 9-5221, June 17, 1980, Allston-Brighton District.

"George was sumethin' else"

One jake killed. Box 3-2124, March 3, 1970, Roxbury District.

Fire attacked from dockside and by lines stretched from fire boat. Italian freighter *Pia Costa,* Pier 5. (This freighter is similar to ship in "A Nice Ship Fire") Box 3-7122, Oct. 30, 1976, South Boston District.

This part of Boston will be missing in the morning. Box 3-1254, Nov. 17, 1979, Quincy Market, Downtown District.

Former Plant Shoe Factory. Occupied by artists' colony. Building was totally destroyed in suspicious fire. Box 5-2411 plus Mutual Aid from several communities. Feb. 1 1976, Jamaica Plain District.

Warm
Weather
Is A Tit

Many serious fires occur during warm weather. Fire fighters suffer from heat exhaustion, dehydration and debilitation. Fire fighters get killed in summer as well as winter and smoke is just as bad in the warm weather as in the cold.

But you don't freeze your ass off in the summer. The ladders aren't covered with ice and neither are the buildings or the hose and you don't end up looking like a popsicle. When you get wet in the summer it actually feels pretty good at a fire, but in the winter, the cold starts to penetrate when you get wet and you're screwed. Once you start shivering, you do not get the option to punch out and go home if you're a jake. No, baby, you gotta hang in there, 'cause everyone else's shivering too.

A guy once said that if a man is a fire fighter in the northern part of the country in the winter, it must be either because he's trapped in the job by economic necessity or he ain't wrapped too tight.

When you talk to fire fighters from Miami or L.A. about slipping and sliding on the ice they always listen politely, but they have no idea what the fuck you're talkin' about. Besides, they're too busy trying to figure out their compass bearings. Chiefs in those towns are always giving them orders to take the north side or the west side or sumthin'. Guys in Boston just say left or right, back or front, 'cause the face of the compass is frosted over with ice.

January 22, 1976. At 1900 hours, Fire Alarm made its customary weather announcement, "The temperature is minus four degrees Fahrenheit. The wind velocity is fifty miles per hour with gusts to sixty-five miles per hour. The snow accumulation is eight inches and blizzard conditions exist. Extreme precautions should be taken to guard against frostbite. KCA 591 at 1900 hours."

Jeez, thought the deputy, ya get cold just listening to that guy. Well, he doesn't havta tell me. We've already had three runs and it's really cold. He was dressed for it though. Thermal underwear, heavy wool socks, navy CPO shirt and wool pants. He had his mittens lying inside his helmet on the hood of the car and had boots on the hood too. You never leave your boots on the garage floor in the winter. If you did you'd start out with cold feet and you'd pay for it later. You'd never get warm for the rest of the fire.

It would be nice to have a quiet night, but it wasn't starting off that way. He was reading a brochure that said there were sixty-three golf courses in San Diego and the average temperature at this time of year was in the seventies. He figured if he lived there now, his handicap would be in the single numbers. Every year when he got down to twelve up here it started to snow and the season ended. Start all over in the spring. Well, two more months we'll be out again, if this goddamn winter ever ends.

He could hear a seven thousand series box striking. Southie. One of his districts, hope they got nothing. First company in reports nothing showing, probably false. Takes a real shithead to pull a false alarm tonight. Wait a minute, what did he say?

"Car 6 to Fire Alarm. We have a corrected location and we are responding to East Sixth near O Street. We're taking the companies with us."

Hm, musta been someone called it in wrong.

"Car 6 to Fire Alarm. We have fire showing on East Sixth."

"O.K., Car 6 reports fire showing on East Sixth," answered the Fire Alarm operator.

In a few minutes, another call: "Car 6 to Fire Alarm, we have a working fire at the location."

"O.K. Car 6, you have a working fire, Operator X."

As the deputy and his aide pulled out of quarters and started toward the fire they could hear the chief ordering a second alarm. He was reporting the fire was in a three-story brick apartment house and was extending. He also reported he had frozen hydrants. Nice.

One frozen hydrant really complicates a fire. Normally, an engine arrives at the scene, hooks a line on the hydrant, and stretches it to the fire. They run a line from the engine into the fire building and start operating the water using the supply from the five hundred gallons they carry in the tank. Meanwhile the guy at the hydrant makes the connection and opens the hydrant, letting the water go into the pump and the pressure is boosted to continue feeding the hose that's operating in the building.

Simple, huh? Sure, if the hydrant ain't frozen. If it is, you got real troubles. You can't add to the supply in the tank and the guys inside the building are gonna run out a water in a minute or so. If they can't get the fire by then, you're gonna have to back them out. If another pump doesn't get water, the fire's gonna keep spreading. The company with the frozen hydrant cannot leave and go to the next hydrant, it may be frozen too, so they gotta stay where they are, and try to free the ice with the thawing device.

One frozen hydrant is a problem and usually results in a multiple alarm fire. On East Sixth Street, the first six hydrants in the area were frozen. The fire had started in the cellar in a small room in the rear. The first company almost caught it with their tank, but they lost their supply as it emptied and had to start backing out.

By the time the deputy arrived all the engines were trying to thaw hydrants and the fire had reached the top floor. He sent the district chief to the rear with instructions to call for whatever was needed. He then struck third, fourth and fifth alarms.

He had to remove his mitten to operate the radio and he tucked it under his arm. He directed all incoming engines to take hydrants, determine if they were working and then bring lines to the fire, notifying him when they got water and where it was. The fire started spreading horizontally across the top, both ways, and soon it was in five buildings and threatening to jump across an alley and a street. Everything in the area had been evacuated.

The smoke was banking down because the wind was blowing so hard and the snow was driving into his face and blinding him. The ladders that the trucks had raised had to be moved because the fire was starting to hit them. If they didn't get water soon, they'd lose a dozen buildings. He ordered the fire boat to respond to one

When the frozen hydrants clear, everything else freezes. Box 5-7447, Jan. 22, 1976, South Boston District.

Some jakes can eat anytime. Box 3-7138, Feb. 7, 1977, South Boston District.

of the yacht clubs but that was over five blocks away and it would take a long time to move water this far. But it might be the only way.

At last, though, he saw a flat line starting to swell as it filled. Soon, another one came. He directed what lines he had to cut off the fire on each end of the block, but at last it started coming in quantity. More and more companies had cleared the ice from the hydrants. They were really hitting it now. But, God, look how quick it froze. The fronts and backs of all the buildings involved formed a glaze which got thicker and thicker. But the men were knocking it down. We're gonna get it.

The lines were taken inside all five buildings and they made excellent progress, great. He reached for his radio to give a report and noticed his hand was still bare and the mitten was frozen in place under his arm. He couldn't get his hand in it. Boy, if the hand's frozen, I'll pay for that later.

As soon as they had the fire under control, he called for several companies to come in and relieve at the scene. The fire fighters had to be gotten back as quickly as possible before they all got frostbite. As each company was relieved, they had to use thousand watt lights from the generators to melt the ice on the windshield so the apparatus could be driven.

Over four thousand feet of hose was left at the scene and it was all destroyed. It froze into the ruts in the street and couldn't be removed. Besides, someone stole all the couplings and sold them for junk a few days later.

When his car backed into quarters, the deputy and his aide raced for the kitchen. Get the mittens on the radiator. Get a cuppa coffee. Run cold water on the hand, jeez that hurts. As he poured another cup, he started hitting the clasps on his fire coat with a spanner wrench. They were covered with ice and he couldn't get the coat off until he unclipped them.

As he was working on the last snap, the guy on patrol yelled in the kitchen, "Deputy, Car 3 is asking for a box on Franklin Street."

Oh, oh, he thought. That's a first alarm response for me. Never even got the coat off.

They drove up the street and swung into Franklin Street. Heavy smoke was pouring from the first floor of a six-story office building. The rescue company arrived at the same time he did and he looked at them. They were still covered with ice, the same as he was, the poor bastards. Even their breathing apparatus was caked. But they got on a line and started in. He could see fire starting to show on the second floor and ordered a second alarm.

Several of the companies that came were just on the way back from Southie, including Engine Three. He sent Three into the second floor with a line, and placed each of the other companies as they arrived. The ceilings in the first floor had to be opened and they were fourteen feet high, metal covered over wood lath. The fire had extended all along the beams. It required long rakes and was a long and exhausting job, but at least they were in out of the wind.

When it was knocked down, he ordered more detail companies in. Some of these guys were gonna get pneumonia if they didn't get back. As he checked out the second floor, he saw the crew of Engine Three, sitting with legs stretched out, soaking wet, frozen and exhausted. "O.K. Lieutenant, make up and get outta here. You guys did a great job at both fires."

When he returned to the street, he could see them driving away, hose piled high on the back step and two fire fighters standing on top of it. "Hey, Chief," one of them yelled, "Lookit the temperature. It's warming up."

He glanced at the neon lights on the bank up the street, "Fifteen below zero, my aching back, what's he mean it warmed up?"

"Yeah," said his aide, "That's Sully. It said minus sixteen a little while ago."

The job continued on Franklin Street and a lot more work had to be done on the second floor. The pump operator on one of the engines yelled to him, "Chief, they just struck a second alarm in District Six again."

Jeez, not again. Well, his counterpart in Division Two would have to take that, we still got too much work here.

He could hear the radio himself now and Fire Alarm was dispatching companies to the fire. "Fire Alarm calling Engine Three."

"Engine Three answering," said a voice with resignation.

"Respond to the fire."

"On the way."

Boy, I really did them a favor sending them back early. Hm, stop helping me please.

The district chief ordered a third alarm. People were trapped in the building, and he called for ambulances. It sounded like another frozen hydrant job and it was. Both fires were finally over as the sky was starting to lighten. One civilian had died in the last fire and several had been rescued.

This time when he got back to quarters, he managed to get the coat off and finish his coffee. But sure enough, another box started striking and out they went again. This time, though, it was a small fire in a high rise in Government Center, the complex of federal, state and city buildings in the heart of downtown. He had the whole first alarm assignment, including himself, get in the lobby out of the wind, while the engine and truck crew completed the job on the tenth floor.

By the time he got back, his relief had arrived. Boy, was he glad to see him. "Hey, you made the front page today. You look like a frozen Eskimo in the *Globe*."

"Ya didn't see anything in there about hiring any deputies for San Diego, didya, John?"

There were one hundred and fifty Boston fire fighters injured on that tour of duty, the most in the history of the department. This did not include all the cases of minor frostbite that were unreported. Frostbite is nice. Every time it gets below freezing from then on, the frostbitten part aches. It conveniently lets you know when winter arrives every year.

A lot of the older men who were thinking about retirement quit after that tour and a lot of younger ones envied them for awhile. But spring comes, the job goes on and pretty soon you forget. The handicap starts coming down again and this is the year you'll end up a nine.

They say this was the worst night ever experienced by the department because of the extreme cold and combination of fires in rapid succession. Maybe it's true. But there's also another thousand nights tied for second.

Yeah, But It Was Only Thirty-Five Cents A Gallon

The expressway that bisects Boston is often described as the world's longest parking lot. It is the scene of horrendous traffic jams during the rush hours, morning and evening, every working day. Commuters usually arrive home tired, pissed off, aggravated and easy to provoke after spending an hour or two inhaling exhaust fumes. It probably should be cited as a contributing factor in the high divorce rate that exists among those who left Boston to find a "better and more meaningful life" in suburbia.

The road was never designed to handle the volume of traffic that travels on it and the breakdown lane is used as a travel lane during peak hours, thus backing up traffic for miles when one car breaks down.

There is also a smaller traffic jam in the skies above due to the fleet of helicopters and small planes from the radio stations that constantly travel the route to gleefully let the poor jerk in the car know why his pork chops are gonna be cold when he gets home. All in all, not exactly like the real estate brochures that say, "Just eighteen minutes drive from downtown Boston."

At 1646 hours, March 3, 1971, Box 1436 was struck for a report of a gasoline tank truck tipped over near Kneeland Street, downtown. The deputy responded with the apparatus from his station and heard Car Four report that it was indeed a tank truck and it was on the exit ramp from the expressway on the northbound side.

When the deputy arrived and started an evaluation with the district chief, it was obvious it was an extremely dangerous situation. He called Boston, MDC and State Police to the scene, three foam companies and truckloads of sand.

There were numerous serious problems confronting him. The truck had turned over when it hit a depression in the road on the ramp. As it capsized, the driver was thrown clear but the tank was severely ruptured with a three foot long jagged hole in its right side. It was lying partially on the ramp and partially in a field. The field was a hill and at the bottom of the hill was one of the Boston Edison main generating plants, about 250 yards from the site. On the left hand side of the ramp and below it was another, circular exit ramp and below that was the expressway itself.

The portion of the expressway was that part that enters the South Station traffic tunnel, which is a quarter mile long. This tunnel passes underneath South Station which is one of the two main train terminals in the city, and the tunnel carries its name. It also serves as an entrance to the Massachusetts Turnpike, which is also one of the major routes used in and out of the city during rush hours. At the bottom of the ramp, in addition to the Edison plant, was Kneeland Street, which is lined with six and eight-story buildings.

The rupture in the tank was pouring raw gasoline, 7800 gallons of it, into the field on one side and down onto the expressway and into the tunnel on the other. Some of the gasoline was also entering the city sewer system as it reached Kneeland Street.

There were several things that had to be done rapidly. Notify the Edison plant that they might have to shut down and evacuate. Get fire companies into the buildings on Kneeland Street, evacuate them and start monitoring the buildings for fumes with explosive meters. Shut off all traffic on the expressway both sides but make sure no cars are stopped inside the tunnel. Close the entrance to the Mass Pike. Get several lines of hose run but keep them dry so they can be moved quickly. Set up foam lines and prepare to use them. Make sure all the apparatus is kept a long distance away in case of ignition. Get the sewer department to find out where the gasoline is going that's running into the system. Notify the owner of the tank truck and the gasoline about the situation and request tow trucks to move the tanker when possible.

Since you don't have a computer for a brain, these factors don't immediately jump into your head and you have to consult with and listen to your subordinates and evaluate their recommendations. But they are all decisions that have to be made at this type of incident and they're all yours, baby. Then there is the difficulty you have from the "Disaster Crowd," people who show up at everything, including some you may have summoned yourself. Oh, not your own fire fighters and not most other officials, but the human element is always present and keeps life interesting.

The major police official from one of the responding departments, when ordered by the deputy to shut off all the traffic on the expressway, said, "Why, Chief, you can't do that. Don't you realize this is the rush hour? You'll tie up traffic for hours, I'm afraid I can't permit that."

"Er, yes, I see. Do you understand that as the fire officer in command, I'm in charge at this scene and am responsible for the safety of the public?"

"Well, yes I do, but — "

"Do as I've ordered you, do ya understand?"

"I'm afraid I can't . . . ."

The deputy turned to a Boston cop, "Officer, will you please arrest this asshole or shoot him?"

"Yessir, Chief," the cop smirked, and the deputy turned away.

Next he was greeted by a reporter, actually smoking a butt, pen and pad in hand.

"What time did this start, Chief?"

The deputy almost fainted. "Lookit, I'm gonna tell you something nice and quietly, O.K.?"

"Yes, go ahead, Chief."

"You are smoking a cigarette and standing in gasoline. Now, hold it, hold it, don't drop it. Just turn around and walk away as quickly as you can." He turned to another cop. "Lissen, follow that shithead and get him away from here. Another thing, I want all spectators kept out of the area from Atlantic Ave. up Kneeland to the other side of the surface artery."

As soon as possible, foam lines were operated to cover the tank truck and the surface of the flowing gasoline. Sand started to arrive from the Massachusetts Public Works and the city. A dike was constructed at the bottom of the hill and the gas was diverted away from the Edison plant and the sewer system first. Next, sand was piled to keep the gas contained so it couldn't run down on the expressways below. The dike had to be over three feet high in spots and the gasoline was up to the fire fighters' knees.

Eventually, the truck owner came with an empty truck but had to stand by because it was not possible to stop the flow and pump out the contents due to the position of the truck and the size of the rupture. Four enormous tow trucks arrived. The contractor who owned them explained to the deputy that they were under contract to the oil companies and that they were frequently used to right turned over tankers.

The problem here was unusual, however, due to the position of the truck, but he was sure they could handle it. After much difficult maneuvering, three of the trucks were placed on the down slope of the left hand side of the ramp. The other truck was placed on the opposite side. A bed of sand was built under the truck on the ramp side to prevent it from sliding when the tow trucks started pulling. Huge cables were run from the tow trucks under and around the tanker and finally everything was ready.

The deputy stationed himself with a foam company up high on the ramp above the truck. He felt if ignition occurred, they could attempt to protect the men in the tow trucks. It was doubtful, but you hadda try anyway. He also figured the company with the foam line was a little safer above than below. If there was a fire, they at least had an outside chance of running up the ramp; down below, with all the gasoline and fumes, no chance at all. He ordered all the companies and all the other personnel away from the area and gave the signal to the contractor to begin the lift. As soon as the slack was taken up on the cables, the truck started sliding along the ramp. "Hit it with the foam," he directed the company.

The tow truck operator shouted, "Hold up, it's sliding!"

God, it was a hairy operation. More sand was added and pressure was put on the cable from the opposite side. This time, the truck didn't slide and it started to come slowly upright. "C'mon baby, come on up!" As it almost reached the vertical, it started to come faster and it hit the ramp upright but started rolling over the other way.

Oh, shit, here it goes, he thought. It rocked back to the right, however, and after a few more quivers, came to rest.

A ragged cheer went up and the deputy sighed. The extra companies were made up and dismissed, the traffic was started again and the tank truck was emptied. The field and the down ramp and a portion of Kneeland Street were closed off for the rest of the night. Fire companies were detailed to the scene to wash away the gasoline and to monitor the building for fumes.

It never was determined what happened to the gasoline that went down the sewers. All the books tell you never to let it happen. That's nice advice, but how do you prevent it? Loads of sand do not magically appear and portable dikes are not lying around in quantity. It's gonna keep running for awhile, baby, and it would be great if you knew where, but in this case no one ever found out.

Experience is a wonderful teacher, someone said, and he was right. Two years after this incident, the deputy had another tank truck tip over and rupture. The conditions were somewhat better though. It was during the rush hour but instead of on the ramp, it was on Kneeland Street itself. It ended up directly over the sewer that got all the gasoline before. The rupture was just as bad and the fluid was pouring out and down the sewer directly. Instead of gasoline, it was number two fuel oil (15 cents a gallon then). Once ignited, it burns just as good as gasoline but has a higher flash point. A lot of the instructions he had given before were helpful and easy to give, and he was almost casual about them this time. It was a much simpler operation since most of the oil ran down the sewers and no dikes were necessary because the surface was flat. The surface artery and a couple of streets were closed and the buildings were monitored but it was nowhere near as hairy.

As with the gasoline, no one ever learned where the oil went. The maps of the system are missing and the old timers who knew everything about it are long dead and gone. Hopefully, it ended up in the ocean, but maybe not. Sometime in the future some poor deputy will find half the town on fire underground and he'll never figure out why. The guys who would know why will be long dead and gone.

They May Be Right Once In A While — Ya Gotta Listen Anyway

The South End of Boston has seen better days. When the buildings were erected just after the Civil War, it was an ideal
place to live. Wealthy families moved into three, four and five-
story town houses and lived in quiet elegance. The streets were
tree-lined and beautiful. It stayed that way until the turn of the
century when blue collar immigrants arrived in great numbers and
moved into the city, while the wealthy headed for the suburbs. The
large single-family houses now were cut up to accommodate several families and this continued for decades. However, after World
War II, these folks also headed out and the area declined rapidly.
Hundreds of buildings were abandoned and thousands of others
were converted into cheap rooming houses so that the places that
once housed only one family now had twenty or more occupants,
all strangers living in squalor. Naturally, when this happens, the
fire business increases dramatically, and the South End had thousands of serious fires during the next couple of decades.

Currently a reversal is taking place, and the army that moved to
suburbia wants back in. The price of gasoline and cars has started
to make the city look attractive again and being near your job ain't
so bad anymore. Professional people have started buying up the
old buildings and converting them back to their original status and
property values have soared. Gentrification is the new catch word.
But the transformation is far from complete and you still can't
walk around at night without getting mugged, raped, murdered or
all three in the South End.

The ladder truck swung into Hanson Street and the men could
see a guy waving from a doorstep half way down the block. As the

lieutenant jumped off he yelled to the Chinese man, "Watcha got?"

"Fliya, second floor, come queek."

The officer nodded to the driver to throw the stick and yelled back to the engine company, "Start a booster line," and they snaked out the hard rubber line and followed him up the front stairs. This is the usual routine if there's nothing showing and it gives you a tremendous advantage if there is a fire. With the aerial to the roof and a line in the building you can check a small fire before it grows or even hold a serious one till you get more help. It's a worthwhile exercise that helps make your aerial operator become so expert, he can throw the stick anywhere and lay it in with precision. However, as he followed the Chinaman up the stairs, the guy said, "Tell men to stop hose, you no need."

"It's a fire, ain't it?"

"Yes but you no need hose here."

"Yeah, yeah, O.K.," said the lieutenant but he winked at the hose man coming behind him; he knew this guy was wrong, so keep it comin'. He had been to so many fires where you got wrong information. Someone was always tellin' ya, "There was this big explosion and the whole place went up." Wrong. Or, "They's two little babies trapped on the top floor." Wrong. Or, "What the fug you guys doin' here, they ain't no fire." Wrong. So follow the routine and you're ready for anything. Right?

In this case, wrong. As they entered the rear apartment on the second floor the guy went to the back window with the lieutenant close behind. He could smell wood burning so he knew he had somethin', but where was it? The Oriental pointed out the window and said, "See?"

"Holy Jeesus, lookit it go!" Across the back alleys he could see the top floor of a building with heavy smoke pushing out the windows. He started running down the stairs, yelling, "Back it down, back it down, it's going like a bastard on Milford Street." He waved the signal to the truck operator to make up the stick and grabbed the mike in the cab. "Ladder 13 to Fire Alarm, strike a box for a fire on Milford Street."

"O.K., you want a box for Milford Street. Is that the same incident you had on Hanson Street?"

"Yeah, and we're responding."

By the time they circled the block and pulled up in front of the fire building, heavy fire was blowing out the front windows. He didn't have to tell the driver to throw the stick, he could hear it coming out of the bed and he could see the engine starting a big line. As he raced up the stairs to the top floor, he met a wino on the third floor who shouted, "There's a coupla my buddies up there, ya gotta get 'em." As he neared the landing the smoke was banking down and he was really puffing. He lay flat on the floor and crawled along, feeling for the doorway to the back room. The door was open and he could hear someone moaning but couldn't see anything. He wriggled along and could feel the heat pushing him down but he hadda keep going. He bumped into something and yeah, it was a body. He grabbed for it and pulled it back out to the landing where the engine men were arriving with the line. "Take him down and tell them to fill the line," and he headed back in.

Now he could make out a glow as the fire spread across the ceiling but he managed to get to the other body which was motionless. This guy was a little smaller though and he moved him out a little quicker. He could hear the air escaping from the end of the nozzle on the line and knew the water was on the way, thank Christ. As he passed the poor guy down he could see he was in tough shape but he seemed to be breathing. Just then the ladderman on the roof crashed his axe through the skylight and the whole damn thing came down, hit the lieutenant on the top of his helmet and knocked him down the stairs. He crashed into the wall at the end of the stairs and lay there panting. Shit, this ain't my day, he thought, but he could hear the line drumming against the ceiling of the back room and knew the engine was moving in on the fire. Another engine company climbed over him and headed up with another line for the front room.

"You screwing off again, Luft?" said one of the hosemen.

"Get lost, you fink."

When it was all over and they finished overhauling, he went down the stairs and out to the street. God, he was pooped. As he threw his light into the front seat he saw the tillerman coming down from the roof. "Hey Joey, for crissakes, when you open the skylight, just make a little hole first, willya, to give us a little warning? You dropped the whole goddamn thing on my head."

"Jeez Luft, you're never satisfied. Last time you said I didn't make a big enough hole, this time it's too big. Make up your mind, willya?"

Oh shit, I'm too tired, I'll have to get to him later. Of course I want it big, but not on my head.

He sat on the running board and pulled his boots off. He had forgotten to pull them up and they were full of water. I guess I'm not too bright, he thought, and he could feel someone's eyes staring at him. He looked up and there was the Chinaman, shaking his head and watching the water pour out of the boots. Finally he spoke. "You flucking asso, I told you not to bring hose over there, you wooden lissen. What the fluck the matta with you? Now you get water over here you fill up your shoes. How much they pay you anyway?"

"Lookit pal, I've had it with you. Why don't ya go play fan tan or iron a shirt or sumthin'?"

As they pulled out of the street on the truck he thought, I shouldn't be too tough on him, we sure didn't need the hose in his house. Hm, maybe they are right once in a while. Jeez, my head is aching. I'm gonna kill that Joey.

A Nice Ship Fire;
Or,
Almost Everyone
Was Happy

Fire fighters hate fires in cellars and in ships. The reasons are fairly obvious. Heat and smoke rise; and at cellar fires they are always coming up at you and the attack is very difficult. Many buildings are destroyed when the fires originate below grade and the seat of the fire can't be reached. Ship fires are somewhat like cellar fires but on a much larger scale. The fires usually originate below decks and a ship is really unfamiliar territory to landlubbers. The most important people at a ship fire are the captain and crew members who can direct you to the fire and provide you with information. You have to be concerned about the cargo and its hazards as well as the stability of the ship. We have managed to sink a few over the years, and while you're sure they're out when they go down, the owners are not thrilled about it. You also have to consider that if you can't control the fire on a ship, it may endanger the docks and buildings or even the entire port, so you may have to have it towed.

Boston, like other major seaports, has had some tragic ship fires, the worst one being the one on the *U.S.S. Leyte*, an aircraft carrier, in 1953. Thirty-seven young sailors died, many of them while trying to get below decks to save trapped shipmates and several Boston jakes were injured. The *Black Falcon* fire at the Boston Army Base in the same year resulted in the deaths of seven longshoremen when the number one hold ignited during unloading operations of that cargo ship.

On March 10, 1974, the department responded to a ship fire at the Mystic Docks in Charlestown at 1039 hours. The fire was in the hold of an old cargo ship, the *S.S. Galacia*, of Panamanian registry. Tourists who follow the Freedom Trail always visit the

Bunker Hill monument and the *USS Constitution* in Charlestown and are never aware of the large complex of piers and wharves in the district, nor the old freighters that are loaded there.

The crew members of the *Galacia* were Greeks with very little knowledge of English. The cargo consisted of oil-soaked metal turnings, loaded from a junk yard in the nearby city of Everett, where they had a machine that ground up used cars. The ship had been moved to Charlestown to pick up additional cargo. The metal turnings included steel, aluminum, copper and magnesium, and when they are oil-soaked they are highly susceptible to spontaneous ignition. The Coast Guard required continuous monitoring of the piles of junk for heating. It is not the type of cargo you would want if you took your wife on one of those romantic, leisurely ocean crossings on a freighter which advertises, "A small number of fun loving passengers who are fond of the sea. Nightly dining with the Captain and ship's officers are featured." Come to think of it, the *S.S. Galacia* wouldn't fit the type of ship you envision for such trips either. It was an old rust bucket with a large population of rats and other vermin.

When the department arrived at the scene, fire was coming from the number four hold and it was quickly knocked down with hose streams. A check of the adjoining holds indicated no extension. The deputy in charge had been to a similar fire a few years earlier, however, and he shut down the lines as soon as possible. He knew from the previous fire that if you flooded the hold with water you still did not extinguish the fire. The spaces between the metal turnings contained air which couldn't be expelled and the fire would continue to smoulder. The water would also turn the outside of the piles to solid slag, which is difficult to penetrate. The only practical thing to do was to unload the cargo into barges, wet it down and take it outside the harbor and dump it. He tried to explain this to the captain of the ship but couldn't make himself understood.

The shipping agent was called to the scene and he called the insurance company in England. A big conference was held the next day while the fire was contained with the judicious use of hose streams. Present were the Coast Guard, the fire commissioner, the chief officer working the fire, the owners, agents, insurance company and a ship fire expert, whatever the hell that is.

The owners, agents and insurers wanted to make every effort to save the cargo. The Coast Guard and the fire department were concerned about the fire, the safety of the ship and the port of Boston. The fire expert recommended sealing the hold and flooding it with carbon dioxide to smother the fire. The fire department was doubtful it would work because it had failed in the past and it seemed too difficult to get a good seal on such an old vessel. The department recommended unloading the ship. However, since it seemed obvious that the fire posed no immediate threat to the vessel at the present time, it was agreed CO_2 would be tried. The fire commissioner insisted that he would not keep the department tied up during this operation since the rest of the city must be protected. A paid detail of off duty fire fighters was set up to maintain round the clock protection.

The operation commenced later that day. The hold was sealed and the CO_2 pumped in from a huge tank truck. More trucks arrived and were used, the ship fire expert watched his monitoring devices and everyone waited. The deputy was pretty skeptical because of his previous experience, but what the hell, he was willing to learn. It looked to him that they'd never get a tight enough seal, though, and he didn't think the CO_2 would displace all the air from the piles. He also wondered how a man became an expert on ship fires. There didn't seem to be that many going on around the world and he knew you only became an expert on anything by doing it often. He remembered listening to a recognized expert speak on fire fighting in Washington one time. The guy had no practical experience and while he was probably a very convincing speaker to the uninitiated, he was a complete asshole as far as the fire fighters listening to him were concerned. But, you gotta keep watchin' and listenin', baby, so pay attention to this operation.

After two days' time, the Expert ordered the hold opened and sure enough, not a wisp of smoke was showing. He entered the hold with the deputy and, using a short probe with a thermometer attached, shoved it into the pile. The temperature showed 90 degrees Fahrenheit and stayed there. "Now, you see, Chief, we have smothered this fire. We will monitor this for twenty-four hours and the ship can depart tomorrow.

"Yeah, well, O.K., if you say so, but I don't think that probe is deep enough, you're only down about three feet. Let's shove it down further."

The probe was extended and pushed in. It stayed at 90 for about fifteen seconds and started to rise. It finally stopped at four hundred fifty degrees. "Apparently it isn't quite out yet," said the expert, "that inner heating is quite suspicious."

"It's not only suspicious pal, the goddamn thing is still burning. Listen, we had one of these before, let's unload it and get it over with."

"No, I don't think so. We didn't hold the seal long enough. We'll seal it up for a week and that should do it." The hold was sealed again and CO_2 pumped in periodically for a week. The paid detail was continued but by this time the fire fighters were starting to look at the expert with jaundiced eyes. At the end of the week the results were the same: "suspicious heating." Another conference, another decision to continue. "Hm," thought the deputy, "this guy may even surpass that asshole in Washington."

By April 24th, over 100,000 tons of CO_2 had been dumped in the hold. A check on that day revealed the pile was still burning so the Expert reluctantly agreed that it might possibly be wise to unload the ship. It was moved to another pier in South Boston and the unloading commenced. Huge barges were brought alongside and a crane started scooping out the piles as fire fighters wet down the material. As each barge was filled, it was towed outside the harbor where the bottom was opened and the still burning metal was dumped. Fire fighters on the fire detail said that when the material hit the water, there would be an explosion that sounded like the atomic bomb. The unloading was completed on May 16th, 1974.

This was a sixty-seven day ship fire, which is certainly a record for Boston and maybe anywhere else. But it wasn't all bad news. Certainly the owners, agents, insurers and the expert were unhappy as you would expect. Those unfortunate Greek crewmen who were mugged or who contracted a slight social disease in the Combat Zone were not thrilled with their stay. However, the captain of the ship fell in love and got married while he was here and he may or may not be happy. Several lasting friendships developed between the fire fighters and crewmen. Some jakes learned how to speak

Greek and some Greeks learned Boston English. The crew got a lot of overtime and the fire fighters on the paid details made good dough. The guy who sold the CO_2 was delirious with joy and wanted to hire the ship fire expert as a consultant. The fire commissioner and the Coast Guard were happy because the ship didn't sink and the port wasn't destroyed. The deputy and the other chief officers were happy because they had recommended unloading in the beginning and the commissioner now thought they were smart, which was not always the case.

All in all, the fire on the *S.S. Galacia* was pretty nice, compared to other ship fires. The only fear the deputy had was that some day, somewhere, he would be introduced as a recognized expert. God, that would be a fate worse than death.

When it reaches the top floor, it goes left and right if you don't get it quick. Box 3-1541, Nov. 9, 1977, South End District.

On New Fire
Lieutenants

The district chief read the latest general orders from the Pentagon. A bunch of fire fighters had just been promoted to lieutenant and one of them was coming to the truck in the chief's
quarters and on his working group. Shit. Well, at least he was
comin' from a pretty good company in Dorchester. Yeah, but this
is the South End, it's a little different. Ah, maybe he'll be O.K. I
just hope he doesn't know everything. Some of them are a pain in
the ass. They just got done studying, they learned every goddamn
form and they're always running into the chief's office, telling you
that you're not doing some foolish thing according to the latest
methods. They probably wondered how a stupid bastard like me
ever made chief anyway. Well, I was pretty good in the books
years ago, but this is the end of the line for me. They can stick the
deputy's job, he's got six districts. One's enough for me. I'm a lot
more interested in how good a jake this guy is than how good his
morning report looks.

He met the new guy in the kitchen and he seemed O.K. but
God was he young. Big and strong with a ruddy complexion, he
looked about fourteen years old. Well, we'll see how it goes. As
long as he has a little common sense and tries hard, it'll be all
right.

The chief was at the other end of his district when he received
an alarm from Box 1552. Hm, Columbus and Holyoke, the new
guy will be first in. Yeah, he could hear him reporting off at the
location, "Ladder 13 to Fire Alarm, smoke showing third floor,
four-story brick on Holyoke." Well, at least he's not screaming.

The lieutenant raced up the stairs and was met by a large middle aged black woman with her arms folded, staring down at him. "It's onny a little fire, don' you break nuthin', Sonny.

He brushed past her and could see an overstuffed chair smouldering in the front room. "Bring the booster in here," he shouted down the stairs and he headed for the front window. He could see the chief pulling in and he yelled down, "It's a chair, Chief, but I wanna check the wall out."

"O.K., Luft, let me know."

This exchange meant the lieutenant wanted to see if the fire had extended into the wall and the chief wanted him to check, and if it hadn't he would hold only two companies and send everyone else back. The black lady yelled from the hall, "What you mean check the wall? I tote you it's only a small fire. You leave dat wall alone, ya hear?"

"Lissen, lady, why don't you be a good girl and go downstairs," said the lieutenant politely.

"Girl, what you mean girl, I'se old 'nuff to be you' muther. You jes get yo ass out my 'partmen."

As he checked the wall, the lieutenant could feel quite a bit of heat. Jeez, he better open it up. "O.K.," he said to his axe man, "open it up."

"Why you mutha fugger, I'll kill yo," she said, and started beating on his arm.

"Now be nice, lady, willya? I gotta open it up." By then, the hole had been made and shit, no fire. But you had to make sure.

She was really pissed now and started to berate him worse than ever. "Look what yo dun now, yo broke dat wall," and she started to advance on him again.

Just then the chief, who had been waiting for the word down in the street, arrived at the top of the stairs. He could hear her chewing out the new guy and he got the pitch. He said to the black woman, "Hey, momma, get the fuck outta here, ya unnerstan'? You get down the street right now or I'll have you arrested. Screw."

She took one look at him and fled. "O.K., Luft, she's bitching 'cause you opened the wall. Did you think it hadda be opened?"

"Yeah, but she — "

"Never mind what she says, you're in charge; just tell her to get lost, ya unnerstand?"

"Yessir."

"O.K., is the fire out now, it didn't get in the wall?"

"Yes, it's out now. No, it didn't get in."

"Then make up and get outta here."

Back in the car the chief thought, well, I dunno, he's not very forceful, but at least he opened the wall. You hafta open plenty of them if you're not sure, but ya gotta do it. We'll see how it goes.

Next tour. A chimney fire, three-story brick. The fire started from a range oil burner in the kitchen stove, third floor, and ignited the soot in the chimney. The routine called for the stick to the roof, booster line over it. Check the chimney breast to see if the fire extended out of it. Put out the fire in the range oil burner. Remove the smoke pipe on the third floor. Block the opening with a plate and play water down the chimney, using a spray to kill the burning soot. The lieutenant gave all the necessary orders. He searched for a plate but he couldn't find one large enough to cover the opening. He looked all over the kitchen but found nothing. Then he saw a big flowerpot that looked about right. It was empty and he placed it over the opening. Boy, it fit just perfect. "O.K., start the water." The next thing he knew the whole room turned black. The force of the water drove the soot into the flower pot and it came through the little hole in the bottom with tremendous force, spreading soot all over the room. "Shut it down, shut it down," he shouted, but it was too late. What a mess.

Once again, the chief was arriving at the top of the stairs. He saw the soot pour out into the hall and was gonna yell down for a line when it stopped. He peered into the room and could see the new lieutenant and his men covered with the stuff, and so was everything else. "What happened?" he asked. When it was explained to him and he understood, he said, "O.K., O.K., make up and get the fuck outta here before the owner comes and has us arrested." Back in the car again. Jeez, I don't know whether he's a shithead or not, but he better start doin' better. He chuckled a little as he watched the poor bastard, black from head to foot, climb into the front seat of the truck.

Next tour. The lieutenant ordered the stick thrown to a roof on

Dwight Street and forgot to make sure everything was clear for the throw. As the chief came down the street, there was his Ace standing in the street, holding up a bunch of telephone wires that the aerial had knocked down. He was trying to let cars drive underneath them. "What now, Luft? "

"I'm sorry, Chief, I thought we had a good fire and it was only a TV set. I got excited and didn't look first."

Back in the car. Jeez, this guy's a menace. If this keeps up, I'll be back on the Maalox like I was when I had that other asshole on Engine 7.

Saturday night, 0200 hours. The chief was once again at the other end of the district and was just leaving a mattress fire in a tenement. He heard the box strike and Fire Alarm announce, "Box 1642, struck for 608 Tremont Street, report of people trapped in the building." As he headed toward the location he thought, my Ace will be first there, I hope he's on the ball. He could hear the radio cut in and the message came, "Ladder 13 to Fire Alarm, strike second alarm, Box 1642." Boy, he's got something all right.

As he swung into Tremont Street, he could see heavy smoke pushing from the top two floors of a four-story brick. Thirteen's stick was in the top floor and two people were just climbing on to it. A ground ladder was being raised to the third floor. As the chief got out of the car, he could see the lieutenant race up and disappear into the smoke, followed by another ladder man.

More people were showing up at windows and the chief ordered a third alarm. He kept looking up at the ladder his new guy had gone up and as the smoke lifted a little, he could see the other guy on the ladder. The lieutenant had gone inside. It was really juicy up there and fire was starting to break out through the next two windows. "Where the hell is he?" the chief shouted up, but just then the lieutenant appeared at the window with a bundle in his arms and handed it to the guy on the ladder. It was a baby, and the guy descended rapidly while the chief waved to a cop. "It's a kid, get it to the hospital." The fire fighter with the baby was giving it mouth to mouth as he jumped into the police car.

The chief looked up and the lieutenant had disappeared again. Another truck was pulling in beside him. "Get the roof," he yelled to the officer, "but send a coupla men up this thirty-five; the officer on Ladder 13's in there."

Two men raced up the ladder and as they neared the top, the lieutenant appeared with a big red haired woman in his arms. He handed her out and scrambled out on the ladder himself. Just as he got clear, the fire burst through the window he had left and enveloped the top of the ladder. He got to the ground, said to the chief, "No one else in there, Chief," and started heading for the front stairs with one of his men. The fire was a very difficult one because so many had to be rescued, but eventually it was knocked down and a detail was called to the scene.

The chief was kinda pooped and he was sitting on the running board of Ladder 13 when the lieutenant stood in front of him. "Er, Chief, Ladder 13's all made up and ready to go. Would ya mind moving to another piece?"

"Not at all, Luft, not at all. Oh, by the way, I've been watching you since ya came here. Ya still got a lot to learn. But about 2 a.m., ya can't be beat. Ya did a hell of a job. Now get outta here before I think of somethin' else for ya to do." As he watched him pull away, he thought, maybe some of the new ones ain't too bad. I dunno, though, I heard Ladder 17's gettin' one next week. He'll probably have two heads and know every goddamn order ever published.

About 2 a.m. ya can't be beat. Box WF-1713, Oct. 9, 1974 Roxbury District.

Lockins,
Lockouts,
Cats In Trees

The department rules wisely forbid the use of the department or its equipment to break into a building to permit someone to enter. This is due to the fact that sometime in the past, some guy told the fire department he was locked out of his apartment, the naive officer of a ladder company believed him and threw a ladder to a window, let the man in and left. The man proceeded to rob the joint, cleaned it out and vanished, since it was not his apartment.

When the owners returned and were informed that the fire department had let someone in, there was hell to pay; hence the rule. But when you're in charge of a company you have to temper justice with mercy at times. In other words, you have to use your head. Consequently, if some poor guy or woman is locked out and has proper identification, or can produce it after you get them in, you judge the case on its merit and make a decision. If you decide to help them you always tell them that the department rules forbid it, but of course if they're locked out and have left their little infant in the crib, the department is duty bound to get in and prevent harm from coming to the poor little tyke. Or, if you locked yourself out and left something cooking, there is a great danger of fire and the department must take the necessary action to prevent it from happening. The lock outee will usually get the message and say, "My little kid's all alone, or I left the chittlin's cookin' ! " Entrance is then gained and the report will state the department responded because of the danger to the child or the building and everyone's happy.

The rules don't mention anything about cats in trees although every article about fire departments always depicts this as a major duty. It is not. First of all, we do not tie up a ladder truck that could be called somewhere to rescue a human, but is delayed because it is rescuing an animal. Secondly, if you climb up a tree to get a cat, he'll probably tear the shit out of you when you get there, while his owner will be screaming at you to stop abusing Tabby. It is far wiser to refuse in the beginning, although it is not good public relations. One officer always had a standard answer for such requests. "Listen, lady," he'd say, "we're not allowed to do that. Besides, I'm an expert on cats and have several at home. When that sweet little thing gets hungry enough it will be down and come back to you. If you look around the neighborhood, you'll know I'm right. Cats are always going up in trees yet you can't see even one cat skeleton up there now, can ya?" This would usually mollify them and you could see them walking away staring upward.

If an officer did decide to let someone into their home, if it was close by, he'd send a couple of men with a ladder to do the job. It was not unusual to see two fire fighters walk down the street with a neighbor, throw up a ladder and climb in a window, and people accepted it.

One night, the district chief in the Tremont Street station had just come on duty for the night tour. He was stacking his papers in order for the fire reports he would have to file before the tour ended when he heard the call over the loudspeaker, "Chief, visitors on the way over." He looked toward the door and saw two well dressed middle-aged black men coming across the main floor. "C'mon in, what can I do for ya?" he asked.

One of them spoke up reluctantly. "Well, Chief, we have always appreciated the firemen around here and having this station nearby, but, uh, we're a couple of musicians and we have a lot of expensive clothes we wear when we perform."

"Yeah, so what?"

"Well, uh, we've been robbed and I hate to say it, but we think the firemen took our stuff."

"What?" the chief was startled, "why do you think so?"

"Well, if you come down to our apartment we'll show you. All our costumes are gone and there's two sets of firemen's coats and hats lying on the floor. Yeah, and there's a ladder up to our back window in the alley."

Oh, baby, thought the chief, we're really in the shit now. "Well sir," he said as calmly as he could, "let's go have a look. We'll get right to the bottom of this." He got his aide and put the two men in his car and took them to their apartment building, all the while thinking, "What the fuck am I gonna do now?" He couldn't believe that a fire fighter would do such a thing. Oh, they're not all angels by any means, but they're not crooks and they're not stupid either.

They entered the building and went up to the second floor. Sure enough, lying on the floor were two fire coats and two fire hats with the owner's names painted inside. The closets in the apartment were empty. Oh, boy, he thought, it sure is our gear. "Er, gentlemen, there's no question that's our gear. Would you please show me where the ladder is now?" He turned to his aide and said, "For cripes sake, go get the cops, will ya?"

The men led him into the room and sure enough, there was a ladder reaching from the alley up to the window. But, thank God, it was an old rickety wooden one and not a fire department aluminum ladder. "Just a minute," he said to the men, "I'd like to talk to the rest of the people in the building and see if they could identify the men who came."

He knocked on the first floor door with the two men crowding behind him. An elderly black lady answered. "Oh, hello, Mr. Fireman, did you come to pick up your ladder?"

"Well, lady, I just wanted to ask ya, did you see the two men put the ladder up there?"

"Oh, yes, this afternoon. They were very nice and polite. Black boys too. I didn't know you had blacks in yo' station. I sees they musta got you two gennlmen into your 'partment. At first I thought it was a fire, but they tole me you was locked out."

"Thank you very much, Ma'm," said the chief, and he breathed a sigh of relief. They went back upstairs just as the cops arrived and the chief asked everyone to sit down. "I know you guys are probably not gonna believe me, but we didn't steal your clothes. That's not one of our ladders out back and we don't have any black fire fighters in this station at the present time. The fire clothes are definitely ours, but the two men whose names are on them are not on duty. I think what happened was this: There were two second alarm fires in the district during the day today and the companies from this station were at both of them. The guys who stole your clothes are probably from the neighborhood and have seen us let people in from time to time. I think they must have got in the fire house, took the fire gear from our lockers and got the ladder somewhere else. Then they just walked down the street, into the alley and threw the ladder up and got in. The neighbors, like the lady downstairs, figured you were locked out. When they cleaned out all your stuff, they just walked out the front door with it, in their own clothes, and dropped the fire clothes."

It sounded plausible, but the two men were skeptical, so the men, chief, aide and cops trooped back to the station. The chief showed them the journal that reported the duties of the companies at the two fires and the time they were absent and then he showed them where the fire clothes were kept, and sure enough, two lockers had been broken into.

The two men finally accepted the story and left with the police to make out a report on the loss, but the chief was pretty sure they had lost a lot of faith in the fire department. He called the officer on the ladder truck into his room and told him the story, and then he said, "If you ever get another lockout, don't send two men with a ladder; take the apparatus every time. Those two poor guys got screwed on account a us. Jeez, are they pissed off. Ya can't blame them. So, let's make sure nuthin' like this ever happens again, O.K.?"

"Yessir," said the lieutenant.

"Oh, yeah, Luft, one more thing. If I see any of those dudes of yours wearing musicians' clothes, I'll have them arrested." The lieutenant stormed out of the room and he could hear the chief laughing as he went, but he didn't think it was so goddamn funny.

A few days later, the cops stopped in to see the chief. "Hey, we got a break on that case, Chief." They showed him mug shots of two young blacks. "The neighbors identified these two clowns and we got one of them. He was tryin' to peddle the clothes to another group. We got everything back." They gave the pictures to the chief and left.

The pictures ended up at the patrol desk with a sign above them, "Wanted, dead or alive. These two men stole the fire clothes of Walter and Joe. Reward, one six pack, see Walter or Joe."

Next Time,
Make It
Longer

As he reported for the night tour, the lieutenant on Ladder 13 thought, Well, at least it's March 1st; spring is just around the corner. The winter had been a bitch. Plenty of cold, plenty of snow and plenty of work. During the last month alone, his truck had been involved in several rescues over ladders and some of them were pretty hairy. At least when spring came, the mounds of snow lining the curbs would disappear and raising ground ladders would be a lot easier.

He thought back to the first fire they'd picked someone off at, four weeks ago. It was during a three bagger at Columbus and Wellington. It had occurred just after a big blizzard and extra men were kept on duty because of the snow. The truck had arrived first, along with Engine 22, and the fire was on the first and second floor of a huge six-story apartment house and spreading rapidly. People were at windows on all the upper floors, screaming for help. The stick was raised to a couple on the top floor and ground ladders were pulled off and thrown as quickly as possible. Without the extra crew on duty they'd have never got them all up and saved so many. But they didn't get them all.

As they laid a fifty foot ladder in to a woman with a baby on the fourth floor, the smoke obscured the two of them momentarily. As it lifted, he could see the woman but not the baby. He heard a sickening crunch and turned around. The baby had been dropped and it landed on the roof of a car. They had to leave it and get the ladder in to the woman. As soon as it was placed he grabbed the baby, but it was obvious it was dead. It was hard to believe what a big dent the poor little kid made in the car roof, but it was dished in deeply. He handed the baby to a cop and returned to raising more ladders. A couple of other people died at the fire but over fifty were saved. The kid bothered all of them though.

The next one was a little weird too. It took place on Holyoke Street at about nine a.m. The temperature was seven below zero, and as they turned into the street from Columbus, he could see heavy smoke coming from the third and fourth floors of a four-story brick. He could also see an elderly black woman and a middle aged black man at the third floor windows. They'd try to get the woman first, and as they pulled up he yelled for a thirty-five. Before they could get it off, though, the man jumped. He landed on an iron picket fence and one of the pickets went in one side of his forearm and out the other. It was a horrible sight and the guy was really screaming, but they had to leave him hanging there and get the old lady because the fire was showing up in the window next to her. "C'mon, c'mon, never mind him, we'll get him later," the lieutenant shouted.

They got the thirty-five up to the woman and a member dashed up and picked her off just as the fire burst through. As soon as she was down, they turned to the poor guy. By this time he was semiconscious but still in a lot of pain. Before they could get him off the fence, the rescue company arrived on the second alarm and the job was turned over to them. The crew of Ladder 13 continued working the fire and found out afterwards that the rescue had been unable to remove the picket without further damaging the man's arm, so they had to cut the picket off with an acetylene torch and take the man and the picket to the hospital. That had been quite a sight and boy was it cold that morning.

The last night they had worked they had also made a couple of rescues but not so dramatically or tragically as the others. They had come into a five-story brick with a one room fire on the second floor. The fire was extending into the stairway so the occupants couldn't get down except by ladder. There was one man on the fifth floor and one on the third. The lieutenant ordered the stick to the man on top because it was the only ladder that would reach him and you always try to get the highest ones with the aerial if possible. He had ordered a thirty-five for the guy on the third and they were coming with it. He was shouting up to the two men, "Don't jump, don't jump, we'll get you both O.K."

As the aerial passed the man on the third floor, he was reaching out to try to grab it but it was too far away. The Lieutenant yelled to him, "Leave it alone, that's going to the guy upstairs, we'll get you, don't worry."

"Yeah, well fug you and the man upstairs, you get that ladder to me you mutha or I'll kill ya!"

The lieutenant kept the stick going up and the stream of invective continued until the thirty-five was laid in beside the guy. He scrambled down unassisted and fled up the street. The man on the fifth floor was brought down and the engine company managed to drive the fire back in the room from the stairway and knock it down.

When it was all over, they found out why the man was in such a hurry. He was afraid he'd get burned but he was more afraid he'd get caught: he was robbing the apartment when the fire started and we helped him get away. No wonder the owner was a little pissed off. But maybe tonight would be easy.

At 0345 hours, Box 1553 was struck and Ladder 13 responded to West Newton and Carleton Streets. As they were en route, the lieutenant could hear the radio squawk, "Box 1553 was struck for 239 West Newton Street. We're receiving calls that people are trapped in the building."

What else is new, thought the lieutenant.

As they turned into the street, sure enough, they saw another fire. They pulled up in front of a four-story brick and wood duplex apartment house. He could see in the front door, which was at street level, that the fire was racing up the main stairway which served both sides of the duplex. He could also see a man hanging from a window on the fourth floor on the right hand side of the duplex and another at a window on the opposite side. "Get the stick to the guy on the right, John," he yelled to the operator. The guy on the right seemed to be in the most trouble.

"Get a fifty," he yelled to the others because it was gonna take that much ladder to reach the one on the left.

As they all pushed on the fifty to get it upright, the engine company started hitting the fire in the front hallway and the smoke started to obscure everything. They turned the ladder to face the building and started to extend it. The lieutenant counted the clicks the pawls made as the tip disappeared into the smoke. Every click was one foot. When he judged they were up high enough, he ordered the men to lower it into the building. The smoke lifted a little and he could see they were just right. But he couldn't see the guy anymore. "Where the hell is he?" "Maybe he fell back in the room." "Get up and see, quick," and a ladder man ran up the ladder with the smoke banking down again.

"Hey," he shouted down, "the guy's on a rope and he's lowering himself down. He's at the third floor now."

"Shit, get a thirty-five."

They raced to the back of the truck, pulled off another ladder and quickly threw it up to the third, but by now the man on the rope had dropped to the second and was still coming down. As he got below the second floor ledge he ran out of rope. "O.K., get a twenty," shouted the lieutenant and he yelled to the man, "Don't let go, hang on for another minute."

Finally, the twenty slid up under him and the guy stepped on and scurried down. The fire was brought under control soon after and the lieutenant sat on the running board of the truck to get a breather. "Hey, fireman, thanks for getting me down."

He looked up and there was the guy with the rope. "Yeah, O.K. pal, I'm glad ya made it. Hey, how come you had that rope?"

"Well, I just got burned out in Somerville last week and I almost got trapped. I swore then that I'd always have a rope with me just in case."

"Well, that's a good idea, I guess, but please, next time, get one that reaches the ground."

George Was
Sumthin'
Else

The average Boston fire fighter is a pretty brave, hardworking guy who likes his job and does it the best he can. He's highly motivated, having studied hard for the position he was appointed to as a result of a competitive exam. Naturally though, the federal courts have muddied the waters in recent years, the same as they have done with every aspect of our lives. But other than their unique motivation, fire fighters are much the same as men everywhere. There are good ones, bad ones, tall ones, short ones, white ones, black ones, yellow ones, Spanish ones, happy ones, sad ones, funny ones, gloomy ones; and any gay ones are still in the closet.

Regardless of which category they are in, they must all acquire the ability to get along with each other. They work a forty-two hour week with the same guys all the time. No matter how busy their station is, they will still be in that station more than they are out. They have to do patrol duty, drills, house work and maintenance. They do not have to eat together or even talk to each other; it's not required by the rules. But from a practical point of view, if you're gonna be together for thirty years, ya better learn to tolerate each other. And they do.

It takes some adjustment, just like in the military service. And like the service, their performance under extreme danger is due more to a desire not to let their partner down than anything else. Pride in yourself and respect for the other guys are major factors in how this strange business works. And it is strange. Objective observers have noted that when people are running out of a building to escape man's most deadly enemy, here comes a bunch of other guys with funny looking hats and suits, running into the same place. The observers have also noted that this doesn't appear to be a wise choice of direction.

There are two groups of fire fighters who don't fit into the average category. One type learns early on that there is less hazardous duty. If you could pick the right political horse and he rides home a winner, there's a good chance you could end up at the Pentagon with a special noncompetitive title and more bread than the guy who's pulling ceilings and dragging lines. Man, you could be a night club or special hazards inspector. The hazards of these types of jobs may be equated to those of a salesgirl in the Windsor Button Shop. Course, every four years, it's back to the starting gate again but you can become adept enough to switch horses without missing a beat if the electorate demands a change. This type is in the minority and represents neither the guy in the field nor the guy at the Pentagon who really is essential.

The other group of guys is also small. This type, the average jake never really understands, but always admires. You could call them super jakes or guys with death wishes or even knights of the round table, but if you did, they'd think you were full of shit.

George was one of these, and he'd probably be representative of the group, although there is not any particular background or ethnic identification that applies. They're just exceptionally brave and talented men who stand out from the crowd. George's father and grandfather had been jakes too, but this also isn't a yardstick.

He was of only average height and build and was appointed shortly after discharge from the service at the end of World War II. There was a tremendous influx of men at that time because of a reduction of hours. All of those appointed were veterans. His assignment was to Engine 3 in the South End and from the first day he loved going to fires. Not in the same sense that arsonists love fires. No, he loved the challenge of it all. The tactics, the strategy, the danger and the dirt. A lot of them thought he had the death wish, but it was far from true. He analyzed the task to be done and took calculated risks based on his evaluation of the situation, although he was not above taking unreasonable chances if another life was in danger.

He had great company pride and always wanted his company to be first in, have the first line, get the best shot at the fire. Oh, the other companies in the district had their pride too, so you weren't trying to beat a bunch of stiffs.

This competition among these young strong guys was great for the chiefs in the district. Their biggest problem was stopping the men from going too far and teaching them when to be aggressive and when to know enough to retreat.

George always believed that you couldn't make up time on the road. You had to get out of the house fast. He had a horizontal white stripe painted on the door jamb. When the automatic door cleared the stripe, the engine could fit out of the door and George was gone and ya better be with him. He made a study of every intersection in the district and knew which ones he could fly through and which ones required caution. He never had an accident, although no one took bets on him.

When he got to a fire he'd do anything to give his company an edge. Try to pass someone on a stairway, shoot a line up the back, over a ladder, through a window, anything. Things always go wrong at fires and the situation is constantly changing. You must be adaptable.

At one fire, a citizen misdirected Engine 3 into the wrong building, the one adjoining the actual fire building. By the time they reached the fourth floor and found nothing, George realized they had gone wrong. He went out the back window and crossed the balcony fire escape into the fire building. He was now two floors above the fire, which was extending rapidly up the stairway. He scooted back, told the officer they could get it by crossing over and he started dragging the line across. When he pulled in enough line, he eased open the hallway door and could see the fire, now at the fourth floor level. The roof man had opened the skylight and was drawing the fire straight up. George requested that the line be filled and asked for extremely high pressure. Before the water arrived he yelled to the company below to back down away from the stairway and stand by. When the water came he directed the wide fog pattern upwards and then down into the stairway, contrary to the normal operating procedure. This action normally would drive the fire downward and cause it to extend, but in this case, it killed the fire almost immediately.

When the chief came up the stairs he was bullshit. "Engine 3, what the hell are ya doin'? Ya came in the wrong building, now ya played down in the fire. Ya trying to kill us all? "

"Well, Chief," said the lieutenant, "We-er — "

"Never mind, Luft, I know this was George's idea. Whaddya got to say, George?"

"Well, Chief, I could see the fire was confined to the stairs when I came across. I told everyone to get off the stairs. We used the fog like a giant sprinkler head. And it worked pretty good, didn't it? Besides if we weren't up here right away, you'd'a lost the top floor. Jeez, ya wouldn't want that to happen, wouldya, Chief?"

"O.K., O.K., knock off the shit. You're getting away with it this time, but only 'cause I'm a nice guy. Next time, pick the right goddamn building and start at the bottom."

"Yessir, Chief," said George, "but you wouldn't want a company in your district to let the second due engine beat it, would ya?"

"Beat it, George, don't push your luck."

He turned another screw up into a good job a little later. They ran a line up to a third floor hallway that was really leaping. As they knocked it down, they could see the fire was not in the rooms, but was racing up the stairway and had entered rooms on the fourth floor. As they worked their way up, they ran out of hose and couldn't go any further. One guy raced back for another length, but George was really frustrated. The fire was lapping out the doorway of a room on the left and entering the ceiling. He crept up the stairway and the heat drove him back, but he had seen something. He turned to the guys on the stairway behind him and said, "Get ready to open the pipe. When I yell, you let it go." With that he jumped up on the landing and grabbed a piece of plywood that was leaning against the wall. "Hit me, hit me," he shouted.

The two men on the stairway looked at each other. "The sumbitch is nuts," but they opened the nozzle and hit the plywood with the stream. George angled it so the water ricocheted off the board and hit the ceiling and the fire coming out of the room.

"Keep it going, you're doin' great."

He kept it up and it really had quite an effect on the fire. It drove it back in the room and caught it as it was crossing the hall in the ceiling. When the extra length came up, they added it on and finished the job.

"For cripes sake, George," said one of the other guys, "how'dja think of that?"

"Oh, I saw the plywood there and we hadda try something. Supposing Seven or Twenty-two or one of them outfits came up with another line and got by us. Ya can't ever let that happen."

You'd think from these descriptions of George that he came on so strong that he was a real pain in the ass, but if you thought so, you'd be wrong. He was what today is called a "workaholic" but the term was unknown at that time. He was always working on someone's car, or fixing the plumbing at someone's house, or helping you move or paint your house or something. He was apparently pretty busy in his own house too, because he managed to have eight kids.

He was constantly making recommendations to improve the job, whether it be color coding ladder tips, conning a manufacturer out of parts for the apparatus, designing a nozzle for rear porch fires or whatever. He was decorated twice for rescues at fires but could not care less. He had talked his superiors out of writing him up for several other jobs.

He always seemed to be working with a burn that was healing or a "blow out" patch covering a few stitches. To him, this was all part of being a fire fighter and you must accept such inconveniences. In 1960, when the new fire house opened at Tremont and Concord Streets, he transferred from Engine 3 to Engine 22. He felt Twenty-two was gonna be the busiest company in the city and he didn't want to miss anything. At that time Engine 3 was responding to over a hundred multiple alarms a year, but he figured Twenty-two was gonna go to more than that because they were assuming two companies' work load.

He adapted easily to the new house. He enjoyed the neighborhood with its parade of hookers, pimps and gays, although he got an eye infection the first week he was there. He said he had blown an eyeball looking at the sights. He said the most exciting thing that happened in Three's area was watching the priests get ready to say Mass at the Cathedral, but it was a lot different over here. It wasn't long before you could hear him yelling at fires, "C'mon, c'mon, ya want three to beat ya?" He was now gonna make sure that Twenty-two was the best in the city.

He never studied for promotion until the mid-sixties when he finally took the advice of everyone and got in the books. He attacked them just like he did everything else and pretty soon he was promoted. Where did he go? Well, with a little maneuvering, he was assigned to the rescue pumper unit in the Roxbury, North Dorchester district. This area was rapidly becoming the busiest in the city and you wouldn't expect him to miss that, would ya? If he was a great fire fighter, he became an even greater fire lieutenant. He taught the men on his shift more about fire fighting than they thought anyone knew. Each one of them has his mark on him and it's easy to recognize one of George's men.

On March 3, 1970, George and his company responded to a difficult fire in a four-story warehouse on Washington Street, Roxbury. The fire started in the cellar and worked its way up through the building, which was loaded with furniture. The battle went on throughout the afternoon. George had used three air bottles so far and was changing to his fourth at his engine. As he pulled the harness on and turned around, he saw the deputy in charge and waved to him.

"How ya doin', George? This is really a bitch isn't it?"

"Yeah, but we're starting to do O.K. We got the cellar knocked down and we're all set upstairs. We'll be outta here in no time.

As he started toward the building he gasped, grabbed his chest and fell toward. He was dead before he hit the street.

George was given an enormous funeral which he no doubt would have disdained. Just part of the job, you know, just part of the job. When it was over, the chief of department spoke to his wife. "Caroline, we're all very sorry. You know how everyone felt about George. Uh, I hate to mention this, but, er, is there anything I can do, you know financially? I know ya got all those kids," he sputtered, embarrassed to be mentioning it.

"No, Chief, thanks a lot. You know, I hate to lose George. I don't know what I'll do without him. But, I've been expecting it for a long, long time. He told me he thought he'd die at a fire sometime and he didn't want me to feel bad about it. It was his whole life and if that's the way it had to end, why it was all right with him. Besides, he ran the house just the same way he did the job. All the bills are paid and he kept a big insurance policy. We'll be O.K., but thank you for the offer."

Guys like George are pretty rare, but we've had more than our share. Some are pensioned, some are dead, and some are still working. Nobody really knows what drives men like these, but everyone knows who they are. No city administration could ever understand such dedication, nor could you expect them to, with their drab, boring, computerized view of life.

The upper walls of Memorial Hall at Fire Headquarters are ringed with the pictures and names of those members who have been killed in the line of duty. As a visitor circles the room, he will notice two names on the list separated by seventy-two years. They read as follows:

GOTTWALD, GEORGE J., LIEUTENANT.

APPOINTED 3/24/1889. KILLED 2/5/1898.

GOTTWALD, GEORGE J., LIEUTENANT.

APPOINTED 1/21/1948. KILLED 3/3/1970.

Bet that first George was sumthin' else, too.

But The Runt
Wasn't Bad
Either

The captain was working on his morning report when the knock
came on his door. "Come in." He heard the door open and
close and he kept on typing. After a minute he looked up and said,
"Oh, hi, Runt, what can I do for ya?"

"Do for me? Didn't you send for me, Cap?"

"No, I didn't, Runt."

"That goddamn Fatback said you wanted me." He stormed out
the door and the captain returned to his report. He could hear Runt
shouting at Joe, or Fatback, as he was called, "He didn't want me
you asshole, he's busy."

"I never said he did, pal. You're just a stool pigeon anyway."

Everything is normal, thought the captain. Just Fatback giving
the shaft to Runt as he did every day, one way or another.

The Runt had come on the job when the hours changed after
the war. He was much older than most who came on at the time
because Civil Service allowed men who were veterans to subtract
their service time from their age to meet the thirty-four year maxi-
mum. Runt was thirty-seven. He was a wiry little guy, five two,
one hundred ten. He was also the most gullible guy in the house
and his trips to the captain's room were quite frequent. The men
were always on him and Fatback was the ringleader. When the
captain had first been assigned to the house, he had watched the
abuse Runt took for a couple of weeks and decided to put a stop to
it. He was not gonna let these jerks lean on one little guy. They
oughta be ashamed. Fatback had tried to explain a few things to
him but he was adamant. Leave Runt alone, period.

Within two weeks, Runt came in to see him. "Er, Cap, can I
talk to ya?"

"Sure, Runt, how's it goin'?"

"Well, I been thinkin' about a transfer over ta Three. Can ya make out a paper for me?"

"Transfer, Runt?" He was startled. "How come you wanna go over there?"

"Well, I dunno. I usta like it here. But it's kinda different."

"Runt, if anyone's botherin' you, I'll . . ."

"No, no, Cap, they ain't, honest. They're all real polite and everythin', but it's a lot different. I'm gonna go over to Three."

After the Runt left, the captain shook his head. You dummy, he thought, the poor little guy thinks they're mad at him. Nice going. You broke his spirit with your bullshit. He called the patrol desk. "Send Fatback to my room, right away." When he knocked on the door the captain said, "O.K. Joe, come in. Sit down. I surrender. Runt wants outa here."

"Naw he doesn't, Cap. He'll be O.K. We learned a long time ago, ya gotta keep on his back. If ya don't, the next thing ya know he's around punching guys on the arm or somethin' just so they'll yell at him. Now that you see the light, things will straighten out. Boy, you learned quicker than the last guy."

Pretty soon the captain could hear a lot of yelling and screaming coming from the kitchen and he relaxed and threw the transfer paper into the wastebasket.

The lunch time activity was a daily ritual with Runt. As soon as he sat down with a cup of coffee and his lunch, someone would jiggle the table with a knee and the coffee would spill on the table. "Hey, Runt, your cup's leaking. That goddamn Clinky bought those cheap cups again."

"Yeah, I know it. And he always makes sure I get a cracked one too. He's a cheap bastid," said Runt.

"Yeah, we pay him every week to run the damn house fund and he's making a bundle off us, right pal?" and Runt would nod in agreement. He'd wipe up the spill and start pulling out his lunch. One sandwich, one chocolate chip cookie.

"What's the matter with you, you little shit? You always bring the same lunch," said Fatback. "One little sandwich, one little cookie. Everything about you is small. You not only got a little lunch, ya got a little wife, a little house and a little car. You're nuthin' but a little pain in the ass and I'm sick of ya."

With that he'd pound on the table, always managing to hit the chocolate chip cookie dead center with his fist. This would create an uproar with Runt trying to punch him and everyone holding him back.

"Another thing. You're only a pump operator. You shouldn't even be eating with the fire fighters."

This would be the last straw. Runt was always sensitive that he was on the pump. At fires everyone else would be on the line and in the building, while he was outside making sure they had water. "I could be in there with ya and I could do a lot better," Runt screamed. "But the captain wants me on the pump 'cause he doesn't trust you. He told me I could get water on the Sahara Desert."

"Well, maybe ya can, but you couldn't get it on Concord Street the other night and we almost got burned to death."

"It was frozen, the damn hydrant was frozen," Runt shouted and the argument went on and on.

The pump operator, of course, is as important as anyone else at the fire and The Runt was about the best one around. If the pump doesn't get water, nothing else is going to work and you're gonna burn down someone's building, baby, so ya better have a reliable guy on the pump. The number of lines run from one pump depends on the size of the pump and the size of the water main, and the department rules limit the number to the capacity. But the right pump in the proper position at a fire is invaluable. If it's close enough to the scene and has a good supply, boy, you can get four or five quick short lines from it.

At a fire one night on Shawmut Avenue, Runt was in perfect position. So much so that he took one more line than the rules permitted, but he fed them all without any difficulty. They really knocked the shit outta the fire and the district chief and deputy were very pleased. As the deputy was about to return to quarters, Fatback grabbed him, "Hey, Deputy, do me a favor, willya? Tell the Runt what a great job he did."

"O.K. Joe, but I know you're probably gonna give him a screwing. I should keep out of it, but I'll speak to him."

Runt was really beaming after the deputy left, but here came the new district chief, also under Fatback's directions. "Er, Runt, you did a nice job."

"Why, thank you, Chief."

"The only thing is, uh, you had too many lines on the pump. You know what the rules say. Good thing we didn't lose the supply. Be more careful next time," and he walked away, thinking to himself, why do I let that Joe talk me into things?

Runt kept staring at his back and Fatback slid up beside him. "How's it goin', pal?"

The Runt was enraged. "That new asshole is yellin' at me because I had an extra line on the pump. He didn't say a goddamn word during the fire. He was tickled to death I give him all that water. Now that it's over, all of a sudden I'm wrong. He don't know shit anyway. The deputy said I did great and he's a lot smarter than this guy."

"Yeah, you're right, Runt. I'll have to speak to this new duck for ya."

"Well, thanks, Joe, I wish ya would. Boy, he's got a lot to learn."

But no matter what Fatback did to him, Runt really loved him, although he'd never admit it. Joe's favorite song was "The Runt Is A Brown Nosed Stool Pigeon" to the tune of "Rudolph The Red Nosed Reindeer," and he'd be singing it or whistling it any time he wanted to get Runt mad. Runt would always take the bait, but with all his lack of smarts, he instinctively knew that if there was real trouble, Fatback would take care of him.

Whenever Joe wanted to get his car washed, he'd take a bucket of water and soap, place it beside the car and lean there, waiting. Pretty soon Runt would come by and ask him what he was doing. It was always the same routine: "Well, Runt, old pal, I'm trying to wash my car but my back is killin' me. 'Member the other night when I was inside breakin' my balls on the line while you were out in the street? I dunno, I think ya gave me too much pressure and I pulled a muscle or sumpthin'." In no time, Runt would be washing the car, giving poor Joe a lift and protesting that he had given him the right pressure. Joe would slip into the bunkroom and lie down. Pretty soon, Runt would come in and let him know he had finished the car.

"Sucker," Fatback would yell as loud as he could and Runt would get furious. But he'd be there the next time.

When he'd get detailed to another fire house because they were shorthanded, the men there would try to get on him too, but he never permitted it. One day the lieutenant from Three called the captain and said, "Jeez, Cap, Runt just quit the job. They were on his back and he stormed out the door. He told me to stick the job up my ass. I don't know where the hell he went!"

"O.K., Luft, don't get excited. He quit on me one day and I don't even know why yet. He'll be back soon."

Runt's hobby was roller skating and he used to go twice a week. Naturally everyone insulted his ability and he was always telling them he'd show them some day. Fatback saw a pair of skates in Runt's locker one morning and pretty soon he was working on him to give a demonstration. He conned him into putting them on, lacing them up and getting on the table in the recreation room to do his stuff. He was really very good and he was leaping and pirouetting around with everyone cheering. At just the right moment, Fatback sounded the house alarm and yelled, "It's a go, it's a go," and everyone raced for the apparatus. Runt was scared to death. He skated across the floor as the motors on the engines started roaring. He couldn't drive the pump with the skates on and the captain would kill him if he got out late. He was pulling at the laces but they kept knotting. He'd never get them off. Suddenly all the motors stopped and he looked up to see Fatback staring at him with a fiendish grin. "Sucker," he yelled, and Runt threw a skate at him. By 1970 Runt had reached his sixtieth birthday and his family talked him into retiring and moving to New Hampshire, or "out in the alfalfa," as Fatback put it. The station ran a going away party for him and off he went. Pretty soon he got a job working in the Fire Alarm Division of a medium sized city. He kept in touch for a little while, but eventually Fatback and the gang lost track of him. About five years later, the captain got a call from the New Hampshire department. They told him that Runt was retiring once and for all and they were having a party for him the following week. If any of the guys would care to come up, they'd be welcome.

Fatback and a carload of the troops headed north, with Joe pointing out the cows, horses, grass and other country stuff all the way up to Runt's adopted home. It was a real cultural thrill for the inner city boys. They arrived just as the banquet started and Runt's face lit up as they marched in and took their seats. When the meal was concluded, several speakers praised him and presented him with gifts and the little guy was thrilled. As the toastmaster concluded the presentations, he said, "Runt, a lot of the men from Boston that you worked with have come all the way up here to be with you. I'm going to ask if one of them could come up and say a few words."

Fatback headed for the podium. "Folks," he said, "we came up here from Boston after receiving your kind invitation. We appreciate your consideration and you probably think we came to wish Runt well. But it isn't true. We really came to let you know, if you don't already, that he was the biggest stool pigeon and the worst pump operator we ever had. We just want to make damn sure he's finally pensioned so he can't ruin your department. We were glad to get rid of him and we're happy you're dumping him too." With that, he turned to Runt and handed him the engraved watch they had brought with them. "Here, you little rat, this is so you'll know when it's time to get out of town."

As Fatback approached his table, one of the guys nudged the man next to him. "Hey lookit, I think Fatback has a tear in his eye. Hey Joe, whaddya doin', bawlin'?"

"Naw, I just feel sorry for all these farmers up here. He's been shittin' them up to the ears tellin' them how many rescues he made in the big city."

Runt got up and made a really voluble speech, talking about his experiences and the friends he had made in both this town and Boston. When he got done he walked down to Fatback's table and kissed him on top of the head. "I don't care what you say Joe, you're still my friend."

"Yeah, and you're still a sucker."

The fire department won't work without men like George Gottwald, but it won't work without men like the Runt either.

The
Leader

There was a fire station that stood in the South End for forty
years on Broadway between Shawmut Avenue and Washington Street. It housed different fire companies at various stages of
its existence, but basically it was the home of Engines 7, 26 and
Ladder 17. It had different names at different times — also being
called "The Big House," "Sing Sing," "The Zoo," "Attica," etc.
But mostly it was called Broadway.

The area was really something. Next door to the house was a
gay bar, although at that time it was called a fag joint. Across the
street was a straight bar, but it was a real bucket of blood. Up the
street was a liquor store which sold mostly wine for the poor
winos who populated the vacant buildings that ringed the South
End in that era. The companies responded to fires downtown and
in Chinatown in one direction, Beacon Hill and Park Square in
another, the South End itself in the third direction and parts of
South Boston to the south.

But while the fires they went to were one thing, the house and
the neighborhood were something else. If you were to walk in cas-
ually in the late evening, the first thing you would notice were the
wine bottles lined up in the toilet on the main floor. These be-
longed to the poor winos. They would leave their bottles in the fire
house for the night so they could get a room at the Pine Street Inn.
The Inn was nearby and was run by people with real compassion
for these unfortunates, but they had an ironclad rule that you
couldn't bring a jug with you. The storage area at the fire house
was inviolate and no wino would ever steal another guy's jug.

In the warm weather they would all sleep in the fire house yard
between the parked cars and cover themselves with newspapers.

They used to say the Sunday *Globe* was the warmest, but they hated the editorials — too liberal for their taste. If they got shut out at the Inn in the winter, they would try to get into a vacant building, and from time to time one or two would get burned to death. They'd always sleep on the top floor of a building in spite of the fire fighters' warnings. The jakes would tell them to stay down below so they could get out easier, but the winos said the kids would beat them up and steal whatever they had if they were on the first floor. There are some tragic sights and stories associated with these derelicts, but you can't get involved in psychoanalysis and still do the job properly, so you just have to accept things the way they are. The fire fighters and winos got along great, with a lot of banter and respect in both directions.

The next thing you might see if you hung around was a hooker coming in to use the same toilet. The hookers in that area had to be the fattest and ugliest and oldest in existence. There was no danger of a fire fighter being tempted too seriously, and no fire fighter would ever personally use that toilet for any reason. It was swamped out with sulpha naphthol every day, but even that strong disinfectant couldn't kill what those dream girls were distributing.

The gays next door kept pretty much to themselves, except on Halloween. At that time it was against the law for a man to wear women's clothes, but on Halloween night it was considered a costume and it was a great night to be working. The parade would start as soon as it got dark and some of them really looked great. They had names like Elizabeth Taylor and Rita Hayworth and other glamour girls. Some of them looked almost as good as the real thing and naturally the fire fighters would let them know about it. They'd end up yelling back and forth and a few times the cops ended up in the act. The joint across the street was often the site of near riots. Some nights it looked like a scene from "Gunsmoke," with chairs flying through the windows, followed by participants. There were also a lot of Chinese in the neighborhood and they were never any problem to the fire fighters. As a matter of fact, great friendships developed between the two groups and it was a very good relationship always.

But of all the characters in the vicinity, the greatest of all was the captain in charge of the ladder truck. He was in the station for fifteen years and, due to his seniority in rank, was the captain of the house. He was six feet four, weighed about two-thirty and was a very impressive looking guy. He had several nicknames, including "Victor McLaglen," "Major Hoople," "Colonel Blimp," and "Slim"; but most frequently he was called "The Leader." He thought he ruled with an iron hand but no one else thought so. He would rant and rave about how he wanted things done, but men instinctively know what a guy is really like and they knew that in spite of all his threats and bluster, The Leader had compassion.

Whenever a new captain came to one of the other companies in the house, The Leader would sit him down and make it clear that he was running the house and the new guy would comply with his instructions. Most of them would nod their heads in agreement until he ran down and then they would proceed to run their companies and their men the way they wanted to. "Slim" would never interfere once he had had his say.

He was always chewing out his men for minor infractions but he would defend them fiercely if anyone else abused them. He considered laddermen to be the cream of the crop and far superior to enginemen. He used to say, "You could replace hosemen with monkeys and they'd do a better job and would give you a lot less trouble. All ya hafta do is feed them bananas once a week and leave them alone. 'Course the bananas cause them to shit all over the floor, but no one's perfect." He used to call one of the engine companies in the house a ditto and the other one a douche bag. One time when the union was threatening a work slowdown in a contract dispute, The Leader said, "A slowdown? Why I have hosemen in this station that I would have to start first before they could slow down."

Following a fire in a dirty bookstore in the Combat Zone, someone asked him how things were going on the next tour of duty. "Oh, I dunno, they got me worried now. They used to call each other pricks and assholes and tell each other to go fuck themselves. After the fire the other night, they grabbed a couple of those books and now they're using words like fornicate, fellatio, menage a trots and I don't know what else. I'm not sure what any of it means, but I think we're gonna have real trouble."

The men used a lot of reverse psychology on him and he was a perfect target. He had always forbidden a television set in the patrol desk, long after every other fire house had one, and he would never let a phone extension be placed in the kitchen which was in the back of the house some distance from the patrol area. The men asked him several times but he always had the same answer. "If I give you a TV at the desk, one of you assholes will be watchin' Howdy Doody and miss an alarm." About the phone he would say, "I have enough trouble keeping you in the desk now. If I put a phone in the kitchen, you'll never be on patrol, it's out of the question."

They tried a few ruses such as outlining a phone jack on the kitchen wall in chalk with the words "cut here for phone" or "bring antenna through here" in the patrol desk, asserting that some guy from the chief of department's office had come down and made the marks, but he was adamant. "If the chief wants to run this joint, let him come down and tell me to my face, I'll straighten him out. I usta do watches with him when he was a private and the sumbitch couldn't even count. If he'd had a TV in there then, he'da screwed up everything."

Finally, a new captain came to one of the engine companies. He and "Slim" were rivals from years ago and there was little love between them. This was just what the men were waiting for. When they heard The Leader approaching the kitchen one morning, they had it all set up. As the captain was coming into the room, one guy said, "Yeah, that new captain's gonna be a pain in the ass, he says he'll never let us have a TV or a phone either."

"What was that?" said "Slim."

"Oh hi, Cap, I didn't see ya. Nuthin', I didn't say nuthin'."

"Yes you did, I heard ya. Let me tell you all somethin', and I'll tell that asshole when I see him. I am the captain here, the rest of them are just on probation and I make all the decisions. You can put that TV in today and we'll have a phone in the kitchen tomorrow, and that's final."

While he was always berating the hosemen, at least they were in Fire Division One. The city was divided into two divisions. He had nothing but contempt for anyone from Division Two and referred to it as "The Other Division." Whenever he returned from a multiple alarm out there, someone would always ask him how it was. "Why, we'd put it out with two damp mops in Division One." When someone once mentioned that a couple of fire fighters had been hurt at a fire he was at he said, "Yeah, they were from Division Two. One got dandruff and the other hurt his feelings." Not very charitable.

The Chinese community loved him. When the company would go through the section on inspections, everyone would stop to talk to him. He didn't understand a word they said but they knew he was their friend. Once he was called to headquarters when a fire prevention problem developed between a Chinese businessman and an inspector. It was really a misunderstanding and in a few minutes "Slim" turned to the Marshal: "Everything is O.K. he's not gonna violate any of your stupid laws, he'll get everything flame proofed, the inspector just didn't pay attention to him. Hey Wong, you're all set. The inspector will see you tomorrow and he won't bother you." The guy bowed his way out of the office. He didn't know what "Slim" was talking about, but he knew his friend was taking care of him.

At the Sherry Biltmore Hotel Fire in 1963, The Leader's truck did an outstanding job and saved twenty-five people over ladders. This fire was one of the worst in years and was publicized for several days because it was a case of arson and a number of people had died. The Leader was interviewed in quarters the next day tour and he regaled the reporter with feats they had performed. When it was written up in the paper he was described as "a strong, handsome looking man with flashing eyes and tattooed, burly forearms. Stern but fair, an ideal leader of men, idolized by his laddermen." From that day on, at every alarm he went to, someone was always asking him to show his tattoos or flash his eyes or even look handsome and "Slim" would really get pissed. He never mentioned it, but he really regretted that interview. The men agreed he was stern and used to ask him when he was gonna start being fair so they could idolize him, but he'd ignore them.

He was a great story teller about World War II. Most of the members of the house were veterans but none were as brave as The Leader. He had served in the Coast Guard and to hear him tell it, they had won the war. He told about suckering Uboats with a ship filled with ping pong balls, invasions in Europe and the Pacific and chasing the Nazis in Greenland. One time, the 82nd Airborne Division held its reunion in Boston and one of the fire fighters had served in the unit, so many extroopers visited the station throughout the week. These guys had all jumped into Normandy on D-Day and Arnhem in Belgium and had fought their way across Germany, but they were no match for "Slim." They came just to hear his tales, although once he got tripped up badly. He was telling one soldier, who was a Filipino, that he had been in the Philippines as well as everywhere else during the war, yeah, he'd been there in 1943. "1943, is that so? Jeez Cap, you must be Japanese then 'cause that's all we had there then." The captain back stepped a little, ignored the guy and went on to the next story.

By the late sixties, plans were announced to build a new house on Columbus Avenue, several blocks from Broadway, and the big house was to be torn down for a new school. "They'll never get away with it while I'm here," said The Leader, and he headed for the Pentagon with those flashing eyes. When he returned he was pretty subdued and he still claimed it would never happen, but privately he knew it was true. Just before the house was to close, he retired, and both events marked the end of an era in the South End.

He had a tremendous retirement party at Florian Hall, which is the Union's building in the Dorchester section. By then he had been retired for a few months and had regained his spirit. When he first rose to make his thank you speech he was overcome by emotion and it looked like he would be speechless. But to everyone's relief, he recovered and started by saying, "You know, I've heard a lot of glowing speeches here tonight about myself and I just want you to know every goddamn word of them is true. Another thing, over the years I may have said things about people that were unkind and cruel, and every goddamn word I said was also true." He then went on to single out many of the guests and berate them in a way that would make Don Rickles look sick. But finally, he ran down and ended with a truly remarkable speech about his years on the job and his love for his men. When he finished he was in tears and so was a lot of the audience. He received a standing ovation that has never been matched in that hall.

A few weeks later, a friend of his who had become the captain drillmaster of the fire academy invited "Slim" to come down for a visit. He arrived for lunch on Wednesday afternoon and entertained the training officers and the new kids with his stories. That started his weekly visits to the place and soon other retirees started dropping in. This was the start of the "Liars Club, " which continues today. "Slim" died a few years ago and the group still meets on Wednesday afternoons, but there was only one Leader of the outfit and that's all there'll ever be.

The
Black
Secret

B ack in the thirties, if a guy managed to get through college, it was quite an achievement, particularly when you see all the dumdums running around with degrees nowadays. The problem back then was that no matter how smart you were when you graduated, there was no work anywhere when you got out. One guy who got out of St. Bonaventure's in Olean, New York, returned to Boston and faced that difficulty just like everyone else. He had been a star athlete in school, but being able to run with a football wasn't gonna help you make a living unless you were Bronko Nagurski or Red Grange.

This guy, though, was a pretty good wrestler. He married soon after he graduated and started raising a family, but finding work was really tough. In desperation he tried out for Paul Bowser's stable. Mr. Bowser was the biggest promoter of wrestling in New England. He had a group of guys who traveled the six state area, filling auditoriums wherever they went. The tryout was a success and the guy joined the troupe. He was always grateful to Mr. Bowser for the chance at a time when he really needed the job. He claimed Mr. Bowser was one of the finest men he ever met. Wrestling, while it is still pretty popular in the area, has never regained the universal appeal it had during the great depression. Sure it's on TV, but on channels that are remote, that you can't get too clear on your set, and you have to wade through roller derby before your heroes come. But back then it was big time stuff. There was no TV or a lot of the other inane types of entertainment presently available. Wrestling and wrestlers were front page news. The Boston Garden, home of the Boston Bruins and Celtics, was always filled for the big matches. It didn't cost much and it was a great show. In those years of America's innocence, some people actually believed it was on the level, but of course it never was.

There was always some masked man, caped challenger or other mystery man appearing on the scene. He would start at the bottom and work his way up through Mr. Bowser's stars, never revealing his identity and attracting larger and larger crowds. If he was popular enough, he would get a championship fight and defeat the reigning champ and be king of the world (or at least New England). When his popularity started to wane, he would be defeated by the next upcoming hero who would unmask him in a dramatic gesture of contempt after pinning him in the final fall. Jeez, guess who it was. The same guy who was the Swedish (or French or Polish or Irish) masked man three years ago. I thought his style was familiar. Mr. Bowser used to rotate the masks so everyone got a crack at the title and the big dough.

As time went on, the guy liked the job well enough, but he knew it had to be temporary. You could only last so long getting thrown into the fifty cent seats and he had to get something steadier 'cause the family was getting pretty large. He took the fire exam, although a bit reluctantly. The money was very bad and the hours were atrocious. Eighty-four hours a week. You were in the fire house every day at eight a.m. either coming on or going off duty, seven days a week. It was no bargain, but it was steady. There were very few appointments at the time, however, so he kept wrestling and traveling the circuit.

Every summer they took a tour of all the state fairs in New England. Four guys would take off in a car and hit the road. When they would get to a town, two would dress like the local farmers and join the audience. The other two would appear in the ring looking fierce and challenging all comers for a one hundred dollar purse. Naturally, the two shills in the audience would be selected and the battle was on. The guys in the ring would always win because, after all, they were champions up in Boston weren't they? Then on to the next town with their reputation enhanced. One time though, they took two cars, and the one with the shills broke down en route to a fair up in Maine. When the two Boston strongmen entered the ring and hurled out their challenge, they started looking around the crowd. "Hey," said the guy, as he stood back to back with his partner, "do ya see Joe or Tiny?"

"No, I thought they were on your side," whispered his partner.

"Jeez, they better be out there. If one of these real plow jockies comes up and gets a headlock on us, he'll kill us."

Sure enough, two well-known locals came up and the match was started. They were very strong and the guy and his partner almost got killed. In the long run, they managed to win, but only because they were very good wrestlers. They kept trying to signal the ref to call foul or something, 'cause he was in on the fix, but the sumbitch never even looked at them. When their arms were raised in victory at last, they were exhausted. They ached all the way home. It was a tough way to make a buck.

The next morning he groaned as he got out of bed. Was he really hurting in that many places at once? He felt about a hundred years old. When his wife brought him the mail there was a letter from Civil Service. Would he accept an appointment as a permanent fire fighter in the city of Boston at a salary of $2100 per year? You bet he would. He came on in the early forties and stayed thirty-five years. It was love at first sight for both him and the fire department. When he reached his first assignment, someone noticed his cauliflower ears and asked him what happened to them. "Aw, ya shoulda seen them before I had them fixed," he replied.

"Hey, wait a minute, I remember you. Yeah, you usta wrestle for Bowser. I seen you at the Garden a coupla times. You were the Black Secret or somethin', right? I was there the night you got unmasked by the big Irish guy."

The title was wrong but the nickname stuck and he was always known as the "Black Secret," or "Secret" for short.

He took to the job like a duck to water and was a terrific jake. Because his family was pretty large, he was not drafted during the war. When the veterans came home, they were given point advantages in promotional exams. This made it difficult for the non-vets to compete, but he never complained about it and kept studying and eventually became a fire captain. He was assigned to the ladder truck in the Harrison Avenue station in the South End and stayed there for many years. He used exceptional judgment both at fires and in the handling of men. His theories for leadership were faultless but aren't found in textbooks. He was a true believer in the dignity of man. He believed when you were given a command over men you were accepting an important responsibility. You were going to be making decisions constantly that could result in serious injury or even death to them, and that could not be taken lightly. But your responsibility did not end when the man went off duty. If he had trouble at home, you were duty bound to help him. After all, he was one of yours, wasn't he?

The Secret did not, however, believe in babying men. He believed that all the average guy wants is a fair shake. He doesn't want to be abused but he doesn't want to be treated like a kid either. He wants direction in his work and it must be firm and decisive. He would much rather get an incorrect order than no order at all. The Secret used to say, "I treat them all the same — rotten." But no one would agree with that last word. He had a voice that could be heard for blocks away and it was a familiar sound in the South End when you heard the Secret yell, "Ladder Three, get the stick up!" One chief always claimed he could hear him before he got to the street the fire was on, and he would start pulling up his boots 'cause he knew he was going to work.

After twenty-five years of continuous fire duty, the Secret almost got killed one afternoon during a fire on East Newton Street. He and another fire fighter were trapped on the fourth floor when a huge quantity of fuel oil ignited in a cellar and drove the fire up the shafts and stairways, cutting off all escape. In the rescue effort that followed, the Secret and his partner couldn't be seen at the window and the men in the street were desperately raising ladders to get the visible fire fighters who were also trapped. The two inside worked their way back to the hallway but couldn't open the door because of the heat. They were getting weaker and weaker. They got back to the window and kept waving their lights. Just when they had given up all hope, an aerial ladder hit the window sill perfectly, right through the dense smoke, and they scrambled on the tip. When it was over, it was a big joke, like it always is when everyone gets out. But the Secret never forgot, and the guy who directed the rescue effort still gets a card every year on the anniversary of the fire that is unsigned but says, "One more year of gravy."

Within a month after the rescue, the Secret was taken from another fire with a cardiac problem, which probably developed from
the narrow escape. He convalesced as the doctor ordered but he
was going nuts at home. When he was well enough, he asked the
chief of department to give him some kind of job, although he
knew his fire fighting days were over. The chief assigned him to
replace the outgoing department drillmaster in training recruit
classes and running the fire academy.

For the next eight years he was responsible for training hundreds of new men and he took that job as seriously as he had taken
his fire company. He instituted several different methods of teaching fire fighters, each one designed to teach what you actually do
at fires, not what the theorists think you do. Among other things,
he arranged with the building department to provide him with a
list of abandoned city-owned buildings. He would take each recruit
class to one and have them spend days cutting holes in roofs,
opening walls and ceilings, chopping floors, throwing ladders, running lines, shutting off utilities. Everything that they would be
doing when they got out in the field. They'd go home filthy and
exhausted, but they were starting to learn the business. Whenever
one of those buildings burned later, and they frequently did, the
Secret would get a call from one of the guys who was at the fire
and he'd say, "We knew it was one of yours, pal, we didn't have
to do a damned thing, everything was open. Thanks a lot." The
Secret liked to hear that.

On the very first day with each new class he made it clear that
they were there to learn. With his gruff voice he'd have them raise
a ladder to the roof of the fire building at the academy. He'd then
have them climb it. They were required to do this every day, twice
a day for the next twelve weeks, rain, snow or shine. The weather
never caused a postponement of this or any other drill. If anyone
complained he was wet or cold the Secret would always reply,
"Whaddya think, we only have fires on good days?"' The kids
never heard the nickname Black Secret. They always called him
"Up and Over" because of his continuous ladder drills. Whenever
he had smoke drills in the fire building, he really made it "juicy"
as he called it. His point always was, this is the way it's gonna be
when you get out there. It's not a job for sissies. The first guy who

ever showed up late in class would cause the Secret to line them all up and give his favorite speech. "This job is not like working in Filene's Basement. It is a twenty-four hour a day service. There is a partner in the house waiting for you to relieve him. You have a responsibility to him. He cannot just walk away when the tour ends. It's a man for man deal. If you can't accept that, maybe you better apply at Filene's cause you ain't gonna graduate here."

But they all graduated all right, and every man had the Secret's stamp of approval on him. He produced some of the best fire fighters the job has ever seen. He always thought he was too hard on them, but they never did. The walls of the fire cademy are lined with plaques. They're all thank you's to the Secret and they're from every class he's ever trained.

The Black Secret retired a few years ago, but he's still around somewhere. Funny thing about the job: when they leave, you always describe them in the past tense, just like they died. It's not really that they died, but something inside you does when the good ones leave.

We'll Never
Get It
Again

The Hotel Roosevelt stood at the corner of Washington Street and Dover Street in the South End. Actually, Dover Street had recently been renamed East Berkeley Street to try to give the area a little class and eliminate the expression, "He was a Dover Street Bum." The attempt was kinda a failure though, because the winos stayed in the area no matter what the street was called.

The Hotel was a fleabag. It was six stories high, had many tiny cubicles — euphemistically called rooms — and about a hundred fifty guests every night. It was situated right next to the elevated railway that bisects the South End and has ruined property values since the turn of the century.

The department responded to the Hotel many times each year, mostly for mattress fires, but once in a while for a room or two. Because of its proximity to the El, the department had preplanned the place and had a pretty good system. In order to get the roof, Ladder Three would come from the west, down Washington Street, and jump the sidewalk just before getting to the building, even hitting a few cars if necessary, if it looked like a good fire. Worry about the accident forms later. From this position, the aerial could be raised to the roof and top floor, but this was the only spot that could accomplish the task. Of course, roof ventilation is essential to effective fire fighting. Just two weeks before they had had a fire on the third floor and everything went all right, strictly routine. Course that damn Clinky on Ladder 13 started raising hell with the hookers. The chief sent him down to the second floor fire escape to clean off some debris they were throwin' outta the third and pretty soon he was yellin', "Chief, Chief, these women are raping me."

The chief dropped down to the second and said, "What the hell are you screamin' about?"

"Honest to God, Chief, they're after my body!"

The chief looked at the two hookers, both in their thirties, both Indian girls from Maine, one with a six inch scar on her cheek. "You girls aren't botherin' one of my men are ya?"

"Naw," one of them said with a grin, "But he invited us back to the fire house. We're comin' too."

He turned to Clinky. "You get the fuck outta here or I'll put ya in on charges. You ain't bringing no one back to the house."

"I wouldn't shit ya, Chief, they tried to attack me. Besides, I gave them directions to Twenty-six's house. You know I'd never bring them to our place; they're pretty tough pieces of work."

Yeah, Clinky's a pisser.

Tonight, though, February 4, 1968, things were a little different. Ladder 3 was at a second alarm in Roxbury along with the engine from their house. An East Boston engine was covering the station, but there was no ladder truck. When the call came in for a fire, the operator telephoned the station and said, "Take Engine 56 to the Hotel Roosevelt." He then called Ladder 17, the next closest station, and gave the same order. As Seventeen left Broadway and turned right onto Washington, they started passing under the elevated railway structure. The lieutenant, since the alarm was only for the truck, assumed they were going to an inhalator case. The structure blocked any view of the Roosevelt, so he couldn't see any sign of fire. As he pulled up in front of the door, he yelled to the men on the back, "Get the inhalator, I'll find out what floor." He ran over, opened the front door and staggered backwards: as far up the stairway as he could see was fire and he could hear people screaming. "Never mind the inhalator, pull by the building and get the stick up." He grabbed the mike in the cab, "Ladder 17 to Fire Alarm, fire in the Roosevelt, strike second alarm, Box 1632." As he got off and looked up, he could see people everywhere and heavy smoke pushing out all the windows. The position of the aerial only permitted it to be placed at the third floor side fire escape, but there was already a crowd there waiting for it. "Get a fifty," he shouted. They were going to have to try to get it straight up between the El and the building because several people were at the fourth floor level.

The district chief pulled up, took one look, and got on the radio. "Car 4 to Fire Alarm, strike third alarm, Box 1632, and send two extra ladder trucks." Fire Alarm acknowledged and he called again, "Strike fourth alarm and send ambulances." They were gonna need them. He started directing all the incoming companies, except the first three engines, to get on ladders. People were everywhere and now fire was showing up behind the heavy smoke on the upper floors. No chance to get the roof. Here came Ladder 3 now, but the position was blocked. He had them take a thirty-five foot ladder right up the elevated stairway and raise it from the platform, but when they got it up in position, they had to pick off a couple of people on the fifth floor and the roof ventilation couldn't be done.

Fire fighters raced along the fire escapes bringing occupants over to ladders, sometimes just beating the flames to the people and getting them to safety. One jake got cut off as the fire broke out behind him but he calmly jumped onto the El and walked down the stairs. The three engines each had lines, two up the front stairway and one over a ladder into the second. The deputy had struck the fifth alarm when he arrived, and as more and more occupants were brought down, lines started stretching up the ladders. The district chief went up a ladder following a line into the fifth. As they tried to climb over the fire escape into the room, a woman victim was blocking the way. They couldn't get by and it was obvious she was dead. The chief looked down to the street, but no one seemed to be watching. "O.K., listen, we gotta get the line in. Get a hold of her and take her back inside."

The officer looked at him. "You mean inside the fire building? "

"Yeah, and make it fast." They gently lifted the woman and moved her out of the way, into the room, and placed her on a bed. "O.K. now, bring the line over here." He was at the door to the corridor and as he eased it open, he could see fire rolling along the hall. The line started hitting it very effectively and they worked their way along, killing fire and getting to the main stairway. Another engine was coming up from below, and between them they advanced up the smouldering stairway toward the top floor. The top floor was tough. It was really juicy 'cause the roof hadn't been opened, but as they worked in, parts of it burned through and it started lifting a little. But they started coming across victims, all badly burned. One in one cubicle, two in another and more as they went forward. The fire was knocked down at last but the toll was pretty high. Six on the top and three down below. All poor unfortunates, most of whom wouldn't ever be identified.

As they were picking up the charred remains of one, the officer said to the chief, "Jeez, that's the first time I ever put one back in a building."

"Yeah, I know it, but for cripes sake, it worked, didn't it?"

"Yeah, I gotta admit we did great once we got by into the hall."

The chief said, "Well, it was the only thing I could think of at the time. But lissen, keep your mouth shut. I don't think the newspapers would unnerstand."

As they lifted the corpse and put it in the flexicot, one fire fighter complained of a piercing pain in his leg. "O.K., send him down, Lieutenant." The man was taken down and removed to the hospital by ambulance. When he was brought in his leg was still killing him. The doctor had him remove his boot carefully, but he could feel his flesh tearing and when his foot came out, he had a long gash on his leg.

"What happened?" said the doctor.

"I dunno, I was just pickin' up this body when the pain started."

The doctor fished around in the boot and brought out a piece of narrow bone splinter, sharp as a razor and about six inches long. He kept staring at it. "How bad was the victim burned?"

"Oh, he was really in tough shape, he was actually falling apart."

"Well, this is part of his leg bone. It tore through your boot and cut you."

"What?" He felt himself getting dizzy. "Ya mean that's the guy's leg?" Nausea swept over him.

The doctor went out in the other room and the fire fighter could hear him saying, "Hey, ya wanna see somethin' funny, come in here for a minute." Jeez, here I am bleedin' to death and that asshole's gonna put me on display. "Hey Doc, never mind the shit, how about fixin' me up?" I'm probably gonna get some kinda poison and he'll write me up in the *New England Journal of Medicine.* "C'mon, willya?"

While the life loss was tragic, the number of rescues had really been astounding under the conditions. Over a hundred had been brought down ladders with no other way of saving them. The chief often wondered if they could have got the ones on the top floor if Ladder Three had been in their own quarters, but no one could really say.

There were a lot of dramatic pictures in the papers the next day, but the best one was of Clinky. There he was on the front page, with the two Indian maidens he had saved, their arms around him, planting a kiss on each cheek. Maidens may not be the correct word, but it's what he told his wife when she threw the frying pan at him.

Space 'Em,
Boys,
Space 'Em

Whenever there is a big fire, a lot of help is going to be necessary. But if the chief orders it all at once, it's not too wise. First of all, too many fire engines are moving at the same time. They're converging on the area from all parts of the city, with sirens blaring, unable to hear anything over the noise they are making themselves. The possibility of a serious accident between responding companies is greatly enhanced. If they all get to the fire at approximately the same time, it is very difficult for the chief in charge to make the proper evaluation and give the correct orders to each fire company. It is much smarter to take a more methodical approach, no matter how serious the fire is. Keep sizing up the situation and adapting to the constant changes, then make a methodical calculation and give crisp, clear orders.

No one believed in this approach more than the district chief in Four. He felt that an unemotional appearance was the best. It not only let you make those proper decisions, it gave your men confidence in you, your orders and your overall ability.

The night tour of March 28-29th, 1968, had been fairly quiet in the district. The usual rubbish fires, abandoned autos and false alarms, but nothing else. The chief was just arranging his hitch near his bed when Box 1537 was struck at 0217 hours. This was on the far end of his district in the Back Bay section. This is the northern half of the district. It is lined with five- and six-story apartment houses, and the occupants are much more affluent than in the southern or South End part. The buildings burn just as briskly, however. The chief and his aide sped down Tremont and swung into Berkeley Street. They were still about a half mile from the box location and the chief was looking up the street. "Jeez, it looks like a lot of lights on up towards Comm. Ave. It's kinda cold for them gays to be demonstrating again isn't it? Yeah, it's kinda late too."

The radio blared, "Engine 10 to Fire Alarm."

"Answering, Engine 10."

"We have a church fully involved, strike second alarm." "Shit, those ain't lights. It must be a pisser."

As they arrived at the scene, it was really a fantastic sight. The entire Unitarian Universalist Church was consumed by fire and it was extending rapidly to other buildings. The left front wall had collapsed into the alley, burying several parked cars and igniting them. The eleven-story office building on the corner had fire on every floor. The rectory in the rear of the church had fire showing on three floors. Sheets of flame were leaping across the alley and licking at the upper floors of eight five-story apartment buildings. Sparks and flying embers were landing on the roofs of several other buildings on Marlborough Street.

As he got out of the car he ordered a third alarm. O.K., now, cool it, cool it. Be methodical, where do you want each company? He had his portable in his hand. Crisp, now, crisp. Strike fourth alarm. Yeah. Bring 'em in the alley from the other end, cut it off. Get a gun hitting the office building. Start evacuating all along the avenue. Yeah. Order fifth alarm, nice and easy. He was standing directly in front of the church, looking up at the enormous circular stained glass window. As he watched, the flames burst through and destroyed it. The wall itself was shaking. Hm, it might come down. A guy grabbed him by the sleeve. It was a civilian. He shook him off. Place another gun here. Start them coming down Marlborough, too. The hand plucked at him again. Why don't this guy get the fuck away from me? He turned to the man and his mouth dropped open. It was the new mayor, Kevin H. White, himself. "Where's Fitzgerald, where's Fitzgerald?" Who the fuck is Fitzgerald, he thought. Oh yeah, that's the fire commissioner. "Uh, he's on his way, yer Honor. Everyone is."

"Are you gonna stop it?"

"Yessir, we will, there's all kinds of help on the way." Why doesn't he get the hell outta here? "Lissen, yer Honor, this front wall is very shaky. It might come down. Will you please move back now, sir?" Jeez, I gotta get more help. Oh, good, here comes the deputy. "Deputy, it's in ten or eleven buildings. We need about ten extra engines after the fifth alarm."

"O.K." Without hesitation the deputy spoke to Fire Alarm. "Send ten extra engines to Box 1537, I'll give them assignments en route. Also, tell all responding ladder trucks to make evacuations on Commonwealth Avenue and be prepared to make rescues. Incoming engines to assume they'll be using heavy stream appliances."

Hey, is he crisp, thought the district chief.

The deputy turned to him, "You take care of the rectory and Marlborough Street, I'll go on the avenue. Keep in touch and call for anything you need, direct to Fire Alarm."

"Yessir. Uh, one other thing. This here guy is the mayor and he wants to talk to you. Yer Honor, this is the deputy and he's in charge now." He could see the deputy glaring at him and he ran as fast as he could to Marlborough Street.

The companies coming in to him were directed to set up guns, protect all the exposures and attack the church itself, while he sent three hand lines into the rectory. Cut it off, cut it off, kept passing through his mind. Don't let it jump the street. After about an hour, they had stopped it on his side and he went around to Comm. Ave. where the battle was much more difficult. The fire had entered the top two floors of all eight buildings that were exposed, plus the eleven floors of the office building. Hand lines had to be used in each building, requiring a tremendous amount of help. As water supplies dipped, pumps had to be used to relay more from blocks away. It was an enormous effort, but it worked. By dawn, there was no question they had stopped it, but the overhauling work would no doubt continue throughout the next tour of duty.

He met the deputy in the middle of the avenue and they both were exhausted. The chief of department, who had arrived in the middle of it, told them both to take a break. They got coffee at the Salvation Army truck and slumped to the curb, feet stretched out in the street. Boy, it felt pretty good. The deputy said, "Well, it was a hell of a stop. I don't know if we ever did any better. Oh, yeah, thanks for dumping the mayor on me."

"Well, jeez, I didn't know what the hell to do with him. He kept yelling for Fitzy. I couldn't even remember who Fitzy is."

"Yeah, that's the way mayors think, ya know? If it's a police problem, the police commissioner's name jumps in their heads. Water department — Smith, public work — Jones, fire — Fitzgerald, and so on. As if Fitzy was gonna make any contribution to this fire. But he's the mayor's guy and that's it. Even the president is like that. Army problem — Secretary of the Army, Navy — Secretary of the Navy. All civilians, all political appointments, but all loyal to him. Yeah, you gotta pay attention. You and I are just a couple flunkies far as the mayor's concerned. Don't forget it. Wait'll we try to negotiate the next raise. He won't even remember this fire."

"What did he say to ya, Deputy?"

"Well, he asked me where I was gonna stop it and I pointed right there." His arm stretched out toward the last building that got damaged. "He really thought it was something when I was right. He doesn't know anything about parapeted fire walls or anything."

The reliefs arrived shortly after 0800, and the district chief returned to quarters. He showered, shaved and really started to feel good. Not a bad job, not a bad job, hm. The phone rang and he scooped it up. It was Tom, his old drill school partner, still a fire fighter and still his most severe critic.

"Hey, big shot. Big deal, you saved all those liberals' homes. Yer picture's in the paper and everything. Boy, you really were cool, weren't ya. Just like you always told me. Be methodical. Space 'em, space 'em, right?"

"Yeah, that's right, Tom. It takes a lot of getting used to but I've been a chief quite a while now," he said.

"Yeah, well how come I heard on the news this was the fastest five alarms in the history of the department? Five minutes from the still alarm to the fifth. Boy are you cool."

Tom hung up and the chief sat staring at the phone. Hm, I thought I took twice that time. Well, there are a few exceptions to every rule, aren't there? Another thing, that wall never fell like I told the mayor it would. It was still standing fifteen years later. Yeah, and so was the mayor.

Sometimes . . .

Sometimes it's just pointing.

Sometimes it's a little more.

Sometimes it's too hot.

Sometimes it's too cold.

Sometimes it snows.

Sometimes it blows.

Sometimes you'll win.

Sometimes you'll lose.

Sometimes you'll make parking lots and there's nuthin' you can do about it.
(See "Advice and Philosophy Unsolicited.")

More jakes . . . More Tools

The door and window grills are modern necessities that hinder the job. Box WF-2219, Feb. 9, 1980, Roxbury District.

All set? Start moving in. Box 6-2124, Nov. 11, 1982, Roxbury District.

Six rescued via ladders. Note snow on big line. Box 2-1873, March 5, 1978, Dorchester District.

If you wanna park in Boston, ya take your chances. Box 3-1354, Nov. 29, 1978, Beacon Hill District.

Who are those space men? Jakes wearing Project FIRES experimental gear. (See "Who Pays for the Shoes?") Box 4-4173, March 20, 1982, Charlestown District.

Note rapid fire spread above ceiling laths. Box 9-5352, Jan. 7, 1981, Brighton District.

Extend tip and drop it through window on the right. Box 7-1383, Nov. 27, 1980, Back Bay District.

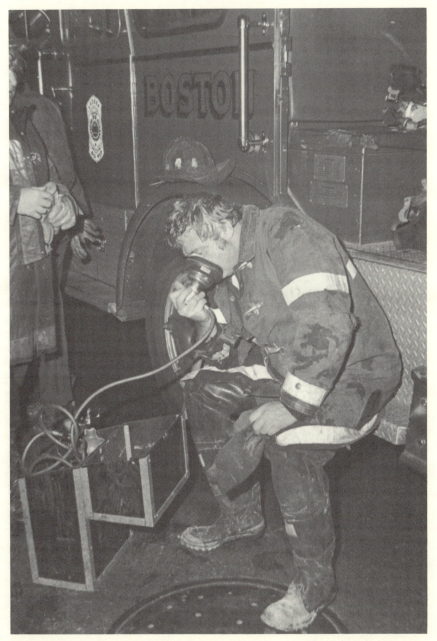

The glamour left a long time ago. Box 3-2124, August. 27, 1981, Roxbury District.

The nearer the peak, the better it vents. Box WF-543, March 28, 1982, Brighton District.

Fire burst through window just after jake made it to the stick. Box 2-5251, June 12, 1979, Brighton District.

Strip siding off when fire gets behind it. Box 2-7322, Sept. 22, 1978, South Boston District.

Moving it up and down — cut the fire off. Box 2-7413, March 16, 1980, South Boston District.

Fill both lines. Box 2-3123, Feb. 1, 1983, Dorchester District.

Yeah, this is part of it, too. Still alarm, 0400, Jul. 12, 1977, Southeast Expressway, Downtown District.

This is one of the big tools. Box 9-7161, June 3, 1982, South Boston District.

Everyone hates cellar fires. Sometimes cellar pipes will catch the fire. Box WF-136, Jan. 29, 1979, West End District.

Overhauling: The part nobody sees. The work doesn't end when the fire isn't visible and all the spectators leave.

More jakes get hurt during overhauling operations than any other.

No fire engines yet. At least the layoffs cut taxes. Box 9-254, June 11, 1982, Jamaica Plain District.

Does
A Ghost
Burn?

The Lockheed L1011, Tri Star Jet has a magnificent record for air safety. Pilots swear by it. It has the most sophisticated equipment imaginable. They say it can fly itself and even land itself under any condition. However, in 1972, one of the first ones built crashed in the Florida Everglades while circling the Miami Airport. It was a tragic accident, and while many people survived, many were killed, including the cockpit crew. A book was written about this crash called *The Ghost of Flight 401* by John Fuller.

Mr. Fuller contends in his book that soon after the accident, the flight engineer who died on 401 started appearing in other Eastern Airlines 1011s, speaking to crew members and warning them about minor defects in the aircraft. He even warned about the possibility of a fire on one plane. He kept appearing until the spring of 1974, according to the story, and at that time some crew members of Eastern who believed in such things performed an exorcism on a 1011 and the ghost has never been seen since.

Mr. Fuller's book also contained a lot of other interesting information, including the fact that a lot of parts were salvaged from the plane that crashed and the parts were used on the planes the ghost appeared on. He also revealed that at that time 1011s were scarce, so when Eastern's Florida runs slowed down in the spring, they'd rent their 1011's to TWA, whose east-west runs increased in the summer. At that time, Eastern had no east-west flights and it didn't affect the competition between them.

Logan Airport in Boston is a great international terminal. It has several runways, handles close to a thousand flights a day, and has several buildings on the property. It has its own fire department, controlled by the Massachusetts Port Authority, which operates the airport. The department is as well equipped as any crash crew force in the country. It also has a mutual aid arrangement with the Boston Department that works very well. Any time there's a serious fire or crash at the airport, the Boston Department will respond, and in return Logan will provide Boston with any help it wants, including their enormous foam delivery capability. Through the years a mutual respect developed between both forces and it still continues.

At 0029 hours, April 20, 1974, Box 612 was struck in Boston. This box is a request for assistance from Logan, and the department sends a larger than normal response because it is probably a plane crash. The deputy responded along with the rescue company from his downtown quarters. While en route through the tunnel to East Boston and then to the security gate at Logan, he was notified by Fire Alarm, "C-6, this box was requested by Logan. They are reporting a fire on an L1011 at the TWA terminal."

"C-6 has that." Jeez, that's a jumbo jet, hope there's no passengers on it. When they arrived at the gate, other Boston apparatus was waiting and they were led by a "Follow me" truck along the taxiways and over to TWA. As they approached, he could see smoke pushing out the doors and he could see the mechanical walkway still attached to the front left door. Smoke was passing through the walkway and into the terminal. He reported to the Logan chief, and after some consultation, decisions were made for the attack. The walkway was pulled away by TWA tractors, and ground ladders were raised to two openings in the plane while pick up trucks with wide ladder stairs were used at the other openings. The fire had originated in the ceiling of the jet and was traveling rapidly in the three foot space. The first attack was made with dry powder chemicals, one thousand pounds of it, driven up into the ceiling from the cockpit end, but it was ineffective. Water lines were then run in through two doors in the middle, and one in the front, and fire fighters started pulling the ceiling. The heat was really intense and an attempt was made to open the roof, but it started to glow cherry red and the jakes on top had to retreat into the bucket of the aerial tower. An attempt also was made to break out the passenger windows but they couldn't be broken with an axe and they were out of the reach of power tools. They were down too low to really provide effective ventilation anyway. When it became unbearable, the lines had to be backed up and the men retreated to the outside. The plane had seven thousand gallons of fuel still aboard but since it was below the fire and in the wings, the danger of ignition seemed remote. The fire burst through the roof and the three hundred passenger seats ignited.

It was a pretty hairy experience. The TWA personnel wanted to pull the plane away from the terminal, but the chiefs from the two departments wanted it kept where it was. The only hydrant available was right near the plane and if the plane was pulled to where the TWA guys wanted it, they'd have no water. Then they'd lose it for sure.

An articulating boom with a nozzle on it called a Squrt was placed inside the vent hole in the roof and it was swung back and forth, front and back, and was very effective. It knocked down a great deal of the fire and cooled the inside so that the interior attack could be resumed. As they entered with the hand lines and started down the aisles, the deputy was moving along, checking the seats and seeing if they were getting the fire. Suddenly there was a deep rumble and he thought, oh, shit, I was wrong again, there go the fuel tanks.

He knew they'd never make it off the plane. Well, at least I won't have to be around to answer why we didn't pull the plane away from the terminal.

As they all started running, the rumbling stopped. What the hell was it? They waited a few minutes and it didn't happen again until they started back down the aisles. The second time, he thought, well, it's not the tanks, must be somethin' else. They finally found a few flight attendants' walk-around oxygen bottles down the back and the safeties on them had let go. That must have been the rumble.

The fire was brought under control at last and the extensive overhauling process began. It had been quite an experience. They'd learned a few things about planes, including the fact that they burn like hell. They also wouldn't mind if they never got another one at the terminal. They had managed to save the cockpit, the wings, engines and undercarriage of the plane but the loss was still around seventeen million dollars. The deputy wrote a report that was later published in the trade journals and sent to the National Transportation Safety Board and the Airline Pilot's Association. The report included recommendations for increasing protection against fire in aircraft.

A few years later, the deputy read Mr. Fuller's book about the ghost and was intrigued enough to write the author and send a copy of his report because the book states that the ghost hasn't been seen since the spring of 1974. He received a reply in which Mr. Fuller stated that the plane that burned at Logan is the same one that got most of the parts from the Eastern L1011 that crashed.

The deputy has never believed in ghosts, but it was so smoky on the plane that night, maybe one left when no one was lookin'.

I Wonder Who
Put Out The
Grass Fire?

It was a beautiful spring day, May 22, 1964. The sun was shining brightly and the humidity was low. It was pretty windy though, but you can't have everything. The captain was whistling as he pulled his car into Andrew Square in South Boston. He parked on Dorchester Ave. and went into the building on the corner. This was a big day. His oldest boy was just completing a series of guitar lessons from the musician in this building. The guy had told him that the kid had a lot of potential and was really quite advanced for thirteen years old. So a few months back he had arranged to buy a pretty expensive electric guitar through the teacher and he had been making weekly payments ever since. Today was the last payment and he was going to pick up the instrument. It would be quite a surprise for his son, but he was a pretty good kid and deserved it. I hope to hell the rest of them take up the kazoo or something cheaper.

He picked it up and it sure looked great ! Oh, boy, case and all. After exchanging pleasantries with the musician, he walked downstairs, opened his trunk and gently placed the guitar inside. As he closed the trunk he looked over the top of the car and could see heavy black smoke rising on the Dorchester side of the square. Hm, looks like a three-decker, maybe two. He started to get in his car and thought, maybe I'll go take a look at it. Well, O.K., but remember dummy, you're working tonight and you're acting chief too, so you hafta get in early. Yeah, yeah, I'm just gonna take a peek. He left his car in the parking space and started walking across the square and up Dorchester Avenue.

The smoke seemed to be really pushing now but he couldn't see the buildings involved because they were blocked by the square and other houses. This area had hundreds of three-deckers lined up street after street. He crossed a small bridge over the Southeast Expressway and continued walking. He looked down toward the expressway and could see several grass fires burning along the embankment. Oh, oh, I better speed it up and tell the chief at this fire that he's got a couple of grassies down there, maybe he can call them in to Fire Alarm. Boy, it sure is windy.

It was 1339 hours. He could hear sirens off in the distance. A chief's car sped by him followed by an engine and a truck. They're just getting here, that's the first due engine. Now he started to run and he reached the corner of Bellflower Street and the Avenue and looked down the street. Three three-deckers were fully involved and the first companies were stretching lines as fast as they could. He could hear a second alarm striking on a radio somewhere and he jumped on a line with one of the engines. They had no officer on this day and one of the men recognized him.

"Hey, Cap, glad to see ya, ya wanna work with us?"

Before he knew it he was helping them move the line and directing them to try to cut off the fire from going into the fourth house in the row. But it was no use, it was just too hot. He could hear other alarms rattling in the background and knew the chief was really "leaning on the hook." Boy he's gonna need it.

The fire not only entered the fourth house in the row; now it started scorching the houses directly across the street. They were driven back and he could feel his arms starting to blister because he was wearing a short sleeved shirt. He kept sticking his hand in the stream coming from the nozzle and the water would splash all over him. As another company arrived, he told them to get a portable gun in addition to their line. When it was set up, they stuck two lines into it and kept hitting into the fire and swinging it back and forth, wetting down the exposures. He saw the deputy arrive and order more help. He went over to him and asked for any orders. "No, just keep doing what you are right now. We gotta try to cut it off. It's starting to spread through the back yards to the other streets." The deputy grabbed his portable and spoke to Fire Alarm, "Strike fifth alarm, Box 7251. We have a potential conflagration. Send me all available help."

The captain went back to the gun. Boy, I never heard an order like that before, I gotta see what's goin' on. He could see that about ten houses were now involved on Bellflower Street alone. He told the company he was with to keep hitting the exposures and he'd be right back. He went back down the street toward the avenue and cut into an alley. He ran down the end and got a look. Wow, he could see why the deputy wanted everything he could get; the fire had now raced through the yards, burning the fences and speeding toward a similar row on the next street over. He counted a half a dozen houses over there going. He could see apparatus hooking up over there too.

Now he crossed to the other side of Bellflower and ran down another alley. Jeez, it was spreading in this direction too. The fire was actually traveling with the wind in one direction and against the wind in another. It was creating a fire storm and developing its own wind. More and more apparatus kept arriving. Mutual aid had been requested when the fifth alarm had struck, but the call for all possible assistance was bringing in even more.

Eventually, fifty-seven engine companies and ten ladder companies worked on the fire. Twenty-six of them were from other cities. The captain and his company got together with another engine and truck and worked throughout the afternoon, constantly operating lines and constantly moving them. The smoke now obscured everything so it was hard to tell how the battle was going. Some three-deckers would start to smoulder and smoulder and suddenly they'd explode in flames. They finally reached one that was not fully involved, although it was next to one that was really going. The captain and one of the officers from the other two companies dashed up the front stairs. They looked into the second floor and could see the fire in the ceilings. The flames were coming across the alley from the burning building next door. They raced up to the top floor. Same thing. Fire in the ceilings. But not too bad yet. With a little luck they might catch it here.

They yelled out the front windows, "Bring a line into the second and third, up the back," because that was the easiest way at the time. "Bring some rakes, too," they yelled to the truckmen. The lines were pulled up the stairs and they started opening the ceilings and hitting the fire. They were holding their own! The captain went up the top and started opening there and here came the other line! "Hit it, hit it," he shouted, "I think we can get it." They were starting to do O.K.

Just then he heard the command, "Everyone outta the building !" It was coming from the back. He ran out onto the porch and in the yard was a chief officer from another city who had come on the mutual aid call. "Hey you, get out of that building, it's gonna explode."

"No it isn't, Chief, we're getting it, honest."

"You're not even a fireman mister, you get outta there or I'll have you arrested."

Jeez, that's right, I'm in my civvies. Hm, no company number on me. "Hey, Chief," he yelled to the visitor, "Go take a shit for yourself," and he ran back inside. He never saw him again, either. Good thing he wasn't from Boston.

When he got back in on the top floor he saw the ladder company officer. "Hey, Cap, I gotta idea."

"What is it, Luft?"

"That building next door is burned so bad I think we can knock the wall down."

"Ya think so? Gee I dunno, these joints are really put together."

"Well, I'm gonna take a shot at it," said the ladder officer.

He got three men with rakes and they stuck them out the window. They started pushing against the wall next door and by God, it moved. They kept pushing and pushing and it started rocking and rocking until it was wavering along its entire length. Finally, with a crash, it fell into the fire. A huge cloud of sparks and smoke went up in the air. But when they settled, the fire quieted right down. No more flames were coming in the window. They caught all the fire that had entered the ceilings and they had cut off the fire on this side. The battle went on for quite a while longer, but each side had similar successes, eventually.

When it looked like it was shaping up O.K., the captain looked at his watch. It was covered with soot but still running. "Oh, Jeez, look what time it is, I gotta get to work." He ran back down the street, pausing only to look back at the devastation. As he crossed the expressway, he suddenly remembered: he never told the chief about the grass fires. He looked along the embankment, and as far as he could see, all the grass was gone and everything was blackened. There was no apparatus in sight. It must have put itself out. Hm, a miracle. We could have used a miracle down the street; it was wasted on the expressway.

When he got in to work, the chief he was to relieve in the South End was not in quarters. He called Fire Alarm on the phone. "Where's District Four?"

"Oh, yeah, Cap, the chief of department just ordered them to the fire. He says everyone there needs a relief, so I guess you'll spend the night at Bellflower Street."

Thanks a lot.

This fire was the biggest in the city since the Great Boston Fire of 1872. It destroyed nineteen three-deckers, badly damaged eleven more and moderately damaged a score of others leaving over a hundred families homeless. The combination of the closely built, combustibly constructed buildings, the high wind and low humidity were the principal contributing factors. The reason the whole section didn't burn down was the actions of the members of the department with assistance from the outside towns. The potential for similar disasters still exists in several districts in the city and for the same reasons.

Who Pays
For The
Shoes?

The Congress created the United States Fire Administration in the mid-seventies following the publishing of the report entitled "America Burning." This was a comprehensive look at what was happening in America's cities due to the great number of fires. The report was prepared by a committee appointed by the president and it was impressive enough to cause the Congress to act. When the Administration started, it set itself a number of goals, one of which was to improve fire fighters' personal protective equipment. NASA had just successfully developed new breathing apparatus by employing a users committee and the Fire Administration proposed to do the same thing. NASA became interested in this project also, and it was decided to tackle the task jointly.

A users committee with members from around the country was selected, once again representing all the fire service, including large and small departments and the volunteers. Boston was requested to serve on the committee and the deputy was assigned the duty. The first meeting took place in Washington in 1976. Decisions were made as to what parts of the equipment were to be redesigned and a time table was established for the various parts. A name for the project was chosen, which is very important to NASA, the Fire Administration or any bureaucracy in that town. This program was named "Project FIRES," which stands for Firefighters Integrated Response Equipment System. Nice. They oughta publish a book with all their initials and project names in Washington. Come to think of it, they probably have. Project FIRES has been delayed due to lack of funds, like so many worthwhile programs, but it's still continuing way behind schedule. At the first meeting, though, the deputy suggested that, as long as our equipment was going to be studied, it might be wise if the scientists visited some cities to see what we do for a living, just the way Harvard had done years ago. It sounded reasonable, so it was accepted and Boston was selected as the first place to visit because stupid didn't keep his mouth shut. When he returned from the meeting he thought, jeez, they'll come in here and we won't even have a run; why don't ya learn to keep quiet? He started looking up all the most recent fires, including the massive one at the Plant Shoe Factory in Jamaica Plain. Well, at least he could show them some burned out buildings and let them talk to the men if nothing else happened.

The big day arrived, April 8th, 1976. The deputy made sure it was a night he was working and the guys in the house agreed to have a spaghetti feed for the visitors. He picked them up at the airport at four and brought them to his station. As they were changing into old clothes, he showed them the release forms they'd have to sign. What for? Well, in case you get killed or injured or anything. It's a requirement of the department. They grinned and signed. Nothing would happen, would it? The three men were from three different backgrounds. Andy from the Fire Administration was a city boy, born and bred with roots in Boston. Harry was a NASA scientist from the deep South, while Ismael, or Ish, was another scientist. He came to NASA via Constantinople and lived in Huntsville, Alabama. He was the project manager.

As soon as they were ready, the deputy took them out to the Plant Shoe because he wanted them to see the place before it got dark. The area he took them to was devastated. The fire had taken place February 1st and had destroyed not only the old factory, which was six stories high, eight hundred feet long and two hundred and forty feet wide, but also several three-story tenements. The place had been occupied most recently by hundreds of artists, workshops and light industry. When the fire began it was raining with temperatures in the forties, but before it was over it turned bitter cold, with snow, ice and wind chill factors of minus forty. It was a bitch. The fire burned for six days and everyone got a crack at it.

After examining the ruins, they headed back through Roxbury

to see a few other burned out hulks, but they had to be back at the station by seven for supper. As they rode along Dudley Street, a box sounded over the department radio. "Box 7236 was struck for a fire at 361 Dorchester Street. We're receiving calls for that location." Whenever Fire Alarm gets more than one call, it's usually something. This location was in the deputy's division and they were headed in the right direction.

"Do you go to that?" asked one of the guests.

"Well, it's in my division, but I don't go unless they ask for help. We'll keep going that way, just in case."

In a couple of minutes an excited voice broke in. "Engine One to Fire Alarm, heavy fire showing on Dorchester Street."

"O.K., Engine One, you report heavy fire on Dorchester Street," answered the operator.

"He's got something all right," said the deputy, "Take a look up in the sky." Clouds of black smoke were appearing over the tops of buildings in the direction they were going. "He should be calling for help."

"Engine One to Fire Alarm, this is a working fire."

"That's it, boys, he's calling for help, so we respond now along with an extra engine, truck and rescue company."

He turned on the siren as his aide hit the lights and started accelerating toward the smoke. The deputy was struggling into his coat and pulling up his boots and he said, "Boy, you guys really cramp my style. There's no room in here."

The next call was from the district chief, Car Six, ordering a second alarm. "That's a call for more help, he really has a good fire." As they turned into Dorchester Street, they could see the fire. Jeez, thought the deputy, at least they're gonna see sumthin'. Hope we don't screw it up. Ah, they wouldn't know the difference if we did.

The fire was in two three-deckers and was spreading rapidly into two more buildings in front and one in the rear across an alley. The companies at the scene had everything going right; lines were entering the buildings, ladders were going up and men were starting to open the roofs, but they needed more help. "C-6 to Fire Alarm, strike third alarm, Box 7236. Send two engines to the rear, via Dorchester Avenue." He lost track of the time and his visitors for quite a while as they worked to cut off the fire. The area had so many three-deckers that it wouldn't take long to get them all going, but progress was good at this fire. The water supply was adequate, all the hydrants worked and it was a generally good performance, thank god.

As soon as he could, he went looking for them and found them with the deputy from the other division. The other deputy knew they were in town and came to the fire. He did a great job of telling them what we were trying to accomplish and how we were doing it. They were thrilled by the whole scene. When the fire was knocked down, the deputy got them each a fire hat and coat and took them into one of the burned out buildings. As they went up the stairs, water was pouring down and they could hear guys yelling back and forth as they opened ceilings and washed down the beams. The stair treads were charred but intact and the smoke had lifted so they got a pretty good look at what was going on. When they were satisfied, he took them outside and as soon as he could leave they returned to his station. It had been quite an experience for them and the deputy was pretty happy himself. It was a good stop, they had seen a little bit of what the job was about and maybe it would help them when they were designing new gear. But mostly he was grateful they had at least had something. It would have been tough if they went through the whole tour with nothing.

When they got back, they washed up and went to the kitchen for supper. The members of the Rescue Company had also just come in, so they sat right down because everything was ready. The engine company from this house hadn't been to the fire so they had gotten the meal ready. It was delicious and the guests did a pretty good job on it. So good that they were offered more. When they said yes, one guy from the Rescue, who hadn't washed up yet, scooped out the spaghetti with his filthy hands and plunked it on their plates. They were appalled, he was so crummy. They didn't know this was his traditional way of serving first time visitors, but they didn't want to offend him so they ate everything, although a bit reluctantly. The rest of the night passed quickly with the scientists visiting different stations, asking questions, making notes and listening to fire fighters talk. They responded to a few more alarms and a couple of fires but nothing like the first one. In the morning, they headed for the airport and back to Washington and Huntsville. The trip had been a huge success.

About two weeks later, the deputy got a call from Huntsville. "Hey, Ish, how's it goin'? You guys recover yet?"

"Yes, Chief, we had a great time. Harry and I were talking on the way home. We had left Huntsville, a nice small little town, flew to Boston, got off the plane and the next thing we knew we were in the middle of a big fire. We thought the whole city was going to go up. It was quite a contrast. We got a kick out of watching the spectators too. There were kids everywhere, all over the fire engines. And a group of young men came out of a barroom with cases of beer and stood around cheering you on. There were a couple of fights too. It sure wasn't like here, or even Constantinople. We were really scared when we went in that building, too. Harry's an engineer and he thought it was going to fall down."

"Naw, those three-deckers are tied together pretty good. They'll be someone living in them in a few months."

"The smoke was pretty bad though, too. We started getting dizzy."

"What smoke, you're nuts. It was clear as a bell in there, I wouldn'tve brought you in otherwise."

"Well, maybe you people thought it was O.K., but not us. We didn't feel good the next day."

"Oh, that wasn't the smoke, it was the spaghetti sauce," said the chief.

"Uh, Chief, one more thing. You know when you took us in the building, you gave us hats and coats but you forgot the boots. I had on my alligator shoes and since I got home, I can't get the stains off them. Er, who pays for them?"

"Well, Ish, old pal, you signed those releases didn't cha? See ya at the next meeting."

What Time's
My Relief
Get In?

It's a business where you can't predict what will happen or when. There is not really any such thing as an average night. The division car responds to about two thousand alarms a year but they're not evenly divided. As the years go by everything kinda runs together and you can't remember what happened when, but there are a few nights that stand out. February 20th, 1979 was worth documenting, and it went like this for the deputy:

1600 hours — Reported for work.
1623 hours — Responded, Box 1443, broken sprinkler pipe — Downtown shopping district.
1638 hours — Responded, Box 1361, mattress fire, apartment house, second floor, four-story — Beacon Hill.
1711 hours — Responded, Box 121568, twelfth floor, hotel, small fire, trash receptacle — Back Bay.
1802 hours — Responded, Box 1471, false alarm — Combat Zone.
1833 hours — Responded, Box 171451, electrical fire, Boylston Street subway, damage minor — Downtown.
1900 hours — Went to District 11 quarters in Brighton, district chief's aide retiring after tonight, congratulated him on reaching mandatory retirement age.
2015 hours — Responded, Box 7112, fire in warehouse, controlled by sprinklers, $10,000 damage — South Boston.
2110 hours — Responded, Box 121356, fire in linen closet, Mass. General Hospital, $1,000 — West End.
2145 hours — Responded, Box 121463, fire in vacant State Theater, orchestra floor, $2,000 — Downtown.
2227 hours — Responded, Box 6173, working fire, duplex,

three-deckers, fire on all floors, both sides, twenty-eight rooms involved. Progress difficult because of unusual double roof construction. Struck second and third alarms. Damage severe, $75,000. Three members injured. Fire under control, left scene at 0040 hours. Fire in East Boston District.

0110 hours — Ate lunch.

0141 hours — Responded, Box 1273. Heavy fire showing from seventh floor, eight-story office building. Man badly burned and bleeding lying inside locked front door, screaming. Door forced, rescue company attended victim. All engine and truckmen put on one big line up stairway. Building not equipped with standpipes. Burned man probably set fire, but was incoherent. Sent two men to hospital with victim with instructions to question him. Reported working fire. Directed additional line be run over aerial to fire floor. District chief reports good progress on fire. Fire under control. Investigation reveals man cut hand breaking into office on fourth floor to get to phone and summon help. Man never spoke, died seventeen days later. Not a thief. Apparently was murdered. Case never solved. Fire damage $50,000. Returned to quarters at 0315 hours. Fire in Downtown district.

0420 hours — Responded, Box 1432, false alarm — garment district.

0515 hours — Responded, Box 1511, rubbish fire against building. Forcible entry, no extension. Damage, $3,500 — Downtown.

0707 hours — Responded, working fire, Box 5331. Second alarm struck by district chief prior to division arrival. Fire involved two-and-a-half-story dwelling subdivided into several dormitories for college students. Several rescues. Fire controlled with six big lines. Damage, $90,000. Reminded chief's aide he was off the payroll at 0800. He stated he didn't mind,

hit a home run last time at bat, just like Ted
Williams. Fire was in Brighton district. Hm, it
really is after 0800, where the hell's my relief?
0840 hours — Arrived back in quarters, relief standing at front
door. "Busy night, huh?"

"Not too bad, at least we didn't have a plane or a ship, but I
think I had everything else. See ya tomorrow."

I Don't
Smell It
Anymore,
Do You?

The department has only one Rescue Company left following the drastic budget cuts that took place in 1981. It responds to every working fire and multiple alarm in the city. It also responds to first alarms in the immediate area of its quarters. But in addition to its fire fighting duties, the company responds to every other type of emergency that occurs, including inhalator cases, auto accidents, people under trains, suicides, baby deliveries, chemical leaks, plane crashes, people caught in elevators, drownings, people falling into holds of ships, off construction sites, etc.

The type of man who's attracted to this company is usually highly motivated and he has to have special qualifications. He has to have an emergency medical technician certificate and eighty hours of training. He also must have some mechanical ability because of the type of tools they carry and use. They carry the jaws of life, cutting torches, power saws, electric drills, survival suits, chemical suits, jack hammers, emergency lights and generators, jacks and all kinds of wrenches, screw drivers, etc. They get all types of unusual calls and must be able to figure out the solutions to many problems, such as how to get someone's hand out of a machine without damaging it more, how to get victims out of cars without killing them, how to deliver a baby without becoming involved in a paternity suit.

They are first and foremost, however, fire fighters. The fact that they go to so many fires is also one of the things that attracts good jakes to this company. When the deputy in charge of a fire arrives at the scene, the Rescue Company is usually not too far behind him because it is dispatched at the same time he is and from the same station. When the deputy is making his evaluation, he is trying to determine what the key is to controlling the fire, and quite often, this can be accomplished with the proper placement of one more line or immediate ventilation of one area or even the rescue of a trapped occupant. As he's making his evaluation, he knows the Rescue Company is coming and he will assign this key duty to the company when it arrives. Since they are a most aggressive group, they will succeed at many of these difficult tasks and will be very effective in bringing the fire under control.

The vehicle they use is a huge box type van. It carries all the tools listed above and breathing apparatus, axes, rakes, Halligan bars, etc., but no hose or ladders. Since it is a van, the men are enclosed, with the driver and officer in front and the rest standing in the box in back.

Since they may be called to any section of the city for their next job, it is not essential that they always be in quarters like an engine or truck which is assigned a specific area. Consequently, it is not unusual to see the Rescue Company at a junk yard, cutting up old cars, using the jaws of life or any other tools to keep their hand in and keep practicing. They also visit refrigeration plants to look for shutoffs, subway stations to practice lifting trains to remove suicides, ships, etc. Anyplace where they think they may find something unusual that they'll have to solve. They have even visited operating rooms of hospitals because once in a while they've had to remove some kind of machine from a victim under the direction of a doctor and operating room staff.

Due to the fact that they travel all over the city, they must have a better knowledge of the streets than anyone else, but it's impossible to learn them all. Consequently, numerous driving drills are necessary to familiarize the members with the city, right? Well, not exactly. Oh, they do the drills all right, and they're out driving around a lot, but the fact that they happen to go by the sandwich shop and pick up lunch, or the super market for tomorrow night's meal, or the fish pier for some haddock, is strictly coincidental, or at least that's what they tell the chiefs when they get caught.

They often look like they know just where they're going when they respond to a multiple alarm, but they have a distinct advantage. You can usually see it in the sky long before you get there.

Many of the fires are quite spectacular and they light up the sky with fire or push clouds of smoke upward and blanket the city. If it's a damp foggy night, though, you may not see them but you can always head in the general direction and smell them. At any serious fire, the most distinct smell is that of burning wood. It smells just like someone's fireplace. As you get closer, it gets stronger, and pretty soon you'll see the smoke and it will be lying close to the ground because of the damp weather, and you'll find your way O.K.

One summer's evening, near midnight, the weather made a dramatic change. It had been warm and dry all night so far, but a front passed and the fog started rolling off the ocean, making it damp and chilly. They were all sitting in the kitchen, having just returned from a false alarm uptown. Naturally, every time they went uptown in the general vicinity of the Combat Zone, they would return to quarters by way of the Zone. This gave them an opportunity to exchange pleasantries with all the hookers.

The Boston Combat Zone is nowhere near as large as Times Square or even North Beach in San Francisco, but it doesn't have to take its hat off to anyone. Compressed into a four block area are more skin flicks, peep shows, nude revues, pimps, hookers, muggers, etc., than you can find in those other towns. There is just as much opportunity to get yourself cleaned and pressed here as anywhere. It is much livelier after midnight than before, but Rescue One would ride through anytime. They're not fussy.

The usual shouting had gone back and forth and Chubby and Harold were riding on the back step waving to the girls. "Hey baby," Chubby yelled, "C'mon aboard, I'll show ya what a real dude is like."

"Shut up, Chub," said Harold, "You wouldn't know what to do with them if you got them. Besides, your wife would kill you."

"Oh, yeah? I'm the hottest jake on this company."

Just then the two girls jumped up beside Chubby, and Harold dashed inside the van and closed the doors. The two girls were all over Chub, hands running up and down his legs, kissing him on the neck and hugging him. Chubby was thrilled but it only lasted a few seconds and they were gone. Harold opened the doors and Chubby jumped inside.

"See, I told ya how good I was. They went right for the old Chubba. They were all over me. They completely ignored you.

"Well, I gotta admit you're right, but that's o.K. with me," said Harold, "They were a coupla dogs anyway."

As they pulled up in front of the fire house, Harold and Chubby jumped off to direct traffic. All of a sudden, Chubby let out a scream. "They rolled me, those dirty hookers grabbed my dough. I had sixty-three bucks in my pocket and they got it." He was really upset and no one had let up on him yet. As a matter of fact, he was starting to get calls from other companies because the word spreads pretty fast in the department. Here he had thought his reputation as a ladies' man would be enhanced, but it wasn't gonna work out that way.

While he was drinking his coffee and turning off all the derogatory remarks, the house gong sounded and the man on patrol announced, "Box 6221, working fire, Division One, Rescue One, Lighting Plant One to fire, Engine 25 covering Engine 9." Thank God, thought Chubby, at least it will take their minds off me for a while.

The fire was in East Boston, and to get there it is necessary to go through the Callahan Tunnel which connects Downtown to Eastie, passing under the harbor. Quite often, as companies speed down the expressway toward the tunnel, it's possible to look across the harbor and see the fire you're responding to. But not tonight, it was just too misty and foggy. The street location was unfamiliar to the Rescue, but they'd get there, they always did. The deputy's car sped away from them and out of sight as it entered the tunnel. He had a pretty good idea of where it was and the car always traveled much faster than the rescue van. Behind the Rescue was the lighting plant. This is a one man truck which carries a variety of fixed and portable searchlights for use at a fire and also carries dry powder in large quantities for use on electrical fires. The dry powder is responsible for the truck's nickname, which is the "Powder Puff." It is dispatched to all working fires and multiples at night and is unmanned during the day.

The man on it this night was Blackie. He was a short, stocky guy who had been around a long time and was finishing out his career on the Plant. He always smoked a stogie cigar. They claimed he couldn't talk without it. He was a pretty gullible fella who would get pissed off easily, so naturally they were on him all the time. But he also was scrupulously honest and on this night it cost them plenty.

When the deputy arrived at the fire, he saw that it was on the first and second floor of a three-decker. The first alarm companies were doing pretty good. Lines had knocked down the fire on the first and were making good progress on the second. The district chief told him he had a line going up the stairway to the third but he didn't think the fire had extended into that floor yet. He needed a company up there for ventilation and opening up purposes and to see if the fire was entering that floor. "O.K., Dick, go ahead up the top with the engine. I'll send the Rescue up to you as soon as they get in, they should be right here. I'll get a couple of lights in the first and second too." He looked up the street, but no Rescue, not yet anyway. They'd be right along, though; they had left quarters the same time he did.

A few more minutes passed, nothing. The district chief called on the portable, "I could use that company, I think it's getting in here."

"Yeah, yeah, in a coupla minutes." Where the hell were they now? He kept looking up the street and pacing back and forth. Maybe they broke down. Well, I can't wait any longer or I'll end up with a second alarm. "C-6 to Fire Alarm, send an extra truck to Box 6221."

"O.K. C-6, you want an extra truck, we're dispatching Ladder One." Ladder One was on the road and in East Boston, as they had been sent to cover the district, so they arrived rapidly and were sent to the top floor. Still no rescue or lighting plant. Ladder One managed to open up in time and the fire was caught with the line from the engine. Meanwhile, the Rescue Company had been speeding along Chelsea Street with the Plant in hot pursuit. In the back, Nellie said, "I can smell it, we must be getting close." The odor of burning wood was pretty strong. They all adjusted their gas mask straps and got ready to go to work. But the van kept going. "Geez, it's out a lot further than I thought," said Nellie. As they moved along, pretty soon the smell disappeared. "Can't smell it anymore, they must be knocking the shit out of it."

"Yeah, either that or we went by it."

"Oh, oh, you might be right." He pounded on the divider between the cab and the van. "Hey, Lieutenant, we can't smell it anymore. Either they got it or we went by."

The lieutenant said, "You might be right. This asshole just told me he's lost. We're gonna turn around. Do any of you clowns know where Byron Street is?"

They turned around in a big empty parking lot and headed back the way they had come. Everyone had a theory which way the street was and every one was wrong. They tried every side street. "Jeez," said Chubby, "If anyone's lookin' out their windows, they'll think there's ten rescue companies goin' to the fire. We been up and down every side street."

Finally, they saw red lights up ahead. "This must be it," said the lieutenant, "put the lights off and we'll creep up the street. If he's really busy, maybe he didn't miss us."

They parked quietly and walked up the opposite side of the street, but their luck had run out. "Lieutenant, where the hell have you been, I almost pulled a second alarm waiting for you. Never mind now, get up the top floor and help Ladder One, and you, Blackie, get a coupla lights in the building.

They dashed up the stairs and went to work. In a short while it was all over and they heard the call on the portable, "C-6 to Car One, I'm gonna start making them up, send the Rescue down to me."

By now they had cooked up a story that sounded plausible and down they came. "Well, Lieutenant, what happened?"

"Well, Chief, er, we came down off the expressway and into the tunnel. When we got part way through, there was an accident up ahead and it tied up everything. We hadda see if anyone was hurt before we got through, isn't that right?" He turned to his crew and they nodded in agreement. What he didn't see was Blackie standing there dumbfounded, with his mouth open.

"Deputy, they're all full of shit. They were late because they missed the street and went to Revere." Revere is the next city to the north of Boston.

"Is that so, Blackie, how do you know?" asked the deputy.

"Well, I followed them. I figured they knew where they were

going. The next thing I knew I saw a sign saying 'Welcome to Revere' and I thought that ain't right. We all turned around in a big parking lot and came back this way."

The deputy turned away to keep from laughing. When he regained his composure he said, "O.K. Rescue, get outta here, next time you go out on a driving drill, you better drill. If I see you coming back with a load of fish, you'll all be in trouble. Blackie, you return with them. I must admit you're the most honest stool pigeon I ever had."

They were all going to kill Blackie when they got back, but they cooled off quick. He was so damn honest what could you do? And he didn't have any idea he was a squealer, he just hadda tell the truth. Besides, there was plenty to do when they got back anyway. There were still plenty of companies they hadn't told about Chubby.

Blackie never did get the chance to finish his career quietly on the Plant. During the Blizzard of '78, he died while responding to a fire and the place has never been the same. Every time a member dies in the line of duty, it takes a piece out of everyone and Blackie's loss was no exception.

Hotel Fires; Or,
A Lot of Guys
Named Smith
Got Rescued

The MGM Grand fire in Las Vegas in 1980 was a terrible tragedy. Over eighty people were killed, most of them from smoke
which traveled from the casino and up the elevator shafts to the
upper floors. The fact that the MGM is so famous and that literally
millions of people have stayed there since its construction, increased the demand for information about the fire and about hotel
safety. Vegas itself attracts so many visitors, and has so many hotels, that a large portion of the population could relate to the fire.
Fortunately with most tragedies, something good usually comes of
them. In the case of the MGM, the state of Nevada changed their
automatic sprinkler laws to make them retroactive, so that now, all
hotels in the state, no matter how old, would have to comply.
Other states are taking similar actions. This is a very wise course
to follow. It is not only good for public safety, it's good for business. Ads are starting to appear with the information that the
building is properly protected, which should prove effective in attracting customers.

The fact that you can get burned to death in a hotel was never
any secret to fire fighters. Whenever a fire fighter goes on vaca-
tion, there's a few things he does automatically, especially if he's
ever been to a hotel fire. He always gets two keys, one for himself
and one for his wife (or whomever). He's also careful to register
under an assumed name if he's with "whomever." He tells his
partner to always keep the key with her, particularly if there's a
fire and they decide to leave the room. If you can't make it to a
stairway and have to retreat, you can at least get back in the room
and to a window, rather than get trapped in the hallway.

When he arrives at his room, he first looks to see if there's a sprinkler head. He also looks out the window to see how high he is and if there's a lower roof he can drop to. If he has a balcony, he knows at least he can get some air if he's trapped in the room. He also looks at the phone and directory so he can call the fire department direct if he can get a dial tone, and he sees how to contact the operator.

Then he takes a walk down the hallway. He wants to see how far it is to the stairway and where the stairway goes. He is also looking for standpipe connections and house lines. A house line is a small line, usually in a cabinet and with enough hose to reach some distance down the hall. This cabinet often has an extinguisher in it and sometimes there is a fire alarm box nearby.

Once he has that information and knows he has a pretty good shot at getting out if there's a fire or taking action to control it, he can relax. This is important in Vegas where you are often distracted and despondent when you return to your room after having been cleaned in the casino. You don't want to have to start thinking when something happens. Be prepared in advance like a boy scout, although scouts don't usually stay in Vegas with Mrs. Smith.

Boston, like most major cities, has had its share of hotel fires, and some of them were tragic. Up until 1979, the most famous ones were:

The Sherry Biltmore Hotel Fire, 0400 hours, March 19, 1963. This fire resulted in four dead, over a hundred rescued over ladders. twenty-three engine companies, ten ladder companies responded, five alarms, Box 2321.

Paramount Hotel, 1841 hours, January 28, 1966. Gas main exploded on Boylston St., downtown. Fire extended to all floors of the hotel. Ten dead, several seriously injured. Temperature 0 degrees F. Five alarms Box 1471.

Hotel Roosevelt, 0347 hours, February 4, 1968. This fire is described elsewhere in the text and resulted in nine dead, 100 rescued over ladders. twenty-two engine companies, ten ladder companies, five alarms, Box 1632.

Copley Square Hotel, December 29, 1976. No deaths, 125 elderly rescued over ladders, aerial towers and stairways. Sixteen engine companies, ten ladder companies responded. Box 1561, four alarms.

At 0104 hours, March 19, 1979, Box 1561 was struck for a fire at the Copley Plaza Hotel. This is a beautiful old hotel which takes up a full block area, is six stories high and faces Copley Square. It has a distinctive clientele but is more liberal than the Ritz Carlton, having permitted Liz and Richard to stay there after the Ritz had denied them a suite because they were unmarried at the time, prior to the sexual revolution.

When the officer of Ladder 15 arrived at the front entrance nothing was showing, but the hotel staff told him there was a fire in the basement. He raced down the stairs with his company and could see a haze of smoke on the lower floor. He called the district chief on his portable and told him there was light smoke and he was investigating. He quickly discovered two separate fires in trash and grabbed a house line to extinguish them. He called the chief and told him what he had. The next order he heard over his portable astounded him: "Car 4 to Fire Alarm, we have a working fire in the Copley Plaza, strike a second alarm."

Oh my God, he musta thought I said two alarms instead of two fires. The chief working tonight was pretty new in the district, although very experienced. He hadda misunderstand the message. "C'mon," he yelled to his men, "we gotta get up there before he hits a third."

He raced through the lobby and could see guests already starting down the stairs. As he ran out to the street, he started to say something to the chief but the chief grabbed him. "They're hanging out everywhere, get all you can," and he turned and ordered a third and fourth alarm. The lieutenant looked up and could see heavy smoke pushing out from every window in the right front side of the third floor. His aerial ladder was being lowered in to some trapped guests on the fourth floor. Thank God, the driver and tillerman were on the ball. He shouted to the others to get a fifty and he raced to the back of the truck to the ladder bed.

The fire had been touched off by a former dishwasher who had recently been fired and he had set several fires, including the two in the basement. The fire fully involved the right front and right side of the third floor, traveling the entire length of the building on the Dartmouth Street side. It was so intense that it started overlapping into the fourth floor. People were trapped on the fourth, fifth and sixth.

When the deputy arrived, he ordered a fifth alarm, two aerial towers and a total of ten ladder trucks, as over five hundred guests were on the upper floors. The laddermen and towermen were picking them off as fast as they could. Hose lines were advanced rapidly up the stairways and they started hitting the fire, but it was like an inferno. More lines were brought over ladders as guests started reaching the ground. But many were still trapped and all the trucks were occupied. Men from the rescue companies and other engines and trucks got up the stairways with masks and started making room by room searches. They brought out countless numbers from the rooms. The only way they could get them out was to share their air supply with them. They did this by holding their face piece in their hand, taking a breath, then clamping it on the victim's face and getting to the stairway and down.

Rescue One had already gotten several out and had cleared the fifth and sixth floors as best they could determine. Their air supplies were starting to run out but they took a peek in the fourth floor. As they did they could hear cries for help so they raced along the corridor. They found two middle aged women in a room and it was heavily charged with smoke. The women were hanging with their heads out of the window but no one could see them from down below because of the fire and smoke. The rescue got their face piece on them and led them over to the stairs. Just as they started down, one of the women said she was pretty sure there was still someone in the next room to theirs. "Oh, Christ," said the captain, "O.K. let's go." Three of them headed back in. They made it back to the room and started a search. By now the alarms on their masks had been sounding for some time and they couldn't see the gauges to tell how much air they had left, but they had to keep searching.

When they were convinced that there was no one there, they headed back. As they crawled along, the fire came in the windows from the overlap and shot out into the corridor, cutting off their escape. They were driven into a room on the inner side of the hallway, facing an inner court. They broke out a window and as they did, their air supplies were exhausted within a minute of each other. They shone their lights down into the court to try to attract attention. There was no one there to see them, but there was a roof on the court about twelve feet down. "Grab the mattresses," said the captain, choking from the heavy smoke. "Drop them on the roof," and they did. "Now, drop the masks on them." They let the air tanks go and they hit the mattresses and rolled onto the roof. "Let's go, hang by your arms as low as you can and hit the mattresses." They went one at a time, and landed all right. They were now down below the fire and the captain got on his portable and told the chief where they were.

As they headed to the stairway, Bob said to Connie, "I think he thinks more of the damn masks than he does of us."

The captain turned to him and said, "If we get killed, I won't hafta make out any papers, but if we lose a mask I'll be in the shit." What compassion.

As the fire gradually was being brought under control and the search for victims continued, a box struck on the department radio. As it finished hitting, Fire Alarm announced, "Box 121568 was struck for a fire at the Sheraton Boston on Belvidere Street. We're receiving calls for the second and third floors. Report of people trapped on upper floors."

Nice. The Sheraton Boston is about three blocks away from the Copley Plaza in the Prudential Center. It is one of the newest hotels in the city, unsprinklered, twenty-nine floors, and it houses about 1500 guests. It is usually fully occupied and this night was no exception. The first company in reported heavy fire showing on the second and third floors and the first chief in ordered a second alarm and then a third.

The fire on the second floor could be attacked by running lines up an escalator from the lobby and the one on the third by lines over an aerial and up the stairs. But the entire hotel had to be evacuated and it was going to be difficult. That's an enormous number of people to get out but it had to be done. The fire probably wouldn't get above the third, but of course you never know and heavy smoke was pushing up the stairways. The elevators were shut off except for fire department use, but with the heavy smoke, they couldn't be used initially anyway. For people other than fire fighters who use elevators in a building, fire is disastrous. About a dozen died at the MGM when they chose this route.

At the Copley Plaza, the commissioner, who was at the scene, was notified of the second fire. Since the Plaza fire was not out but they were pretty sure the occupants were, he started dismissing as many companies as was possible, and Fire Alarm dispatched them to the other fire. Under the circumstances, it was a tremendous achievement. As the lines started hitting the fire at the Sheraton, arriving companies were sent up all the stairways to assist the guests and search the rooms, and once again, air supplies were shared. The fire was rapidly knocked down, but the evacuation took quite a while. The deputy from the Copley Plaza was sent to the Sheraton fire and assumed command until it was over.

By dawn, things were in pretty good shape. Both fires were in the overhauling stages and an assessment was being made of both buildings. One guest was dead at the Copley, another died later, and several had been injured. At the Sheraton, several guests suffered smoke inhalation injuries but no one died. The same little dishwasher who set the Copley set the Sheraton. He had also been fired there. He's serving life for murder at present. The damage at the Copley ran into the millions and a couple of hundred thousand at the Sheraton.

While these fires did not result in a new sprinkler law in Massachusetts, legislation was passed that required smoke detectors throughout all hotels, better alarm systems and a generally safer setup for guests.

Mr. Smith can perform his nefarious nocturnal activities with the knowledge that he is a little safer in case of fire, but this will not help him with either the muggers or Mrs. Smith's real husband.

Fill The Line Quick, We Gotta Hold It!

As long as anyone could remember, the Boston Fire Department had operated under a five alarm response system. This means that five was the highest number of alarms that could be transmitted from a particular box. This would bring in a tremendous force to fight a fire; if necessary, additional help could be requested but no more alarms would be transmitted. It must have been pretty successful because it lasted so long, but it did have a few drawbacks. When the chief in charge ordered a second or greater alarm, each alarm would bring him at least four more engines. This was fine most of the time, but occasionally, he didn't really want all four engines. He might only require one or two, but the system provided him with four anyway.

In 1979, the department decided it was time for an improvement. So the headquarters staff started working on a nine alarm response to replace the five alarm system. This would provide the officer in charge with just as much help as he could command before, but with a more piecemeal delivery. Now he would get only two engines on each alarm from the third to the ninth. He could get a small amount if that's all he needed but the larger amount would always be available by striking additional alarms. Not bad, not bad at all! Maybe there's hope for the Enchanted Kingdom after all. The system was initiated on February 4th, 1980, and is working very well.

But far more important than the technical improvements was the fact that the new system created an opportunity for a pool. Like most people, fire fighters will bet on anything. The last box struck each year, the first one New Year's Day, the first multiple alarm, the last one, anything. Now here was a golden opportunity.

A pool that could run for awhile until the first nine alarm fire in the history of the department took place. Oh, baby. It was not a pool that was run department wide or anything like that. Each house ran its own and each tour ran its own. The pool had eight combinations depending on what group was working and which fire division the nine bagger occurred in. So eight guys at a deuce a week came to sixteen bucks a week. Not bad. It probably wouldn't go too long 'cause hell, we usually had about eight to ten five-baggers a year, so logically, it won't take too long for nine. Right? Wrong. What no one realized when the system went in was that there were not gonna be too many nine alarm fires. The piece-meal response worked very well and the deputy chiefs had a better opportunity to place apparatus than under the old system. Oh, there were plenty of fires all right, just like always. But they were being handled with five, six, seven, and eight alarm responses. Hey, man, there's some pretty serious bread in there. By the middle of June, there was $288 bucks in each pool.

Rescue One, like everyone else, had a pool, and Lieutenant Jack was in charge of it. He felt pretty sure he was gonna win because he had another group in Division 2 in the pool. They were always losing buildings out in that division, so he had a good shot at it. He knew it wouldn't happen on his group or his division, Group One, Division One, because his pal, the deputy, or old dad, usually knew what he was doin' and he knew he'd keep anything below nine.

June 17th, 1980, was a warm, sunny day. The humidity was low and it was pretty windy, with a gusty twenty-five mile an hour breeze. Group One was on duty and Rescue One was having a cookout for the evening meal. Ah, steaks, thought Jack. He was making the salad because they never let him touch the meat. He always burned it. He was getting a little concerned about the pool because it was getting up there. Unfortunately, he had been tapping it now and then and owed about two hundred bucks. But, what the hell, Division Two would come through for him. Mm, smell those steaks, won't be long now.

At 1820 hours, Box 5221 was struck for a fire in the Brighton district, but no one paid much attention. Keep an eye on the steaks, start adding dressing to the salad. How's the baked potatoes comin'? "Engine 41 to Fire Alarm," squeaked the speaker in the kitchen.

"Go ahead Forty-one."

"We have a working fire in a warehouse at 70 Western Avenue."

"O.K. Forty-one, you're reporting a working fire Box 5221, Operator One."

Oops, that's us. Hey, Twenty-five, take care of our suppers will ya? they yelled to the engine company in the house as they sped out the door.

The Brighton district is at the extreme end of the division, isolated from the rest of the city. It has about 80,000 residents, thousands of three-deckers and apartment houses, and many warehouses, trucking firms, chemical plants, etc. It is so far from downtown that the best way to get there quickly is on the Massachusetts Turnpike, and Rescue One and the deputy responded by that route. As they started on the toll road they could hear the chief of the district ordering second and third alarms. They could see a huge column of black smoke rising in the distance.

The fire was in a one story warehouse about one thousand feet long. It was in a complex that had several other identical structures and a freight yard, truck facility and other businesses. It had its own water system, privately owned and maintained. It was connected to the city system, but the property owners were responsible for its care and maintenance.

As the first in companies dropped lines at the hydrants and stretched in to the fire, they could see that about one third of the warehouse was involved and the fire was spreading rapidly. As they committed themselves to strategic locations for heavy stream operations, they ordered the lines to be filled. Then they found out! Most of the hydrants on the system were defective. Oh, oh. Here they were right in position but no water. Gonna be a long night.

As soon as the district chief realized the extent of the problem, he started transmitting messages to incoming companies to keep off the yard system and start relaying from the city hydrants which were a quarter to a half mile away. When the deputy arrived he ordered fourth, fifth and sixth alarms and sent the district chief to the rear of the complex. The fire was now over halfway through the building and had ignited about fifteen trailer trucks in front and several freight cars in the rear. It was also threatening to jump to another warehouse unless they could cut it off.

When Rescue One arrived, Jack and his crew helped an engine company stretch in their long lines and they were all waiting for water. The fire in the rear was now exposing some freight cars with hazardous cargoes and some tank cars with flammable and explosive solvents. The deputy had contacted the railroad and they were bringing in an engine to try to pull out the most dangerous cargoes but it was gonna be close. Better get water quick. At last it started arriving but they were gonna need a lot more. Seventh alarm, eighth alarm, keep stretching, keep relaying.

Jack was working himself into a frenzy. He and his crew had a portable deluge set and he was having them actually carry it and keep hitting the fire. Jack was always a good worker, but this was ridiculous. What the hell's the matter with him? They were starting to make progress, weren't they? Hey, ya can't do the whole thing by yourself when it's this big. "Keep it movin'. Come on. We're starting to get it." He had his portable radio slung around his neck and he could hear the messages going back and forth.

"Car Eleven to C-6. We have the railroad here now and they're hooking onto the tank cars."

Good, good, thought Jack.

"But we're starting to lose pressure on our lines and need a relay. Can you send me some more help?"

For cripes sake, shut up. The deputy didn't answer. Great, thought Jack, his radio's broken again. He cut around the end of the building with his crew and found a flat line with a nozzle attached. He grabbed one of his men and said, "Quick, follow this back and get it filled. Chief, Chief," he yelled to the chief of Eleven, "here's a line; where do ya want it? " But the chief was talking to the deputy on the radio again.

Then he heard the message he had been dreading: "C-6 to Fire Alarm."

"Go ahead, C-6."

"Strike ninth alarm Box 5221."

He sagged visibly. It was all over, the pool was gone. Yeah, and he was missing two hundred bucks. The additional help did the trick. Now the supplies kept increasing and the fire was gradually coming under control. But it was long after midnight before a fire detail could be set up to complete extinguishment. The deputy dismissed as many companies as he could, including the Rescue Company, but Lieutenant Jack seemed in no rush to leave.

"What's the matter, Jack? You look down in the dumps. You guys did a terrific job, I was watching you. Go ahead, now, make up and get home. You deserve a rest."

"Yeah, O.K. Deputy," he mumbled and got into the front seat.

As the Rescue drove back along the Turnpike, the driver said to Lieutenant Jack, "Hey, Luft, guess who won the pool? "

"Aw, who gives a shit?"

"It was Moe."

"Moe, the deputy's driver?"

"Yeah, how many Moes do ya know?"

"Why that's collusion. He'd a never hit nine alarms on that fire. I'm not gonna pay. It's fraud, that's what it is."

"Jeez, Luft, I dunno, it was sure a good fire. And besides, Moe's a big guy. You better pay up."

Soon after, the deputy was riding back along the Turnpike and he was feeling pretty good. It had been a good job. Yeah, the loss was in the millions, but they had done the best they could with the water problems and everything. Thank God, none of the tank cars let go. Quite a few men were hurt but nothing really serious. Just the usual cuts, bruises and sprains they get at every fire. Jeez, another thing, that was the first nine alarms in the history of the department. Hey, not bad. That gave him two records that could never be broken. The fastest five alarms years ago on Berkeley Street and now this. Years from now, when people who enjoyed such inconsequentia looked at the record, they'd probably say, "Hey, lookit this guy, he must have been a pisser. He really blew a few, didn't he?"

He glanced over at his aide and saw him smiling. "Whaddya so happy about, ya oughta be pooped."

"Well, Chief, I had the pool. Yahoo, two hundred eighty-eight balloons."

"What? You mean to tell me you had this group on Division One? They'll say we bagged it. Shit."

When they backed into quarters, Lieutenant Jack was waiting for them. "Hi, Deputy. Nice job, huh? Uh, Moe, could I see ya for a few minutes?"

As the deputy went over toward the stairs, he could see the pair of them walking toward the kitchen. Lieutenant Jack had his arm around Moe's shoulder and was talking earnestly to him. Hm, wonder what that's all about?

Thirteen
Three-Deckers,
Vertical

There is a healthy rivalry that exists between fire fighters from different parts of the city. The three-decker areas are busier, the downtown and South End fires are tougher, and the grass fires drive you nuts out in the sticks; Roxbury and Dorchester, the kids bomb you with rocks, there's more drunk drivers crashing into you in the city, etc. Anything to make your area tougher and your company the best. The funniest part of it all is that the way the department operates, a serious fire in a particular area brings help from the other areas, so the work is tough no matter where you are. It's not uncommon though, to hear one jake yell to another, "Jeez, these three-deckers are a tit, lookit all the windows; boy, plenty of ventilation."

The reply is usually, "Yeah, you hadda come out here to get some work. You guys ain't done shit in a month. Besides, the sprinklers put out everything you get downtown."

"Yeah, bullshit. Next time ya come in bring your long rakes," referring to the much higher ceilings in the in town areas.

At 0630 hours, January 23, 1982, Box 1338 was struck for a fire at #4 Longfellow Place, Downtown. The building is an apartment house for the affluent, thirty-nine stories high. The temperature was six degrees F with a wind chill factor of minus twenty. Upon arrival, the department was notified by the maintenance staff that all the elevators were out of commission and that the fire was on the roof. Nice. The department's high rise procedure requires companies to carry 2 1/2 inch donut rolls and other equipment and everyone equipped with masks, the same as at any building fire. Both the deputy and district chief had run into similar experience in the past and knew how difficult it was to walk that many flights. They also understood that there was no way they could effectively get the donut rolls up there. Since the previous April, due to budget cuts, the department had been systematically emasculated with hundreds of the youngest men laid off so that now the average age of the department was forty-three.

The deputy reached a decision. "O.K. Joe, it must be in the elevator penthouse and all the controls are burned out. Remember when we walked up the Prudential and how pooped we were. I think we can handle the fire with inch and a half, so take four companies and four fifty foot lengths. Take about four masks with ya and keep rotating the gear as they get tired. If there's any fire below the roof, I'll get a lot more help and send up the two and a halfs. Let me know quick, when you get up there." He turned to the company officers and men. "I'm sending all but one company. Now listen to me. Take your time. If you've never done it before, you gotta be careful. Keep passing the gear back and forth. If you get tired, stop. If your feet start to blister, take your boots off. It sounds like it's just the penthouse but watch yourselves when you get up there."

They set off climbing. In spite of the warnings a few of them raced ahead, but after about a dozen stories, they slowed down. The deputy was thinking, jeez, I wish I could have kept the older ones down here, but we haven't got any young ones left. He had the company that he kept in the lobby run a line into the standpipe inlet outside, in case they had a water problem. His aide went into the adjacent building with a maintenance man and took the elevator to the roof. In a short while he called and said, "I can see the fire; it is in the penthouse and it's going good. The smoke is banking down into the top floor but no fire that I can see there."

"O.K., stay up there and let me know."

The building staff told him he could communicate with the tenants by the PA system but when he tried it, it failed. "It's out of business, I guess. Listen, call each room on the phone and tell them the fire's on the roof. Have everyone from the thirty-fifth to the top drop down to the thirty-fourth. There's no need for them to walk all the way down." But a lot of the tenants came anyway — no "towering infernos" for them.

The chief kept in touch with the men on the stairway by

radio, keeping them informed about what his aide could see from the other roof. The radios kept cutting out. God, they worked lousy, particularly in high rise buildings. Wish someone would invent a good one for fire fighting. He could write a book about broken messages. He got more calls that said " ————more help," "Strike————," "Send up———— away," "Urgent————," "They're————out the wind————." Well, the guy who makes these can kiss my ass.

At last, though, he got a message he had been waiting for. "Ladder 24 to C6."

"Go ahead, Jack."

"We're on the top floor, we have heavy smoke in the corridors. Can't feel any heat. We're waiting for a coupla masks. All the tenants are outta here, we passed them on the stairs."

"O.K., keep me informed." The next call he got was from the district chief. "Four's stretching the inch and a half to the roof. I'm pretty sure that's just smoke backing down into the top floor but Ladder 24's checking it out now."

The lieutenant on the truck called him again and his voice was muffled, so the deputy knew he had his face piece on and was holding his mike on the regulator. "We made it across the top floor: no fire, just pent up smoke. We're gettin' the windows now."

Jeez, that's good news. Another engine company took a couple of dry powder extinguishers up to the roof. The door of the penthouse was badly warped by the fire, but they managed to swing it open after forcing it with a tool. The fire came racing out at them. The extinguishers couldn't make a dent in it. The deputy had the maintenance man standing by in the lobby. "They'll be asking for water shortly, make sure all the power's off up there." The juice was killed but it also shut off all the power to the building, including the fire pump. They called for the water but got no pressure. He turned to the fire company standing by in the lobby. "Fill the standpipe inlet hose, " and they raced to comply. But as it was about to be filled, he got a call from the roof, "O.K. we got pressure now, and we're hitting the fire." The auxiliary generator had cut in.

It was all over in a few minutes once they got a really good flow. But the tenants kept coming down. Some of them had gone outside but it was freezing out. Some had gone into the lobby of the next building. The place was jammed. The deputy told them, "Everything is O.K. now, you'll have to walk back up, though, the elevators will be out for quite a while."

One tenant told him, "After we got the call, we were gonna stay, but there was a lady racing through all the corridors yelling fire. She was at the MGM Grand when it burned and she must have knocked on every apartment door. When she got done telling us about that fire, we decided to come down."

As the fire fighters came down the stairs, lugging all the gear, one fire fighter, who had been transferred in town after his company had been deactivated in the force reduction, said to another, "You in town jakes call this a fire; why, we'd pissed on it out in Roxbury."

"Yeah, if that outfit of yours was so good, how come they did away with it? Besides, this was thirty-nine floors. That's like thirteen of those shitty little three-deckers piled one on top of the other." The officer on the last company on the roof called via the portable, "Engine 10 to C-6." "Yeah, go ahead." "Do you want us to blow the tanks before we come down?" "What tanks?" "The water tanks. You know, like Steve McQueen did in 'The Towering Inferno'." "O.K. Mike, don't be a wise guy or I'll leave you as fire detail. Make up and come down."

When the deputy returned to quarters and was washing up he heard one of the local radio stations giving the news. As the broadcast neared completion the announcer said, "We've just received word that there was a fire on the roof of the Longfellow Place Apartment House this morning. The fire is now under control. The fire department spokesman said it was confined to that section and that it was strictly routine."

Strictly routine, thought the deputy. I bet that asshole never walked thirty-nine floors.

Advice
and
Philosophy
Unsolicited

Jeez, it's been quiet, he thought as he stirred restlessly. You dummy, you're lying here still awake, thinkin' about all that old stuff. Why dontcha think about what you'd tell some guy who's getting promoted to chief. There are so many things that sink into your thick skull by osmosis that are never written down in all those books you study. Nobody learns them the first day in spite of the fact they think you get a new head at the Pentagon when someone pins a gold badge on ya.

Fire fighters are unique because of the nature of the business. They cannot be compared to any other military or semi-military organizations. A soldier may serve for thirty years and never fire a shot in anger. A police officer may do the same. The weapons they use in their businesses are deadly and if the soldier were constantly at war and the officer constantly using his gun, society would be destroyed. Consequently, the fact that they are not required to do so is hopeful. The soldier does not therefore face danger daily, and while the threat to the police officer is ever present, he does not have to use force or his weapon at every incident.

A fire fighter is in constant danger at every fire he goes to and he uses the weapons of his trade continuously throughout his career. His enemy is the most frightening natural force and has been throughout history. So, while the new chief has been working his way up through the ranks, he has learned a lot about the trade but now his viewpoint is going to be somewhat different. He now becomes the guy who has to decide how a fire is going to be fought, and the orders he gives are often going to be the factors that determine who's gonna get hurt and who isn't and even who's gonna live and who's gonna die. The responsibility you accept is awesome at times, but that's the reason they lay the heavy bread on you on payday. The gold badge and buttons don't mean anything.

The first thing you hafta do right is select an aide. Your aide must be a good enough driver to get you to the fire without killing you, but it is not his most important asset. He must first and foremost be an experienced fire fighter with good judgment. He must have a basic understanding of how fire travels and where to look for extension of fire. He must also understand how *you* think and how *you* handle a fire. When he is sending you information from inside a fire building, he must know what you are usually looking for and limit his report to those essentials. To fit these requirements he must have a good knowledge of building construction, electricity, plumbing, heating, etc. You should be flexible enough in your decisions to give serious consideration to any recommendations he makes from his vantage point tempered by whatever other information you may have relative to the overall strategy at the fire. It's also a great advantage if he gets along well with you personally. You are going to see him as much as your wife and you may even get to know him better, but not in the biblical sense, it is hoped. It is not essential that he be good on paperwork. If you have a choice of a good fire fighter or a good clerk, take the fire fighter every time. He'll keep you out of trouble a lot more than a guy with neat margins. You also do not want a stool pigeon, but he must be loyal enough to you to let you know if anything that could really prove detrimental to you is going on, without dealing in specifics. A good aide can make or break you.

The next thing you must do is learn the judgment of your subordinates. This can't be done overnight. When you first start in a district or division, you must use your previous experience as a guideline for awhile. You can't put complete faith in what is reported to you at a fire until you learn the source of the information. As time goes on you go to more and more fires with the same men and you will learn whose judgment is good and whose is bad. If a man has consistently used poor judgment, you can keep trying to teach him and advise him, but you're probably not gonna change him very much. You can't really fire him, he's civil service just like you are and if you get him transferred, you're just dumping him on someone else. So, you might as well hang in there, keep tryin' with him, and accept him as punishment for your past sins. But the fact that you have learned he has bad judgment gives you an advantage. You can base your decisions on the fact that he doesn't have the proper understanding of the job and can discount most of what he says, but keep an open mind as much as you can. When a guy has good judgment, though, boy, it's great! He makes your job so much easier. When he gives you information you can take it as gospel. Remember, when you're in charge of a fire, most of your decisions are based on things you can't see happening yourself, so you are the captive of the information you receive from others.

You must also learn as much as you can about the buildings in your district or division. This is an ongoing process, and in a city as old and large as Boston, you will never learn them all, but you have to keep absorbing like a sponge. Knowledge of when buildings were·built is as important as the materials used because different periods of history utilized different methods of construction. In the older cities, like Boston, the value of complete fire walls or divisions between adjoining buildings was not properly understood a hundred or more years ago. Consequently, it often happens that when a fire originates in one building, it often spreads to two others in a short period of time. The officer in charge must consider this possibility and take the necessary actions. It must be great to work in a town where all the buildings are new, properly constructed and protected, detached and above grade, but that's not how it is here, baby. The age of the buildings also means that they've probably been remodeled several times through the years, often by people unqualified for the job who may remove vital supports without anyone, including themselves, being aware of it. Such alterations are often concealed, increasing the danger of collapse. Ceilings are often lowered to conserve heat and it's not unusual to find three ceilings in old buildings. When the fire gets above them, they all have to be pulled and the fire keeps traveling and getting ahead of you. It requires a lot of help and a lot of hard work to make the stop.

In the last twenty years, four collapses of fire buildings cost the lives of seventeen Boston fire fighters. Each one was due to a flaw in the building that could not be detected. The chief officers in charge were blameless, but try telling that to them sometime. That's another reason they lay the bread on ya, but no one ever talks about it.

There have been very few changes in the methods of fighting fires in the older cities. This is not because fire fighters are too stubborn or too stupid to change, as the experts often state. It is because the extinguishing methods are usually governed by the buildings themselves. Whenever you see spectacular pictures of fires with gleaming fire engines delivering huge streams of water into buildings, they are very impressive and make the six o'clock news worthwhile, in full living color. But what you really are viewing, more often than not, is a battle that has been lost. The building involved is rapidly becoming a crane job. A lot of the water being delivered is not able to hit the seat of the fire and the building will probably be destroyed. Oh, the relatively new aerial towers and snorkels with their buckets that permit men to deliver water more accurately and work with greater safety at heights, are wonderful. Such innovations have improved things somewhat, but not even they are always successful.

The real job has to be done on the inside. Departments are often criticized when tragedies occur with fire fighters working in buildings. People actually believe that it is some macho challenge that you are fulfilling. While there is no doubt that it plays some part in what a fire fighter does, as a chief, you should be long gone from that kind of thinking. You are the guy who must decide when to take them out during an interior attack or keep them out after a knockdown from the outside. No one else. You will get very little help in making this decision.

If you could extinguish all fires from the outside it would be nice. If you used this method in the older cities, you would have no city. The "surround and drown" theory doesn't often work here. Fire travels most rapidly in concealed spaces and old buildings constructed mostly of wood are honeycombed with such areas. A visiting Australian fire chief, after viewing a four alarm fire in five three-deckers, remarked to the chief in charge, "Ya know somethin'? You bloody Yanks fooked up the whole country."

"Whaddya mean, I thought you liked it here."

"Well I do, but that's not what I meant. You built the whole damn thing of wood, ya shuda used cement! That's what we did in Australia."

"Sure, that's because you ain't got any wood down there. We got plenty here, and that's what we use."

Yeah, that is the problem. There's three major ways to save lives and property from fire. Eliminating wooden buildings is one of them but that ain't gonna happen as long as we got Oregon, and all those other states with big forests. The other two things could be done though, and maybe the new Federal Emergency Management Agency will accomplish them in time. The first thing and the least expensive is to put smoke detectors in every building. This practice has started to spread across the country and has already saved many lives. It notifies people to get out of buildings. But it doesn't do anything to put out a fire. Automatic sprinklers do. The agency is experimenting with home sprinkler systems and if they ever become mandatory for new construction, fire deaths in dwellings will be practically eliminated in about fifty years.

This is now, though, and not future dreamlands. When fires are knocked down from the outside, they are never completely extinguished and the chief in charge must decide whether to finish the job from the inside. This is one of his two hardest decisions, the other being at what point to pull men out of a building during an interior attack. One method of deciding if they can enter is when you have knocked down the visible fire with heavy streams from the outside, shut everything down. You then enter the building yourself with a district chief and an aide and make as thorough a survey as you can, going from floor to floor, if possible, checking to see what has burned, what kind of supports are intact, what has to be opened up and overhauled, listening for unusual sounds or any defects you can find. Take your time doing this. A gallon of water weighs about eight pounds. The longer you take on your survey, the more water is running out of the building, taking weight and pressure off the structure. Don't be influenced by the fire fighters outside. They are eager to get in and complete the attack. They know that if they can get inside and kill it, they'll get back to quarters sooner, so they're raring to go. They also know if they can't get inside, it's gonna be a much longer job. But you're the one to decide. If you end up putting them in as a result of your survey, use as few men as possible, stay with them, get the job done and get out. If you decide the longer route, keep them out, set up enough heavy streams to insure containment and get the building department to call a crane. Keep the minimum number you can get by with at the scene and relieve them periodically. It's sometimes a frustrating decision and sometimes you're wrong about keeping them out, as events may later prove, but that should not stop you. Whichever decision you make you are doing it based on your best judgment with the information you have available at the time.

Many of the decisions you make will be criticized, usually by people who have never been in charge of a fire. You may have rabbit ears at first, but the longer you're at it and realize just how much responsibility you are carrying, the less important the criticisms become. Taking men out after commencing an initial attack is also agonizing at times. You have to base it on a few important things. The type of building, the location and extent of the fire, progress and time. You must constantly watch the building itself for signs of anything unusual. During your initial size up, you should be looking at the walls for cracks, bulges or any other defects. but you don't look only once. The building is burning and is subject to changes so you gotta keep watching until it's under control. If you don't start making real progress shortly after you get water and the attack commences, start thinking about whether you are gonna get the fire or not. If the fire is traveling and you're not getting ahead of it, you may have to pull them out. The time will vary with the type of fire and the construction, but if you don't start doing good within twenty or thirty minutes and can't take action to improve conditions, get them out. Make certain everyone gets the word and make certain everyone gets out.

While you're running the show, you have to keep moving. You are generally stationed in front for easy access of others to you, but you are not a statue. Keep watching the building all the time. Don't run unless you have to. You probably will pace miles back and forth and you have to conserve yourself. You may be there all night. You can always bring in extra companies to relieve the men, but no one relieves you until the fire or your tour is over.

As you know, fire fighting should be a relatively simple task, but it's complicated by many factors. The most important, of course, is when human life is in danger. The theorists often write that if you come in to a fire and the people are hanging out the windows, it is better to leave them hanging, raise your ladder to the roof, and perform prompt and proper ventilation, thus drawing the fire up and away from the people hanging. It will also save all those others in the building that you can't see. That's wrong. When they're hanging, grab them quick, by any available method. Most of them are scared to death and ready to jump. If you go by them with your ladders, they may jump for them. Just pick them off as quick as you can. Besides, your second truck may be able to get the roof open from the back. You really don't know if there's anyone else in the building that you can't see, but you know the ones you can see are there. Venting will have to wait. Try to get an engine company to get a line on the fire and let them ignore the people, but not the truckies. A line may cut off a fire or hold it until everyone's out of the building. However, in desperate situations, forget the fire and use everyone on ladders. Once you get them all, the attack returns to normal, but the fact that there were people still in the building when you got there means your search for victims will have to be more thorough than usual.

One other thing ya gotta keep in mind when you're a chief. There are times when you get to a fire and everything goes wrong. No matter how smart you think you are and how experienced, it's not gonna be a good day. You can go to a dozen fires in a row and do what you think is a pretty good job and pat yourself on the back. Then you go to one and feel like quitting: every action you take and every order you give, doesn't seem to make any difference, it's just a bad scene from start to finish. Try not to let it get ya because, if you're a chief long enough, sometimes you'll make parking lots, baby, and there ain't nuthin' you can do about it.

He dropped off to sleep finally, probably putting to sleep the imaginary guy he was giving advice to as well.

The lights came on and the house gong was sounding, and as he jumped into his hitch, he could hear the terse announcement on the P.A. system, "Second Alarm, Box 1662, Mass. Ave. and

Washington, Deputy and Rescue One, Tower One, respond to the fire, report of people in the building."

I guess I better go see if I know what I'm talking about, he thought as he slammed the car door and his aide drove him out of the fire house.

Epilogue

On February 1, 1924, the Boston Fire Department reduced the work schedule of fire fighters from one day off in fifteen to an eighty-four hour work week. This progressive adjustment created many appointments for young veterans of World War I, and my father was among them.

He was an auto mechanic at the time and his job was not steady so he viewed the fire department position as a chance for permanent employment. While he liked the work from the start, he seriously considered quitting during his first year on the force. He was single then and the long hours and confinement in the station didn't give him the same freedom he had had when he was greasing cars.

But love, marriage and children soon wiped out any thoughts of leaving and he settled into a thirty-two year career that culminated with him serving as Chief of Department during his final six years in the department.

He grew to love the job as do many others, and his dedication to his men and the department resulted in the Boston Fire Fighters Local creating an award in his name. It is the highest award the Union presents each year and it is given to the member who best exemplifies the qualities of humility, integrity, loyalty and fortitude. We consider it to be a great honor to him. Each year until his death, he took pleasure in writing a congratulatory note to the recipient, although he was much too modest to attend the presentation.

As kids growing up, we seldom saw him. The eighty-four hour week may have been a great boon back in 1924 but it still meant a fire fighter was in the firehouse every day at 0800. He was either going on duty or going off, but he was there just the same. Of course, if there was a serious fire in progress, or a snowstorm or other emergency, he never got home and there was no such thing as overtime pay in those days.

In November, 1942 a building collapsed during a five alarm fire in the East Boston district, killing six fire fighters. Forty others were seriously injured, including my father, who was a fire captain at the time. His injuries were so severe that he was unconscious for a week and he was hospitalized for three months. When he finally came home, it was another three months before he could leave the house. I know this sounds like a really tragic story, and I guess in some ways it was. But his long stay at home was the first time we really got to know him. We older sons were just finishing up high school and gearing up for the war, like everyone else, but in spite of our youth we could see he was fighting a great mental and physical battle although he was always trying to conceal it. At first, he was always under tension and he had absolutely no interest in the department anymore. He was taking his pension and that was that. He wouldn't even look out the window when the fire apparatus passed en route to a fire. He was cutting it out of his life. In spite of his nerves, he became very interested in what his family was doing. He'd help us with our homework each night, listen to the radio mystery stories with us, teach us how to play poker, checkers and other things that fathers who were home every night did. He tried to get interested in some hobbies. He would go in a room with a radio kit and try to build a set that would reach China but he never got a sound out of it and there were parts everywhere.

He started doing some of the cooking but we could see that wasn't his best subject and we'd all find excuses to eat somewhere else when he started getting out his pots and pans. He did a little painting as his physical condition improved. No, not like Rembrandt, just a few walls and ceilings.

Then, one day, as the summer started approaching, he read a recipe for making root beer in the paper. Boy, he loved the stuff. Now he was going to be able to make a whole year's supply. He sent everyone out searching for empty bottles and he started buying yeast and other ingredients. It was quite a project. When it was done, we had bottles of root beer everywhere. It had to be properly aged, of course, before we could touch it. We could hardly wait. The day before the great opening, something went wrong with the batch and the bottles started to pop. Pretty soon, bottles, caps and root beer were flying all over the kitchen and pantry. It sounded like the German subs lying outside Boston harbor had finally attacked.

God, what a mess. He came charging into the kitchen when it started. He slipped on the wet linoleum and fell flat on his face. He lay there for a few minutes and soon we could see his shoulders starting to shake. Oh, jeez, he's crying, we better get outta here. But as we turned to go he sat up, and he wasn't crying at all. He was laughing. It was the first time he had laughed since he came home from the hospital. Pretty soon he was hysterical and so were we. The neighbors must have thought we were all nuts because the house was jumpin'.

When it was over he said, "You know, kids, I think it's time I stopped kidding myself. About the only thing I ever did right was fire fighting. If I take my pension now, I don't know what I'll do. I could never work as a clerk in an office and it's a cinch I'll never be a good painter or cook, and no one's going to hire me to make root beer."

As soon as he made that decision the tension seemed to drain out of him. He started going for long walks to get his legs back in shape. As time went on, he'd be gone for longer and longer periods of time. He'd walk everywhere. At night he'd be tired but he was always cheerful. Now, he laughed all the time. He was driving the shadows away.

One day he was gone when we got up in the morning. When we asked mom where he was she said he just left a note saying he'd be home late. Around ten at night, he staggered in the door and collapsed in an arm chair. "Johnnie, where on earth have you been? You're exhausted, " said my mother. "Well, you know I've been getting ready to go back and I figured I should have a goal to prove I'm capable. So, this morning I took a bus to Providence, Rhode Island and walked back. Not bad, huh? Forty miles in, oh, about thirteen hours. Florence, I'm ready to go. I'm gonna see the doctor next week and tell him to put me back!"

When he first went back, he was pretty nervous for awhile but after a few fires he settled down and was O.K. He told me years later that the memory of the East Boston fire eventually faded completely and he couldn't remember responding to the alarm at all. The only thing he remembered was an auto fire he went to earlier in the evening.

The period that he was home was a great joy for all of us, and was also the most we saw of him in his lifetime. It was an unexpected gift for us. This myth of a guy who had never been home was around all the time now and he turned out to be much different than we imagined. He had a great sense of humor and could laugh at himself even when covered with root beer. He taught us not to take ourselves too seriously and how to enjoy life. But he also taught us to be loyal to each other and to try to do our best for something that's worth doing. Whether it be studying for an advancement or just doing a job, put everything you have into it because it gives you great satisfaction.

Soon after he went back to work, we went in the service and he wrote to us every week. By the time we came back he was a district chief and soon became a deputy. He was made chief in 1950. It was pretty hard to believe this was the same guy who wouldn't look out the window at a fire engine just eight years before. One thing, though, he never really encouraged any of us to take the job. I think there was always something lingering in the back of his mind about his experience and he didn't want us exposed to the same thing. But love, marriage and kids aren't restricted to one generation and pretty soon I found myself on the job, although I was the only kid in the family to try it.

I entered the department with mixed emotions. Oh, I wanted a good steady job but I didn't know if this was the one for me. At first I was pretty scared. Hey, I remembered seeing him unconscious for days, didn't I? Aw, so what? Is that all you're gonna think about the rest of your life? People get hurt and killed all kinds of ways, don't they? Jeez, ya gotta get outta this world somehow. I'll probably get beaned with a golf ball anyway.

Once I got through that initial period, I began to discover that being a fire fighter is actually a whole way of life. The fires and dangers are just parts of it. It's a combination of a lot of things:

friendship, pride, satisfaction, spirit and loyalty. Oh, not all fire fighters love each other but they stick together in a closed shop type of thing. It does have something to do with constantly facing danger and surviving it. The exhilaration afterwards really can't be put in words. It probably helps to explain, though, why the fire fighters hung together so well and fought so hard to get all the young guys back during the layoffs. Hey, they're all part of us, ain't they? Now that the union got them all back, the morale is improving and the future looks promising. Nobody who hasn't done any fire duty is going to break us.

My father lived to see two of his grandsons become fire fighters. I'm glad he never lived to see them laid off. But they came back with all the rest. So, if you have a fire, give us a call. We'll always give it our best shot.

Whenever there's an unusual incident on the job or whenever something funny happens, some firehouse kitchen lawyer always says, "Why don't anyone write a book about this crazy job?" I thought I'd give it a try.

No Magic

Chief of Department John V. Stapleton. Box 5-1323, Feb. 1, 1954, Downtown District.

Has Arrived Yet

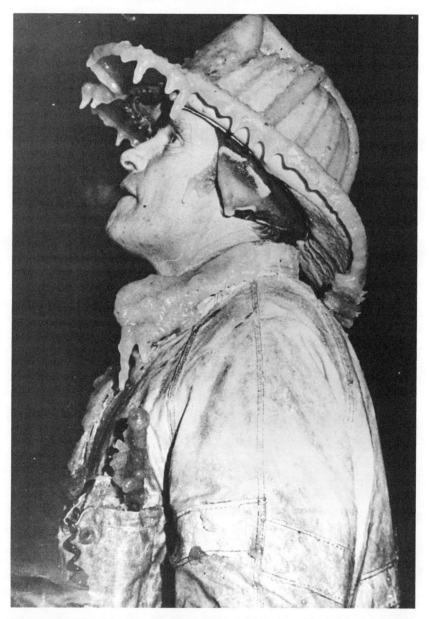

Deputy Fire Chief Leo D. Stapleton. Box 5-7441, Jan. 22, 1976, South Boston District.